THE HUSTLER & THE CHAMP

WILLIE MOSCONI, MINNESOTA FATS,
AND THE RIVALRY THAT DEFINED POOL

R.A. DYER

THE LYONS PRESS
Guilford, CT
An imprint of The Globe Pequot Press

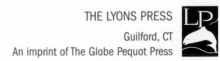

The Lyons Press is an imprint of The Globe Pequot Press.

10 9 8 7 6 5 4 3 2 1

Printed in the United States of America

Designed by Kim Burdick

Library of Congress Cataloging-in-Publication Data

Dyer, R. A. (Richard A.)
    The hustler & the champ : Willie Mosconi, Minnesota Fats, and the rivalry
that defined pool / R. A. Dyer.
          p. cm.
    Includes bibliographical references and index.
    ISBN 978-1-59228-883-0 (alk. paper)
    1. Mosconi, Willie. 2. Minnesota Fats, 1913-1996. 3. Billiard players—
United States—Biography. 4. Pool (Game)—United States—History.
    I. Title. II. Title: Hustler and the Champ.
    GV892.D93 2007
    794.73'30922—dc22
    [B]
                                                    2007021034

For Dad

AUTHOR'S NOTE

It's a lovely blue-sky Saturday afternoon, the sort meant for lounging and listening to music. And that's exactly what I'm doing as I sit here thinking back at the roughly three years I've spent writing and researching *The Hustler & The Champ*. I'm at one of my favorite Austin coffee shops, on the patio with my laptop open on a wobbly picnic table. The sun is hot on my back, but there's also a light breeze and that comforting buzz of people with nowhere to be and who laugh and chat with what can only be described as the opposite of urgency. This book is at least partially the product of both the happy times I've spent here, but also some frustrating ones as well. It's here, for instance, that I exhausted my weekends highlighting sections of old columns by *Pool & Billiard Magazine*'s Tom Shaw, and transcripts of my interviews with Karen Fox and Evelyn Wanderone, and pouring through hundreds of newspaper clippings. I would find needed quotes and then lose them. I went through that ever-growing pile of newspaper clippings and magazine articles and transcripts so many times I thought my eyes would fail.

But it's also here at this coffee shop where I spent one lovely afternoon in the company of Bill and Judy Mosconi, their son Chris, and Chris's girlfriend Evelyn. They had come in from New Jersey, they called my cell, and so we meandered away a couple of hours on this patio doing one of the things I love most: talking about Bill's father, the great William Joseph Mosconi. This book is the product of those difficult record searches, but also the delightful conversations I had with the Mosconis and others at this coffee shop and elsewhere. It's a product of all the fascinating people I met and the people I read about. Without all those I met along the way, this book would be nothing.

One can live an entire lifetime and not find a family so gracious and charming as the Mosconis. Bill and Judy invited me into their home as did Bill's wonderful mother, Flora. She even fed me cookies. Bill steered me around south Philly one afternoon, showing me all the old haunts. We explored the neighborhood together like fascinated kids. And Candace Fritch consented to an interview, giving me real insight into her father's character. I cannot thank the family enough.

And then there's Charles Ursitti, the colorful ringmaster at the center of The Great Pool Shoot-Out. Having first befriended Fats and then Willie Mosconi his story in some ways also is the glue that binds together this book. With patience and good humor Charlie recounted for me his story and theirs, from beginning to end. I cannot express all my appreciation for his patience and for the courtesy he extended by inviting me into his home. I still marvel when I think back at his extensive collection of photographs, old books, and antique sports magazines. You'll find much of that material referenced in *The Hustler & The Champ*.

Neither would this book exist if not for the research of historians like Mike Shamos, curator of the Billiards Archives, and Stanley Cohen, author of the estimable *Willie's Game*. Shamos provided photos, gave me context, and through his wisdom and study illuminated a bright-line path for this book. The long and detailed interviews Cohen conducted with Mosconi before his death—they form the marrow of his excellent 1993 book—must now be seen as one of pool history's most important troves of information about the great champion. I want to also thank the editors and writers at *Billiards Digest*, but most especially Mike Panozzo, Mason King, George Fels, and Audra Quinn. There's also the eerily talented Jon Resh, the graphic artist and former *Billiards Digest* editor who created the cover for my first book and the cover of this one too. I am his number one fan.

Many other people provided me invaluable assistance, including my sister Cathy who selflessly read through and edited more than one draft of *The Hustler & The Champ;* my mother Aida Dyer, who found a passel of dumb mistakes; and my sister Carolina Cordero Dyer and my sister-in-law Claudia Glazer, who put me up at their house during my research trips to New York. Carolina and Claudia even left me the key to their family car. How cool is that? Also my day-job colleagues somehow tolerated my endless mewling about this project. For that they deserve hero medals. They are Jay Root, John Moritz, Steve Campbell, and John Gravois—each of them close and valued friends.

I also must thank Karen Fox, the widow of Tom Fox, who provided me with great insight into those early Johnston City days; and professional friends and colleagues, past and present, some in the pool world, some in my newspaper tribe. They include Chris Doyle, *Around the Bloc* author Stephanie Elizondo Griest, Brandi Grissom, Claudia Kolker, playwright Clair Lavaye, Jennifer Liebrum, Julie Mason, Tara Parker Pope, Ned Pickler, Jack Plunkett, and Armando Villafranca. There are many others, including April Castro, Jim Vertuno, Liz Austin Peterson, and Kelly Shannon who work across the hall at the Associated Press. From the publishing world, I want to thank my agent Dan Mandel and my editor at Lyons, Christine Duffy.

In the category of those who I don't see nearly enough, but who are never far from my thoughts, I include my brother Jim and sister-in-law Shelley, and my very good friends George Crain, Doug and Debbie Posso, Devon and Andrea Fletcher, Keith and Melanie Fletcher, and of course Armando "Re-group" Taborda. Also, Devon was a great help with last-minute edits.

And then of course there's my immediate family. They have put up with more than any family should. For that I will always be grateful. They are my lovely wife Grettel, my handsome son Alec—he always makes me proud—and my daughter Sofia, who likewise happens to be my number one research assistant.

And finally I want to thank my father. He's been with me every step of the way.

Someone once said that those who write history must stand upon the shoulders of others. That dictum comes to mind on this beautiful Saturday afternoon as I listen to the easy chatter of contented people.

Again: thank you.

CONTENTS

CONTENTS

Chapter 1

THE CHAMP

Odysseus, now, was a man who could defend his house
against the spoiler. . . .

—The *Odyssey*

It is October 22, 1977, and the grey-haired Willie Mosconi sits regally
in a high-backed chair. The chair is long-legged and tall, like a bar
stool, except it has padded arm rests and an elevated, cushioned seat.
It is the sort of chair from which men who play pool can watch their
lives unfold. It is the sort of chair designed for men like Willie
Mosconi—had there been other men like Willie Mosconi.

But since there were none, it is more like a throne.

In the course of his sixty-four years, Willie Mosconi had won the
world championship fifteen times. He held the record for the highest
number of successive balls pocketed in straight pool, 526—more than
thirty-five racks without a single miss. Like Joe DiMaggio's fifty-six-game
hitting streak, this is a feat that may never be surpassed.[1] Mosconi so
dominated the field during the first of his championships that the
newspaper men immediately proclaimed him one of the best players
ever. This was not hyperbole nor breathless hype. It was prescient. No

---

[1]There are a few reports of higher runs but none confirmed by witnesses. Willie's official record
may remain standing until the end of time because straight pool has nearly disappeared from the
American scene.

one then living had ever witnessed a performance like the one Mosconi delivered during the first of his world championships. And for nearly two decades more, that spectacular performance would continue.

And so, sitting in that high-backed chair on October 22, 1977, Willie had become the living embodiment of pocket billiards, the man who had become bigger than his sport. He was the king in the yellow sports jacket. This is why the network producers had hired him that day, why he was on hand to provide expert analysis for a pool match, why he was accompanied by the most famous of sportscasters, Howard Cosell. The venue was a ballroom in an elegant New York City hotel.

So come now and listen to this story, the story of how the grey-haired king got suckered into redefining his very kingdom. For on October 22, 1977, the great Willie Mosconi was *hustled* and *duped* and goaded by the taunts of America's greatest hustler. The champion *exploded* into a blind rage! October 22, 1977, was not a great day for pool—not in itself—but it set the stage for one of the greatest days of pocket billiards. For Willie Mosconi, Willie the Great, Willie the Wondrous, Willie the Most Kick-Ass Pool Player Ever to Walk the Earth, before a live audience and a broken camera, Willie Joseph Mosconi on that day lost control of his wits. He ranted, and he waved his cue as if his very kingdom had come under assault.

This is the story of pool's greatest champion, a man born under a special star, a man who conquered and ruled but who then became separated from his kingdom. He was terrible and cruel but great also. He lived by a code, and he defended it.

And this also is the story of American pocket billiards, a game of unfolding patterns, mesmerizing colors, balls interlocking and scattered. The game is played by thieves and marked by cruelty, but its heroes possess untold skill.

And finally this is the story of a trickster, one of the greatest in the history of American sport. For one cannot tell the story of the great champion Willie Mosconi and that of modern American pocket billiards without also telling the story of its court jester, a hustler named Minnesota Fats.

Chapter 2

THE USURPERS

This is not a hoodlums' game played behind green-painted windows.

— Willie Mosconi

"This is the God's honest truth." Charles Ursitti holds up his right hand and then solemnly places it over his heart. "As Fatty would say, I will sit in a lie detector and put my head in a guillotine if I lie."

A portly man, bearded, gregarious, and above all, a New Yorker, Charles Ursitti fits the central-casting bill for the poolroom loafer. But while he may be the only man in America actually flattered by such a description, it is one that rather widely misses the mark. "I guess I didn't want it bad enough," he would say, without a hint of irony. "But I'm happy with the route I took."

Yes, Ursitti has spent his share of days in poolrooms, playing, practicing, falling into the hypnotic trance of colored balls, but the idleness of that world does not define him. As much as he wishes that it would, it simply cannot. Rather, Charles Ursitti is a student and promoter of the sport. The route of Charles Ursitti's life passed not through back room wagers but through TV deals and bookish research. He is a passionate historian, a gregarious raconteur, and above all, a lover of pool. His life's route led through the organization of ambitious tournaments, through a single-minded collection of books and magazines, and on to the very startling affair of October 22, 1977, when Willie Mosconi sat with Howard Cosell and two hustlers went head to head.

The whole thing, after all, was Ursitti's idea.

Put my head in the guillotine if I lie.

Ursitti's family back then owned a printing plant at 285 Lafayette Street, in downtown Manhattan, just a block away from his home in Soho. It was at this plant that Ursitti met a supposed pool hustler by the name of Bruce "Superstroke" Christopher, who was blond, in his twenties and movie-star handsome. He showed up at Ursitti's door some months before the events of October 22 and brought with him photographs and press clippings. One recorded an alleged victory by Superstroke over a maharaja from India. It alleged that Superstroke won $70,000. A related photograph showed Superstroke victoriously raising a cue above his head.

Christopher also explained that he was in the *Guinness Book of World Records* for having pocketed more than five thousand balls in a single day. He said the feat was unprecedented. He told Ursitti that he wanted some promotional posters printed.

"So I said, 'Sure: we'll do a layout of the poster, and then I'll print them,'" Ursitti recalls of that first meeting. "And then Christopher comes back later, and he wants to do a book called *Superstroke*. It had a lot of pictures of him, with a lot of celebrities and a lot of hype. And you know I wasn't then involved in pool, and so [Christopher walking in the front door] is how my whole career got started. And that's when we started hanging out."

Now somewhere in there—again, this was 1977—the great hustler Minnesota Fats had been scheduled to come to town for a pocket-billiards exhibition. At the time, Fats was quite famous: he frequently appeared on *The Tonight Show* with Johnny Carson; he hosted several TV programs; he had became the subject of flattering profiles in *Sports Illustrated* and *Esquire*. In short, Fats possessed the sort of fame to which Bruce Christopher could then only aspire. In the public's mind, Fats had come to represent everything that pocket billiards stood for: men behaving badly, gambling, and excess.

"We should go see him," said Christopher.

Ursitti explains what happened next:

"So Fatty comes into town, and we meet him, and of course, he's very jovial and cordial and funny. I think Fats is in town for a day or two, [and so] we go have dinner with him. We're laughing and talking and I says to Fatty, I says, 'Fatty, I have this idea, you're the legendary hustler, right? And the kid here is now in the *Guinness Book of World Records*, and he just beat a maharaja. He's the young hustler of today. What if I did a match between the two of youse and try to get it on TV?'

"And Fats says, 'Okay, Junior'—he called everybody Junior—he said, 'Okay, Junior, you got my permission. Go ahead and use my name.' And with that I start to feel out the [billiards] industry. I make phone calls. I call the industry guys up. I call the cue companies. But nobody wants to have anything to do with me. I'm thinking Jesus Christ—there must something wrong here, they must be jealous. I have no idear what's going on. . . .

"And so finally I call the Guinness people. I tell them, 'I have this fella who's in your book with this tremendous run, and I want to get him to play Minnesota Fats.' I says, 'You get your *Guinness Book of World Records*, you open it up, and his name is right there.' And they say that all our television is handled by an outfit called Big Fights—call for Bill Cayton or Jim Jacobs at Big Fights. And so I call and . . . I spoke to Jacobs, and we get the match between Fats and Christopher. We book the Waldorf-Astoria ballroom, and there's a lot of hype."

Ursitti is a colorful man and gregarious. He adroitly uses the well-known plural of "you" as he tells stories ("How's 'bout I set up a match between the two of youse?"), and he tags all friends, enemies, and cab drivers with the same moniker: Buddy. But when Ursitti tells this next part, the *buddies* and *youses* and all his other words escape him. All Ursitti can manage is a heavenward glance, a shrug of the shoulders.

"Now you remember," he says, "that Bruce Christopher had gotten himself in the *Guinness Book of World Records* for having run 5,688 balls without a miss. . . ."

Without a miss?

5

This is when the pained expression comes and the shrug.

"The book said he *pocketed* those balls," Ursitti says finally. "That's the way it was phrased in the book: 5,688 balls *pocketed* without a miss, in twenty-four hours. I was saying this guy must be unbelievable. I mean, I had never seen him play yet, but I heard that Mosconi's record was 526. Unbelievable, right? It was something else. What did I know?"

Ursitti set up a practice room in the five-thousand-square-foot loft of his printing press. He sectioned off part, installed a gorgeous antique table, and invited Christopher up to practice before the big match. Ursitti was a capable amateur, claiming lifetime high runs in straight pool at fifty or sixty—which was pretty good but far from what might be expected from a professional.

"So I says to Bruce, I say, 'I'm not much of a player, but at least I can spar with you.'

"The first couple of days go by, and we're sparring back and forth, and we're playing short sets, and I'm holding my own. I'm holding my own, and then I'm beating him. And then, in three or four days of me playing hard, he can't beat me. I mean, he'll beat me a game, but he's not winning the sets. So finally I says to Bruce, I say: 'Bruce, your match is three or four weeks away and you can't beat me? Try real hard. Try your best.'"

And this was the reply of Bruce "Superstroke" Christopher, the beater of maharajas and the runner of more than five thousand balls: "I *am* trying my best."

And it was then that Ursitti came to the sickening realization that his whole world was turning to crap. It was one of those *oh-shit* kind of moments, the sort that inspires panicked flight by the lesser beasts.

"What are you going to do?" Ursitti asked, pleadingly. "If you can't beat me, and if this guy plays just one-tenth of your legend, then he's going to kill you."

How did Bruce Christopher get into the *Guinness Book of World Records*? Ursitti says there are twenty different stories. First off, Christopher wasn't playing straight pool, where one plays rack after rack and cue-ball control is essential. That's the game Mosconi played; that's the game that defined pool's greatest champions. But Superstroke "was just pocketing balls," said Ursitti. "I found out they were just putting balls in front of the pockets in front of him. It was bogus."[2]

But, really, does it matter? The fact that Bruce Christopher managed to get himself in the *Guinness Book of World Records* was the real feat. It might have been pure hype, pure showbiz, *pure bullshit*— but remember this: only because of Bruce Christopher's appearance in the *Guinness Book of World Records* did Big Fights take an interest. The billiards industry, by itself, could never have gotten Howard Cosell and the network on board. Hell, they'd have had nothing to do with Superstroke Christopher and his fishy world record.

"I guess they just didn't like it when I was showboating," said Superstroke.

•   •   •

Not with hustlers, but with men of excellence did Willie Mosconi identify himself. "When I was a kid, it was played in plush billiard academies," Willie once said, speaking with a reporter from Texas. "I'm not talking about poolhalls—little places that front for bookies, but plush billiard parlors where gentlemen played." The true champions were old-time stage magicians. They seemed always and forever to be striding about in their dark tuxedos and creaky leather shoes. They were aristocrats.

And so the history of billiards, as told by the industry and embraced by Mosconi, begins with European royalty. According to Brunswick,

---

[2] Christopher, for his part, says that only through his own tenacity did he make it into the *Guinness Book of World Records*. He said he had a contact there, one whom he frequently needled. Guinness was neglecting the cue sports, Christopher recalled telling him: "I said, 'Put something in there about pool, and make it more popular' and [the Guinness contact] told me, 'Go and run some balls for twenty-four hours, and we'll put you in there." And so that's what Christopher did. How exactly did he run all those 5,688 balls? Christopher doesn't say exactly. The 1977 and 1978 editions of the *Guinness Book* include a jubilant picture of Christopher having presumably just completed his astronomical run.

pool evolved from a lawn sport that was popular with the old-world kings during the fourteenth century. One hundred years later a man who was probably French created a flat table so he could play the game indoors. The table received green cloth to represent the green of the grass, and it received banks to keep balls from rolling off the edges.[3] The precursor of the modern pool table also had a wooden target and wickets, and instead of using cues, players struck balls with odd-shaped maces that might remind one of croquet mallets.[4]

The first recorded instance of anyone, anywhere, owning a table comes to us from a 1470 palace inventory of King Louis XI of France. According to Brunswick Billiards, this table included a bed of stone, a cloth covering, and a hole in the middle of the playing field. Marie Antoinette and Louis XVI also delighted in the game and even played one another on the eve of their imprisonment. Likewise, the separated head and body of Mary Queen of Scots was entombed in the cloth of her beloved table.

From France[5] the game spread throughout Europe, to England,[6] and eventually to the American colonies, where the old-world aristocracy had been replaced with a new-world one. And so it was with these new American men of excellence that the industry and Mosconi associated the sport.

Ask industry reps to identify the first American players, and their eager answer is "The presidents!" According to information provided by Brunswick, George Washington won a game in 1748; John Quincy

---

[3] In fact, the sides were referred to as "banks" because they reminded one of a river bank.

[4] According to Brunswick Billiards, "The word 'cue' is derived from the French queue, meaning tail. Before the cue stick was designed, billiards was played with a mace. The mace consisted of a curved wooden (or metal) head used to push the ball forward, attached to a narrow handle. Since the bulkiness of the mace head made shots along the rail difficult, it was often turned around and the 'tail' end was used. Players eventually realized this method was far more effective, and the cue as a separate instrument grew out of the mace's tail."

[5] The inventor of the leather cue tip, Captain Mingaud, was imprisoned during the French revolution for political reasons. He became obsessed with the game after managing to get a table installed in his cell. Mingaud perfected his invention during his incarceration and actually asked for more prison time so as to complete his studies.

[6] In the seventeenth century, William Shakespeare included a reference to billiards in Act II, Scene V of *Antony and Cleopatra*.

Adams installed a table in the presidential quarters in 1828; and Abraham Lincoln extolled pool as a "scientific game lending recreation to the otherwise fatigued mind."

Other privileged players included Colonial explorer William Byrd, who was said to have laid his wife on a table; Thomas Jefferson, who installed a secret billiards room at Monticello; and millionaires Andrew Carnegie and John D. Rockefeller. Likewise, sociologist Ned Polsky tells us that during its earliest years American billiards "consisted of 'respectable' playing by the upper class, which flourished especially in country houses."

Clearly, then, billiards has its roots not with the great mass of the unwashed, the hoi polloi, but rather society's most excellent members. For Willie Mosconi, the noble home of pocket billiards was furnished with crystal chandeliers and burnished wood; its practioners conducted themselves with dignity and grace; its champions possessed a relentless, brooding seriousness. This is how Willie Mosconi identified pocket billiards because this is how he saw himself.

"Ours is an honorable game," he would say.

And yet, yet . . . there was that *other* history. . . .

THE TV DISASTER

The camera has broken down, and so I says to Fatty, I
say, 'Fatty, why don't you entertain the audience?'
— Promoter Charles Ursitti

This is true: most of our early knowledge of pool comes from the written and pictorial accounts of royalty. This is also true: upper-class European emigrants introduced pool to the New World, where it quickly took root with a similar upper class in America. Pocket billiards' long aristocratic tradition in the United States and Europe is simply a fact. As Mosconi once said: "All the cities once had beautiful billiards rooms. Gorgeous places." But Superstroke and Fats and all the rest were there too, just as they've been in poolrooms for centuries. The leeching suitors were *always* there, waiting in the courtyards and drinking the wine.

"It has been known as the 'Noble Game of Billiards' since the early 1800s, but there is evidence that people from all walks of life have played the game since its inception," billiards historian Mike Shamos wrote in a 1992 essay. Likewise, Ned Polsky, author of *Hustlers, Beats and Others,* tells us that pocket billiards predominated in homes and country estates prior to the 1600s but that another, more tawdry tradition took hold in later years. "In America, public poolrooms . . . were always associated with gambling and various forms of low-life."

Polsky's book, one of the most important in the literature of pocket billiards, marks the game's parallel tradition: one of the stodgy gentleman, the other of the working man. He details the transmigration of tables from the richly apportioned private billiard rooms of European aristocracy, then to the upper-class private clubs where gentlemen could gather in exclusion, and finally to the coffeehouses and other venues open to the broader public.

And with the emergence of this strictly public pool playing, the game's dodgier reputation began. Insulated from middle-class morality, the sporting fringe of the upper class could mingle with the sporting fringe of the working class—and together, in the poolroom, they could drink, gamble, and hobnob with the hookers. Like the racetrack, it was the gathering place for hell-raisers.

This trickling down of pool's popularity from the upper class to the lower took root by at least the seventeenth century. And in almost inverse proportion, the stigma attached to pocket billiards began to bubble up. Pastors would rail against the sport. Women deplored its undue influence. Polsky even finds evidence of early legal clampdowns—he cites one in Dublin in 1744,[7] for instance.

"If billiards could be played in public places frequented by the gentleman, there was little to prevent it being played in public places by the not-so-gentlemanly; and little did prevent it," writes Polsky. "As this second tradition developed, the 'respectable' upper class who played at home or in meeting places restricted to their own kind were immediately concerned to distinguish themselves from it, and in doing so they conceived it as morally deviant.

"In their view, it was bad enough that *hoi aristoi* had occasionally spent too much time and money gambling at billiards amongst themselves, but much worse that hoi polloi should now become

---

[7] As cited by Polksy, from a 1744 edition of *Gentleman's Magazine*, "At the Court of King's Bench, in Ireland, were convicted 15 of the Billiard Tables, presented by the Grand Jury of Dublin, (who had traversed) The Citizens have determin'd to prosecute, in the same Manner, all Billiard Tables that shall be erected for the Future, or those which now remain, if kept open after 9 o'Clock at Night, or knowingly suffer Merchants, Apprentices or Clerks belonging to Gentlemen of any Businesses, to play in their Houses."

wastrels over it and (worst of all) sometimes seduce weaker-minded bettors into joining with them in a life of dissolute gaming."

When the European upper class brought the game with them to America, that tawdry stigma came with it like a stowaway rat. It's true that American presidents and aristocracy were the earliest practitioners of pool in the New World. It's true that Thomas Jefferson had a billiard room. But Jefferson's table at Monticello was a *secret* one. The game then was illegal. Yes, John Quincy Adams put a pool table in the presidential quarters, but not without a great hue and cry from the political opposition. And that awful, sorry element—the blacklegs and the ruffians, the Superstrokes and the Minnesota Fats—they have been part of American pool from almost the beginning.

In 1808 there were perhaps eight public tables in New York. They were then set up in coffeehouses and hotels. In 1816 there was evidence of two bona fide poolhalls in the city, but they were likewise connected to other businesses. In 1824 a New Yorker could find as many as twenty-four tables. And then by the 1850s public pool playing had become quite common indeed. Melvin Adelman, author of *A Sporting Time: New York City and the Rise of Modern Athletics,* writes that with the rise of this public pool playing there came so-called "leading" players: men who were superior at the game, who would regularly compete with others, who were possibly professional, but not necessarily so.

These were the progenitors of Minnesota Fats *and* Willie Mosconi, of the great champions and the hustlers.[8] Theirs was a common ancestry.

•　　•　　•

---

[8] By the mid-1840s, according to *The Clipper* magazine (and as cited by Adelman), "blacklegs and professional sharpers, those vampires of the sporting world, had begun to frequent the public billiard rooms, and men of respectability and integrity were driven from it." Adelman contends that the atmosphere of the American poolroom then changed—it then became much more associated with the lower class, and the stigma increased.

"This is so unbelievable, but it's true." Charles Ursitti again is our man on the scene. He was bespectacled in 1977, dark haired and goatee bearded. On the day of the big hustlers' duel Ursitti wore a black tuxedo, a black bow tie, a crisp white shirt. "You've seen those players' seats, right?" says Ursitti. "You know the ones I'm talking about? They're up fairly high; they are like these huge massive thrones. Well, Willie was sitting in one and happened to be holding a cue. It was a house cue."

Ursitti describes more seats on one side of the room for audience members, a sound booth for the commentators, and TV cameras— maybe two or three. The room was crammed with spectators, all of whom had paid $200 to gain entry. Technicians with headsets and clipboards milled about; Willie and Howard whispered side by side, their heads slightly inclined, Willie in a sports coat, Howard in his trademark yellow ABC blazer. By then the audience had settled in, drinks and programs in hand; Fats and Christopher were ready with their cues. Ursitti flitted about, blindly attempting to keep everything in order: the players, the lights, the cameras. . . .

The cameras.

Ursitti doesn't quite remember what it was. Maybe a wire came loose. Or a lens fell off. Or maybe it was a burned-out transistor. But what's clear is that one of the cameras broke down, just totally stopped working—*shit!*—causing the whole Fats-Superstroke production to come to a grinding, screeching, horrific halt.

Imagine this scene: Ursitti has brought Howard Cosell and Willie Mosconi on board for a challenge match with a pool player who couldn't play pool, before TV equipment that didn't work, before an increasingly impatient crowd.

With no camera and an anxious crowd, Ursitti turns to Fats. *Please do something—I'm dying here!*

Capricious fate always seems to turn with Minnesota Fats. Fats says—and you know Fats, he sounded just like W. C. Fields—so Fats says, "Don't you worry 'bout nothing."

Here it comes.

"Anybody have any questions?" Fats becomes the carnival barker, working the crowd. He's a showman, so it comes easy. He'll entertain the crowd while the camera gets fixed.

Someone calls out, "What's the most you ever played for?"

"I played Happy the Chinaman for $50,000!"

Someone else calls out, "What about Ralph Greenleaf?"

"I played Ralph a thousand nights in a row, and I beat him every night!"

Someone asks about Andrew Ponzi, Mosconi's old rival.

"Andrew Ponzi was a girl. I beat him like a drum!"

This unfolds in slow motion, like memories of a car wreck. Mosconi sits off to one side, in his high-backed chair, while Fats rattles off, one by one, the names of green-felt gladiators he's supposedly left for dead. Ponzi? *Greenleaf??* These are some of the greatest in American history. These are men that Mosconi respected, heroes, champions.

"Why are you letting him go on like that?" Mosconi seethes, turning to Ursitti. Mosconi cannot stand this. He absolutely cannot. And it was then, just as a vein had begun to pop out on Willie's forehead, that Ursitti remembered the magic words. They came from a member of the audience, another question for the Fatman.

"Did you ever play . . . *Mosconi?*"

The silence lasted a moment and just a moment. It was like a sudden whooshing vacuum had enveloped the room, like the air had been sucked out—leaving only an unsettling anticipation of what might come next to fill the void. Ursitti remembered it. Christopher remembered it. The audience must have felt it.

Did . . . you . . . ever . . . play . . . Mosconi?

Fats, incredibly, seemed to have lost his voice. Incredibly, he seemed to have been taken aback. Here, he must choose his words carefully. Mosconi, the Old Lion, sat at his back, glowering; his eager fans sat before him, waiting. It was a moment fraught with both peril and promise for Minnesota Fats, Willie Mosconi, and all of American pool.

Fats took a breath and then answered indirectly: "I played 'em all and I beat 'em all." It was a rare moment of discretion for the hustling storyteller, but it did not matter.

"It was like Carl Lewis off the starting blocks," recalled Ursitti. "I swear to Christ—for a guy sixty-something years old he would have beat Carl Lewis for the first thirty feet."

Mosconi was *off*. He had his cue in one hand; he looked as if he might strike Fats with it. His eyes were ablaze. The speed with which Mosconi had lost himself to the anger stunned Ursitti, Howard Cosell, Bruce Christopher, and, probably most of all, Minnesota Fats.

"You beat *me*? You beat *me*? *You beat me??*"

"They're face to face, toe to toe, belly to belly," recalled Ursitti. "Willie is sixty-four years old, and Fatty is sixty-four years old, and they're screaming. They're waving their cues. 'You *bum*,' Willie says, 'You *never* beat anybody in your *life*. . . . I played you in Philadelphia, and I beat you five games in a row. . . .'"

Willie is going crazy.

"We played your game, one-pocket, and I had to give you train fare home!" He was ranting. He was screaming.

"My dad was doing color for that match on TV, and Fats was going on like Fats usually did, and my father just *exploded*—they had to restrain him," Willie's son Bill recalled years later. "'I'll play you right now,' he said. 'I've been trying to play you for years, to shut you up.' My dad couldn't stand anyone saying they could beat him, let alone Fats. He was beside himself, wanting to play him.

"Fats was a great talker, and he was an entertainer, which my father was not. My father was very quiet and modest. He was the antithesis of Minnesota Fats. The only thing my father cared about was winning. And if anybody said they could beat him, his first reaction was, 'Let's get on the table.' That's what he always did."

And so it was during that moment—a moment prompted by a loose wire or a blown fuse—that the spark took. Ursitti stood between Willie and Fats, and he watched them rant and rave and wave their cues, and for a moment Ursitti thought that he might lose an eye. There could be blood drawn that day. Willie was *that*

16

angry. It was a moment of dead TV air but electrified with promise. *Let them have at it,* thought Ursitti. *Let them show the world who really is best!*

The idea came like a thunderbolt, as epiphanies often do.

"Man, they were screaming," Ursitti recalled. "I've never seen Mosconi so mad. 'You bum, you never beat anybody in your *life.*' That's what he said. His jugular was popping out. And it was then that the idea hit me to have Willie play Fats. The lightbulb went off over my head: this was the next match."

The match between Minnesota Fats and Bruce "Superstroke" Christopher never made it onto TV, and the world was no more a sad place for it. Although technicians got the camera working, and they got Mosconi settled down, and Fats did his trick shots, the made-for-TV train wreck continued unabated. Days after shooting wrapped, technicians hit another snag in the editing room. The resulting footage was unusable, the show stillborn, dead.

It was a bona fide TV disaster. But that's not important. This is what's important: without that broken camera, without Mosconi's towering ego, without that fight that no one would see, without Ursitti's thunderstroke of an idea, without the frauds that were Superstroke Christopher and Minnesota Fats—there would never have been that later pool match, the most celebrated in the history of the sport. What Ursitti had created was the most important TV disaster in the history of American pocket billiards.

But what's important is what came next.

Chapter 4

THE KINGDOM

This dwelling of Odysseus is noble, easily picked out
and recognizable amongst many. See how it rises stage
beyond stage with its courts all properly walled and
coped, and its double doors so securely hung. No man
could reckon it cheap. And I can tell there are many
men banqueting within, and the smell of meat hangs
round, and loudly rings the lyre which the Gods have
made to chime so well with feasts.

— The *Odyssey*

Extraordinary and marvelous academies, earnest newspaper write-ups, professionals reigning like kings—these things marked American pocket billiards in 1887. The game had not peaked, not yet, but clearly it was a fine and beautiful time. Historian Melvin Adelman[9] tells us that pocket billiards was on the move then, growing from a sometimes-confused pastime into a modern sport. There were already professional events in 1887, and magazines and books . . . and even a first-ever national tournament at New York's Racquet and Tennis Club. The *New York Times* that year ran sixty-one separate items about billiards.

For students of pocket billiards, 1887 was also notable for another reason. It was in that year, on September 17, that there appears the

---

[9] Melvin Adelman, author of *A Sporting Time: New York City and the Rise of Modern Athletics.*

first recorded documentation of one of Willie Mosconi's line in America. According to family genealogy records Domencio Moscone (the family then spelled its name with an "e") forsook in 1887 all allegiance to the king of Italy and in so doing was given U.S. citizenship. Domencio was Willie Mosconi's grandfather. He lived in Philadelphia[10] and like most Mosconis was a hardworking Roman Catholic.

Not much is known about Domencio. According to family stories, he emigrated from the Italian village of Fontana Rossa, just outside Genoa, probably around 1877.[11] In the United States he married Maria Galuppo, perhaps of Medica, Italy. Family records do not reveal when or where the marriage took place, the age of the couple, their residence, or even their occupations. What's clear, however, is that Domencio and Maria sired Guiseppe Mosconi, better known as Joseph, who was born on February 8, 1891, and who was baptized at Philadelphia's St. Mary DePazzi's Catholic Church three weeks later.

Joseph was a rough kid and though small got a bully's reputation. He played baseball and like all kids shot some pool, but mostly Joseph boxed. And he had some success at it. Family records indicate that Joseph went pro early in life, quickly racked up a winning record, and at one time was ranked third in the country. He fought under the professional name "Charlie Russell" as a bantamweight. "Everybody was afraid of him," recalled his grandson Bill. "I don't know how good he was as a boxer—you know, Philadelphia has a long tradition of boxers, and he was a small guy. But he was tough, so nobody messed with him."

Joseph managed to find a good woman, Helen C. Riley, the daughter of an Irish grocer. He lived in an Italian neighborhood; she lived with

---

[10] Part of the family settled in Calfiornia and continued spelling their name "Moscone," with an "e" on the end. They eventually produced a famous big-city mayor, George Moscone of San Francisco. Moscone perhaps gained his greatest fame in death: he was assassinated (along with city supervisor Harvey Milk) by supervisor Dan White on November 27, 1978. Before his murder, Mayor Moscone would sometimes entertain his world-champion relative during the pool player's tournament stops in San Francisco.

[11] This perhaps was not his first appearance in America, as there is some evidence that Domencio also came earlier to the United States in the company of several brothers, and then together they returned to Italy before coming back a second time to settle for good. On the return trip the brothers went west to Denver and Domencio east to Philly.

the Irish. It was a South Philly working-class Montague and Capulet courtship and one probably frowned upon then by friends and family. But no matter: they married on May 7, 1912, and then Helen, within that first year of marriage, gave birth to twin boys. Records show the twins died shortly after childbirth or died as infants.

By this time Joseph likely would have retired from the ring and was either doing "dental work" (there is some reference to that in one family document) or running his gym in South Philly, on Eighth and Wharton. There, sweaty men would pound leather bags, skip rope, and curse violently. The gym also included pool tables—four, set up near the front—where the fighters could unwind with a few games, or where Joseph himself would play, probably straight pool but maybe rotation,[12] because that game then was also popular. Combining pool with boxing was a money-making stroke of pure genius, as bachelor pursuits were then near the height of their popularity in America.

The reason: there were simply more bachelors then, at least as measured as a proportion of the overall population. Likewise, those men who eventually did marry would do so later in life. And all these men needed gathering places, retreats from feminized society, and so a sort of bachelor culture appeared in places like taverns and barber shops. But boxing gynmasiums also served the purpose and most especially poolrooms. Instinctively, Joseph Mosconi understood the age.

• • •

Industry reps agree that the game was then in full bloom—but they place the time of its peak even more precisely. According to Brunswick, the number-one year for pool in America, the year when manufacturers sold the most tables and the game reached its highest pinnacle, was 1913. If ever a special star appeared over the noble sport of pocket billiards, it came then. Bachelor men flooded into the rooms; tournaments received front-page coverage in the *New York Times;* A. C. McClung &

---

[12] In rotation games, balls are pocketed in numerical order.

Company published *Daly's Billiards Book* that year, which achieved a larger sale in its first decade than had ever been achieved by *any* other book on sports or gaming.

Without a doubt, 1913 was a magical year. Alfredo De Oro, Jerome Keogh,[13] Charles "Cowboy" Weston—the names of these pool champions were on the lips of men and boys alike; their fame outstripped that of most professional sports figures, including those who played baseball. Pool in 1913 was glitzy show business and hard-knuckled sports and New York–nights pizzazz.

But mostly, professional pocket billiards, in 1913, was just *big*.

And so it must have seemed right and just, and a sure sign that the pocket-billiard stars had just then aligned, that in 1913 there came the birth of a man who stood above the ruck of others, a man who could outstrip De Oro and Jerome Keogh and Cowboy Weston and every other American pool player ever born: it was the half-Irish/half-Italian son of Joseph Mosconi and Helen Riley, and his name was Willie, and one day he would lord over all.

•　•　•

Willie appears to have been brought into this world by either a midwife or what then would have been a great rarity, a female physician. The date was June 27. Family records do not reveal the exact moment of Willie's birth or its location or provide further details of the labor and delivery. One document simply notes that William Mosconi was the third child born living to Helen Riley (by then, the older twin brothers were dead) and that the professional woman Ellen Beck assisted with the delivery.[14]

---

[13] Jerome Keogh, who won his first world championship during a New York City straight-pool tournament in 1897, said this about the poolhalls of that time: "Despite the vaunted glamour of the great billiard academies of the gay nineties . . . the fact was that during this period 'nice' young men stole surreptitiously through the by-ways of the night to enter them, lest detection should result in the stigma of being 'fast.' . . . The game struggled against the dictates of society, the raising of eyebrows, and the word 'pool' uttered with caustic venom."

[14] His Roman Catholic baptism came a month later, on July 31, at the Church of Annunciation, Tenth and Dickenson, in Philadelphia.

Sometime before Willie's fourth or fifth birthday, his father closed the boxing gym and opened (in a nearby American Legion Hall) a small poolroom. The Mosconis lived on the second floor. The poolhall was on the first, and the building had three floors in all. The room had several tables, probably 5 by 10s, but also some pocketless tables for billiards, as that game was then quite popular. Willie always recalled hearing the collision of balls from his upstairs bedroom.

He was a boy, just five or so, but already a seed had been planted. The *smack* of ivory against ivory. The shouts of big men. The glimpse of bright color on dark felt. Willie Mosconi may never really have *loved* pool, never adored it like other players, but the sport was undeniably part of who Willie Mosconi was. It was like family, religion, ethnicity—things that take root in a man before he's fully formed. It was like a childhood neighborhood that one grows to despise but can never really leave. It was like . . . *blood,* and for Willie Mosconi it preceded memory. It preceded identity.[15]

Mosconi never could remember all the stories. His uncles had reminded him how he was, or he'd get a glimpse of himself from something his father told him about, and sometimes the stories were contradictory, with Willie retelling them one way to one journalist and then another to someone else. But what seems certain is that Willie saw plenty of pool as he scampered about his father's poolroom, rolling balls, bugging customers, torturing his father. Willie also told of sneaking into the poolroom at night, of scrambling barefoot down a rain pipe that ran just outside his window. He said it may have been the poolhall concession stand that drew him, the pies and sweets there, but it was pocket billiards that kept him rooted. "You know how kids are; I used to raid the place for pie, candy, and chewing gum," Willie said in a 1984 interview. "And I'd sneak down and try to play. I was fascinated just by the balls rolling on the table. I used to play for hours, just rolling the balls back and forth." Eventually he took up a cue,

---

[15] Plenty of the all-time greats were the children of poolhall owners, including former world champion Babe Cranfield, whose dad owned the famous Cranfield Room near Yankee Stadium, and Jean Balukas, one of America's greatest-ever woman players.

which at fifty-seven or fifty-eight inches tall would have been a foot taller than Willie himself.

Now Joseph Mosconi, the fiery and intimidating former bantamweight, was none too pleased with these moonlight excursions and so locked the balls and cues in a cabinet at night. But it made no difference. Instead of a cue, Willie would use a broomstick. Instead of balls, Willie would use potatoes, the roundest ones he could find—all stolen from his mother's cupboard. "I knocked them all over the table, but of course they left their mark," Mosconi said in his autobiography, written with Stanley Cohen. "One time the skins started peeling, and the juice smeared the cloth so bad I couldn't clean it, and boy, did I catch hell. But I still hung around there whenever I could, and I was watching the players more and more intently." Willie confessed that he also once ripped a deep gash in the cloth of one of the tables, right precisely at the center, and did about $40 worth of damage.

What's a father to do? How could he keep his son away from the sport, away from pool? Willie's dad loved the game, played it well, probably gambled even—but associated the sport, quite rightly, with the working class. As with boxing, pool seemed a tawdry pursuit. What he wanted for Willie was a life more delicate. Better to get him out of the poolhall altogether, better to encourage some other interest, better *anything* than letting him keep company with old men all day.

Uncle Charlie, Joseph's brother, ran the South Philadelphia Dance Academy, a dance studio, and was the father of several accomplished vaudeville dancers. These talented cousins toured with the Ziegfeld Follies, tapped and ballroom danced, performed acrobatic stunts; and even shared the bill on occasion with Fred and Astele Astaire.[16] "The Dancing Mosconis" were successful. They were big time. What else do you call a troupe that headlined the Palace Theater fifty-eight times? Clearly, professional dancing was a lucrative business for the family—

---

[16] Fred Astaire was a lifelong friend of Willie Mosconi and the Mosconi clan generally. Astaire was also said to play a fair game of pool.

and one in which Joseph's son might find a place. It was the summer of 1919, and the boy was just barely six years old.

But again, it made no difference.

First off, Willie made a piss-poor dancer. Awful. "I tripped all over the place," he recalled of his days at the South Philadelphia Dance Academy. There was a cigar store out front, the rehearsal studio was out back, and there was a single pool table there in the studio, where Uncle Charlie practiced by himself. Willie would take his joyless tap lessons and then predictably wander off to the pool table, where he would wait for his father to pick him up. Sometimes he waited a long time.

"I soon found there was much more to the game of pool; you have to attain a knowledge of the game, you have to be a good shot maker, but that's not all. Study the bank shots, learn how to get around the balls and become a good position player, work on all the shots that give you trouble." He learned some of this from his Uncle Charlie, who himself was a fairly decent player, and some by practicing shots he witnessed in his father's poolroom.

After about a month, he could run a rack. Before long, he could run even more. Uncle Charlie witnessed some of this, actually watched the boy run off fifteen balls before his very eyes, and then watched as he freakishly began a second run. Uncle Charlie was flabbergasted. He shook his head. He told Willie's Dad: *Your kid's got talent. Real talent.* Joseph Mosconi refused to encourage the boy, would not even consider it; but Willie kept practicing, kept playing, and then one day the inevitable occurred. A man came into his father's poolroom, a grown-up man, and he was looking for a game. Willie's dad wouldn't play him—he was preoccupied with bills or paperwork, or maybe he was reading the newspaper, but neither did he notice when his son took up the challenge.

The stranger was amused. *Let's see what you can do, young feller.* And so Willie got up, little Willie, no older than seven, and he pocketed one ball and then another and another and another. He ran five balls, six balls, seven balls. He kept running: 11, 12, 13, 14, *rack! 15, 16, 17, 18, 19, 20, 21.* The run went on and on, it just kept going, and it went quick, with Willie slowed only by the inconvenience of the large wooden box, the one he shuffled back and forth to stand upon so he could properly reach the table. *Holy Christ.* The man stood wide eyed, amazed. He could only laugh. And it was then that his father looked up from his paperwork.

•   •   •

In 1919, when Joseph Mosconi first took note of his son's preternatural talent, the game then taking root in America was 14.1 Continuous—also known as straight pool.[17] It had become the official game of pocket billiards the year before Willie's birth, and as the boy grew to dominance, so too did the game. Prior to the 1960s, straight pool would define the game's greatest champions; it was the only game featured in national-class tournaments; it was the only sort seen on TV. Not eight-ball, not nine-ball. For fifty years at least, straight pool *was* pocket billiards.

The rules are simple, austerely so. In straight pool, the player can select any ball—solid or stripes—and send it to any pocket. Every pocketed ball counts for exactly one point. It is called "continuous" because of a rule unique in cue sports,[18] the so-called "key ball" rule. Under it the last ball of every rack gets left on the table before the next rack begins. This is far different from, say, nine-ball or eight-ball, in which the competition ends when the last object ball goes down. In 14.1 Continuous the player must always consider the final resting place of that one last ball because he'll need it to break open the next rack.

---

[17] Straight pool was invented by champion Jerome Keogh in 1910 as a variation of the then-dominant tournament game, Continuous Pool, which in turn was a variation of another game known as Fifteen-Ball Pool. In 1911, a year after straight pool's introduction, the *New York Times* observed that the then-new format "warrants any amount of maneuvering for position on the last ball, which provided a decidedly interesting factor in the game." Mike Shamos, in his *New Illustrated Encyclopedia of Billiards*, shares several interesting and bizarre facts about straight pool, including this one: the number of possible initial racking arrangements in the game is 6,227,020,800.

[18] For the official rules of straight pool, eight-ball, and other pocket-billiard games, check out the *BCA Official Rule and Record Book*, available at your local bookstore.

So, for example, a player runs one, two, three, four, five balls, runs them all except one—and that last ball he leaves on the table. He reracks the remaining fourteen and then attempts to continue the run. Now, if he has left that final ball well positioned, he can use a single stroke to simultaneously pocket it and open up the new rack. A single stroke, and the cue ball slams into the last ball, pockets it, and then the cue ball ricochets away to slam into the rack of fourteen, opening it like a flower. That leaves more target balls and the run can continue. Hence the name "continuous."

The first player to reach some predetermined number of points (remember, one ball equals one point) wins the game. This may seem simple, this notion of potting any ball into any pocket, but it is not. Achieving even modest runs can be crazy-making difficult. "It requires intense concentration, superb position play, defensive maneuvering, and all-around shot-making ability," explains billiards historian Mike Shamos. "Luck is virtually no factor." The fairly serious amateur may go through life never having run much more than a couple of racks and typically running quite a bit less. Willie Mosconi was freakishly running multiple racks by age seven. It was like attaining master-class status in chess while still in grade school.

And so with the pool gods looking favorably upon the eldest son of Joseph Mosconi, so finally too did Joseph Mosconi himself. He suddenly realized the boy's potential. Practice, he said. Practice as much as you like. And practice Willie did: running rack after rack, day after day, colored balls and bank shots, knee pants and an apple crate. It was mesmerizing, magical, captivating, watching this boy, so small, so young, but with such unexpected grace. And it wasn't just the proud father who thought so. In trying to separate his son from the poolroom, Joseph Mosconi had gone about it all wrong. Rather than driving customers away, Little Willie actually attracted business. This boy wasn't a pest, he was a *gold mine*.

Joseph contacted Uncle Charlie, a man well acquainted with show business, and this is what Charlie suggested: posters, a fancy made-up title, and exhibitions. Remember, there was no TV in 1919, no

TV sports—but pocket billiards at that time was near the height of its popularity. Charlie said there was money to make off this boy. *He'll take Philly by storm!* Hence, the creation of the young "Child Prodigy" of pool—except prodigy somehow got misspelled as "protege" on the posters.

The first exhibitions were in Joseph Mosconi's own room, but before long he was performing them elsewhere. The posters went up, word of mouth spread. At $25 per appearance, Willie was making enough to buy his family's groceries, although Willie, personally, received little or nothing. In his autobiography he listed his typical "take" as an iced soda and a pat on the back.

Willie also suggested in his memoirs that he gained the approval of his fiery-tempered father through this father-and-son enterprise, as if they then and there forged a wonderful lifelong bond. But this belies the testimony of others and even Willie's own words, published elsewhere, hinting at a long-lived and deep-seated friction between Willie and Joseph Mosconi. Ironically enough, pool itself may have been the source of some of that ill will.

Willie's dad made pool something other than fun for the boy. No longer goofing off on Uncle Charlie's back table, no longer slinging balls on his father's pool tables, suddenly pocket billiards became get-up-in-the-morning work. "First my dad was trying to stop me from learning the game," he said, "but now he was trying to ram it down my throat." Instead of being kept off the tables, Willie was *forced* to practice. The exhibitions became a never-ending carousel, enticing, exciting, torturous, exhausting. Poolhalls were everywhere, pool players were everywhere, money was everywhere. Young Willie performed like a trained monkey.

And what did Willie's mother Helen think of all this? Was she alarmed that her little boy spent so much time in the exclusive refuge of old men with their cursing and their gambling? Was she distraught at the performance schedule, the pressure? Maybe her familiarity with the Dancing Mosconis made it seem less surreal. But what of the police raids? There were *laws* against children in poolhalls. And yet there he was, her precious son dressed in knee pants and a giant bow tie, just eight, just nine—and sometimes the terrified main attraction when the harness bulls came stampeding up the stairs. Once at the old National Billiard Academy, Thirteenth and Market, the cops shut down the whole show. It was a two-day exhibition with fellow child star Ruth McGinness. Willie was seven, she was ten. He ran forty balls the first day; the police threatened everybody's arrest the second.

Helen Riley could not have liked it—but she may have kept her mouth shut. Joseph Mosconi was a hard man and possibly abusive. Here's a story: Once when Willie Mosconi was an old man he fell apart in a heap, sobbing, right there in front of his son. Willie Mosconi was never one to open up much, but sometimes, at the end of a man's life, the torture of it breaks through. Suddenly Willie was that little boy again, helpless, the child prodigy, and he remembered his father being so mean, so *angry*. He bullied Willie's mother mercilessly. And he demanded every penny Willie made from playing pool. And there was nothing, nothing, the boy could do about it.

"Remember, he was very tough, he was an ex-professional boxer—and all my father's brothers were scared of him," said Bill Mosconi, Willie's son. "And when my dad was much older, during the end of his life, he got really sobby with me one day in the car. He said that his father had been so mean to his mother; he was sorry that he was never able to do anything. He was [just a little kid], and he never had a home life because he was out working."

By 1922 Willie no longer loved the game, nor even really liked it much, and so this boy who would one day become the sport's greatest champion found the courage to give up pocket billiards. He was just nine years old when he announced his first retirement. "I was sick of the game," he said. Joseph Mosconi's disappointment must have been unbearable.

Chapter 5

ODYSSEUS AND EURYMACHUS

I want to be a Sultan!
— Young Minnesota Fats in a comment to his father

He would have been fatter than Willie Mosconi, and louder, and, if possible, even more aggravatingly nervous. He required less order in his life (and after growing to manhood was less controlling of others). He was a vulgar child, filthy and foul-mouthed. He was slatternly, while Willie was fastidious. He was affable, while Willie was ill-tempered. He could not stop eating. He never told the truth. He was, in style and substance, as far removed from the Child Prodigy of Pool as a pauper to a young prince.

And yet Rudolf Walter Wanderone would nonetheless follow a strikingly similar path. The two boys would not have met one another, not then, not when Willie was abandoning pool and Rudolf was just then taking it up. They would never have seen each other at exhibitions, or traded racks in straight pool, or even played stickball together. They lived miles apart—Willie in South Philly and Rudolf in the Washington Heights neighborhood of New York City. But their lives kept to a parallel course nonetheless. It was as if they walked together upon the twin rails of a railroad track: never crossing yet plowing ahead to the same destination.

Both, for instance, had fathers who nudged them into show business. For Mosconi, it was the Dancing Mosconis; for Wanderone it was the vaudeville strongman act. In his autobiography, Wanderone says his father, a Swiss immigrant, would sometimes entertain the crowd during neighborhood festivals with prodigious feats of strength. And then Rudolf Jr. said he'd go on stage and lift weights like they were basketballs. "I always brought down the house because I was like six or eight years old with the most beautiful reddish blond curly hair you ever saw," he said.

But the vaudeville circuit didn't take, either for Mosconi or Wanderone—and so both fell to pool instead. Willie shot his exhibitions in Philly, escorted by his father; Wanderone performed them in the New York City neighborhoods, likely at poolhalls also introduced to him by his father. And both appeared with (and sometimes were matched up against) top-notch talent. For instance, early photos of Willie Mosconi show him with the great Ralph Greenleaf, the only American with a pocket-billiards legacy that would rival his own.[19] Wanderone, who would have been at least a young teenager when he played his exhibitions, faced the so-called masked-marvel players, who were pros typically hired by the Coca-Cola Company.[20] Wanderone also claimed to have beat Cowboy Weston, a former nine-ball champion, in a much-heralded Washington Heights exhibition.

Further similarities: Both Mosconi and Wanderone came from Roman Catholic families with strong ties to old Europe. For Mosconi it was Italy. For Wanderone it was Switzerland, which was the birthplace of both his parents and at least one of his half sisters. Although it's unclear when Wanderone's father arrived in the United States, evidence suggests that his then twenty-seven-year-old mother Rosa came through Ellis Island in 1909 as a passenger aboard the 607-foot-long

---

[19] One promotional poster notes that young Willie pocketed forty-six balls to Greenleaf's fifty in an exhibition of straight pool. Greenleaf predicted the boy would one day become a world champion.

[20] Masked players would appear unannounced in neighborhood rooms, challenge the best players, typically beat them, and then slip away mysteriously. Coca-Cola reps followed the exhibition with a round of soda. Among these players was Andrew St. Jean, a monster of straight pool and an expert banker. The gimmick was further evidence of the insane popularity that pool then enjoyed.

King Alexander, a vessel then flying under the German flag. The ship manifest shows that the vessel arrived on July 25.[21]

Likewise, both Mosconi and Wanderone grew up in three-story tenement buildings in big-city ethnic neighborhoods. In Wanderone's case it was a brownstone at 403 West 148th Street in Washington Heights, which was that part of upper Manhattan then popular among Swiss immigrants.[22] Wanderone shared the home near St. Nicholaus Avenue with his three half sisters and a brother-in-law.

But beyond all that—beyond similarities in the course of their early lives, and their family backgrounds, and the influence of their fathers—there is the strange accident of their very births. Remember, the billiards industry calls 1913 the sport's greatest year. The media loved pool then. Poolrooms blanketed the nation; instructional books became top sellers. And for some strange reason, 1913 was also the birth year of these two great men. Rudolf Wanderone was born January 19. Willie Mosconi was born five months later.

These two men would grow up. They would accomplish great things. They would come to embody this sport of emperors and scoundrels like no one else, before or since. Mosconi would become the sport's greatest champion. He would, in fact, become one of the most dominating players *in all of sports*. Wanderone became pool's most famous hustler —one of the great trickster figures of the twentieth century.

---

[21] Records further indicate that Rosa paid her own fare, that she was in possession of $50, and that she had visited the United States at least one time previously. Her height was listed as five feet ten inches, her complexion as fair, her hair as blonde, and her eyes as blue. The purpose of her voyage was to visit Rudolf Sr., whom she oddly listed as her brother, not her spouse. Other evidence suggests she may have told this lie to sidestep some problem with immigration.

[22] The building is listed (along with the names of his parents, Rosa and Rudolf Sr.) in 1930 business and probate announcements from the *New York Times*. Census data from 1930 also shows seven lodgers apparently not associated with the Wanderone clan at 403 West 148th Street. What it does not list, however, is Wanderone's father, Rudolf Sr. Instead it references Rosa as the head of the household. This means either that the census workers made a mistake or that the couple suffered a rocky relationship (and Rudolf Sr. then lived outside the home), or that Rudolf Sr. did not have his immigration papers in order, so hid from the government census workers.

Chapter 6

ROADMEN
1977

I never wanted to go into pool as a lifelong profession.
— Willie Mosconi

Jim Jacobs, back then, had an office at 9 East Fortieth Street, in Manhattan. He shared it with Bill Cayton, fifty-nine years old, and together they managed Big Fights, a production company behind the televised *Guinness Book of World Record* events but also responsible for some of the biggest boxing events of the 1970s and '80s. Cayton, for instance, managed Mike Tyson early in his career and also took on Wilfred Benitez and Edwin Rosario. But on October 22, when Willie and Fats were squaring off and losing their minds in the Hilton Room of the Waldorf-Astoria, Cayton was neither promoting nor managing—he was home in traction. He had suffered a serious back injury some weeks earlier, and so Ursitti then was dealing mostly with Jacobs.

"Did you see—did you see what happened?" Ursitti had gotten Jacobs on the phone. "All hell was breaking loose. Those guys were going to *kill* each other."

"I saw," said Jacobs.

"Jimmy—do you realize what you've got here?" Ursitti was talking fast now. He gets that way when he's excited. "You've got the two greatest names in the sport. You've got the legendary hustler in Fats. And you have the legendary champion of all times in Mosconi. . . ."

"I saw. . . ."

"This could be something *big*. . . ."

As a fight promoter Jacobs knew there was money to be made from rancor and bile—and both flowed forth in beautiful abundance when Fats and Mosconi were together. It was well-known that Fats spoke only one language: trash talk. Even his prodigous appetite and inhuman snoring became the subject of it. As for bile—that was all Willie Mosconi. It was as if he had reached down into some deep dark recess of his soul and come up with the pure stuff. So . . . put them together in front of a national audience, give them cue sticks and microphones. With the proper mix of hype and production values, Mosconi and Fats would create piles of money. "It didn't take a brain surgeon," said Ursitti.

The problem is there had been talk for years of such a matchup, and so far it had never happened. Jacobs said it himself: *Can we lure them out? Can we get them to play?* Once, with the backing of a Philadelphia investor, Mosconi had extended an open and public challenge to Fats—$20,000, winner takes all—but Fats either never received the challenge or chose to ignore it. Mosconi even spent one afternoon in a West Philly exhibition hall waiting for Fats to show. "I've offered to spot him 250 balls in a championship match of straight pool," Mosconi had recalled. And now Mosconi was in retirement. How to get Fats to play now? How to get Fats to the table? Skeptics said it would never happen. They actually placed wagers against it.

To Jim Jacobs and his partner Bill Cayton (still recuperating then from the debilitating back injury) fell the responsibility of making the pitch. First they called Mosconi, then Fats, then their TV connections, and then one called Mosconi again, and then Fats. There was haggling over contracts, times, and venue. "Fats was quicker to respond," recalled Ursitti. "He said, 'I'll play. I'm the best player in the world—I'll play."

But what finally drew Mosconi out of retirement was the money. "That's the cold hard fact of it," said Ursitti. The agreed-upon fee for Mosconi was $60,000. It was the biggest payday in Willie's career.

With the haggling done, Jacobs and Cayton then summoned Ursitti to their Manhattan office at 9 East Fortieth Street. There he received a contract, a check, and a mission: drive down to Haddon Heights, New Jersey, and deliver a $15,000 deposit and a contract to Willie. And this Ursitti dutifully accomplished the next day. He motored ninety minutes down the New Jersey Turnpike in his giant two-door Lincoln Towne Car. It was a cool autumn morning, but Willie and his wife Flora were waiting in the front yard. Flora brewed up a pot of coffee, and Willie signed the papers. Ursitti produced the deposit check from his briefcase, and then he was on his way.

Two days later Ursitti boarded a plane for Chicago. The weather by then had changed violently—the snow was coming down, the visibility was nothing, but Fats was there waiting at O'Hare. The fat pool hustler had motored all the way up from his home in Dowell, in southern Illinois, about three hours away. He wanted his damn money. "I remember it took maybe ten minutes, and then his name was on that contract, too," said Ursitti. "I got on a pay phone and called Big Fights immediately. I said 'It's inked; I have it.' We had a deal."

Chapter 7

A NATION OF ROTTWEILERS

I'm not a poolhall guy.

— Willie Mosconi

Here, then, enthusiasm mounts, and state after state cedes its authority, and America remakes itself as a nation without liquor. Saloons close. Beer comes off store shelves. Gangsterism explodes. On January 16, 1920, just as the Child Prodigy of Pool launched his short-lived exhibition career and Rudolf Wanderone was lifting barbells in Manhattan, America ratified the Eighteenth Amendment to its Constitution. America had become a nation of battling Rottweilers.

During those days between January 16, 1920, and December 5, 1933, during Prohibition, one finds the pure embodiment of America's unending Culture War. But look hard at this failed experiment that was Prohibition—at the placard-carrying moralists and the violence and the drunkeness and the whole sorry contradictory state of things—and also find the conflict that resides within the soul of pocket billiards, a sport that has never truly understood itself. The teetotalers went to war with the hell-raisers. Self-mastery and saturnalia vied for the upper hand. And like a tiny reflection of this great national zeitgeist, we find a contradictory sport marked both by excessive appetites and puritanical aspirations. As with Prohibition generally, the great protagonists of pool waged tireless war against the improper. Like the age itself, pool is marked by rogues and by those who would exert over themselves towering levels of control.

Was it mere coincidence or was there some cause-and-effect reason behind the curious fact that pool was then near the height of its popularity? Was it mere coincidence that its two most celebrated players, Willie Mosconi and Minnesota Fats, both came of age during Prohibition? Was it mere coincidence that we find that same startling dichotomy of high-minded ideals and wanton recklessness in the characters of these two players? No other age better exemplifies America's unending Culture War, and no other age better exemplifies the noble sport of pocket billiards. It is as if the age served as both the game's mother and its father.

In his *Only Yesterday: An Informal History of the 1920s,* historian Frederick Allen Lewis theorizes that Americans molded their Eighteenth Amendment from the same uncompromising spartanism that had brought them victory over Germany. Americans credited their abstinence during World War I with their success abroad and so figured the nation could become more successful still with a total and permanent ban on booze. Lewis said Americans had become well acquainted with Wilsonian notions of Utopia and self-sacrifice during World War I, and so this New Spartanism seemed not too great a leap.

But of course it was. It was madness. No whiskey, no beer, no carousing, *no fun.* As one *New York Tribune* reporter put it, it was as if the nation had been swept away on a windless ocean, compelled by some lunatic force no one could see. It was a state of affairs that simply could not last. And so by 1925 the secret speakeasies were doing brisk business, and the casinos had spread to cities large and small, and American crime lords were murdering each other with great abandon. The dirty politicians took over; the dirty cops kept order.

Wrote Lewis: "The prohibition law—that curious final product of the revolt of the American conscience—had not been long on the books before people began to flout it right and left; pretty soon a great many men and women who had always considered themselves patterns of law-abiding respectability began to patronize bootleggers, or home brew very peculiar beer, or concoct even queerer bathtub gin, or wear hip-pocket flasks to parties."

Much of the fuel of that mad decade (an exploding postwar economy, a multitude of worldly bachelors, a revolution of morality and manners) made for a vibrant poolroom scene. They were everywhere, the poolrooms with their dark burnished woods, their clouds of wafting smoke, the soft clicking of ivory upstairs and down. According to sociologist Ned Polsky, there existed ten times as many poolhalls per capita then as existed during the last years of the twentieth century. And these were big rooms with scores and scores of tables: places like Allingers in Philadelphia, or Fox Billiard Academy, or Jullians in New York.

"The war introduced a lot of the rural population to cities. That had as much influence on the rising popularity of pool as anything else," said Polsky. "Keep in mind that a tremendous part of the population back then was farm raised, and so the war got a lot of farm kids introduced to the cities. These kids had not been off the farm, even in their own state, before they got shippped overseas."

The poolrooms typically operated separately from the secret speakeasies, but both establishments vied for the same just-back-from-the-war clientele and became targets for the preachers, for the moralists, and for meddlesome women. In Texas in 1919, women pressured the legislature to ban poolrooms altogether. The Woman's Christian Temperance Union,[23] an organization formed in 1874 to combat alcohol, also went on the rampage against poolrooms in New York, Ohio, Illinois, and other states.

According to billiards historian Mike Shamos, one of the Temperance Union's followers was so "profoundly impressed with the idea that the billiard table is a toboggan slide to perdition, and that whoever plays thereon is destined to an eternity of exceeding discomfort" that she attacked a room single-handedly. "To do what she could in her feeble way toward the suppression of this evil, she entered a billiard saloon alone, gathered a pyramid of pool balls in her overskirt, and proceeded

---

[23] The Woman's Christian Temperance Union considers itself to be the oldest continuing nonsectarian woman's organization in the world. According to information provided by the group, it grew out of an effort by Mrs. Esther McNeil, an early prohibitionist, who led a group of disruptive but high-minded ladies into a Fredonia, New York, saloon on December 22, 1873.

to make some fancy shots. Her proficiency was so great that she smashed everything in the place, and then went her way sustained and soothed by an unfaltering trust in the wisdom and propriety of her action." [24]

Shamos likewise notes that a group of fifty or so revivalists raided a poolroom on Sixty-third Street in New York City in January of 1911. "Singing hymns, the raiders descended on the players," the historian reported, quoting a contemporary newspaper account of the assault. "In a few moments pool tables were deserted and the room converted into a meeting house. By prayer and preaching the erstwhile pool players were led to see the error of their ways and left the place."

Of course, there is nothing inherently wrong with the game, nothing about pool balls and billiard tables and break shots that should inspire such wrath. Far from being a "toboggan slide to perdition," pool, when played correctly, represents excellence, self-mastery, and the *ultimate* in subordination. Consider this: In what other sport does a human being exert more control over a ball? Not basketball, baseball, or golf. Not bowling. It's straight pool, nine-ball and eight-ball. It's the pocketless variety of billiards, where a great player must have a sense, *and a very clear sense*, of where and how three balls will move and cease to move. Muscle memory, touch, speed control—as much as the scoundrels and the speakeasies, these things define pocket billiards.

Like the decade itself (and even the American people and the nation's history), the American poolroom is defined by subjugation and wildness, good breeding and bad. Mosconi played one side of that equation; Rudolf Wanderone hustled the other. Both men grew to adulthood during the thirteen years of Prohibition, with Fats boasting of saloons and whores and "making . . . whoopie from morning to night." Mosconi told of sacrifice and deprivation.

•   •   •

---

[24] As cited by Shamos in an April 2004 *Billiards Digest* article about an autobiography of Temperance Union founder Carry A. Nation. But perhaps the six-foot, 180-pound Carry A. Nation would have been better called "Carry A. Hatchet." According to Shamos, the temperance union warrior would sometimes physically attack saloons with an axe, often leaving them in shambles.

Mosconi started out as Philadelphia's adorable and proper "Child Prodigy" of pool, or even the "Juvenile Champion," playing exhibitions through 1924 with the likes of Ruth McGinniss and the great Ralph Greenleaf. But by age eleven he was sick of it. Utterly sick. So Willie exchanged that life for one of stickball and public school. "It was like having a weight lifted from my shoulders," he said. After Barrett Junior High, Mosconi went to South Philadelphia High, where, like Wanderone, he dropped out early—probably by his sophomore year. He said he did this at his father's insistence, and that he was then enrolled, more or less against his will, in business school. He did not graduate.[25]

On October 17, 1929, the stock market collapsed and along with it the American economy. More than $100 billion vanished in an instant. Factories closed. Millions lost their jobs. Misfortune never comes when it's convenient, but for the Mosconis it came just as the family was dealing with horrible deprivations of its own. For it was during the Great Depression that Willie's father got pnuemonia and then suffered a heart attack. The poolhall at Wharton and Eighth closed. Willie's mother also became gravely ill.[26]

Unable to work and with the economy in shambles, Willie's father retreated from the world. There were children to feed, rent to pay, electric bills, and clothing expenses—and the often angry and controlling Joseph Mosconi had become utterly helpless. He was an ex-boxer convalescing at home without money, prospects, or dignity. He was a shell of his former self. And so he turned to his eldest son Willie, not just to support the family but literally to save it.

This is a seminal moment in Willie's life and the key to understanding the man he would later become. But it's also here—at this point to which Willie would return over and over again to explain

---

[25] Late in life, Mosconi claimed to have completed high school. However, he acknowledged in early interviews that he was a dropout.

[26] Helen C. Riley died tragically young at age 43, on December 23, 1935, according to genealogical information provided by the Mosconi family.

himself—that one finds important differences between his official sanitized version of his past and the reality of it. Willie didn't lie about these years; he didn't make things up. It's just that he would emphasize certain events and conveniently forget or sugarcoat others. He saw himself in a certain light, and he wanted to project that light to others. *How* he told his story said as much about him as the story itself. And again, the contradictions in the story of Willie Mosconi parallel in surprising ways the contradictions in the story of the Culture War in America itself.

This much is entirely clear: Prohibition and the mean overlapping days of the Depression would mold the man who would become America's greatest-ever pool player. The roaring good times had come to a roaring end, and really because of it the march of Mosconi's historic career began. His father got sick, desperation set in . . . and young Willie returned to the poolroom. "It was his *duty*, he said. "I was the oldest, and we all had to eat." It's in the details of Mosconi's story that important contradictions emerge.

Now the sanitized version opens with Mosconi not as a pool player but as a working man. The story goes that the collapse of the economy and his parents' illness pushed Willie into a straight job at Beinfield's Upholsterers, where he ultimately received $35 and $40 per week stretching cloth over couches and chairs. If not exactly a princely sum, it was at least enough to feed the family and pay the bills. And so he said he would have held tight to that job if not for the unreasonableness of Boss Beinfield's very unreasonable son.

Again, according to the official story, Willie's Uncle Johnny had obtained for him a more-precious-than-gold ticket to the World Series (the Philadelphia Athletics faced the St. Louis Cardinals), and Willie wanted to get off work early and head to Shibe Park. He flew through work and got it done quickly, but then Beinfield's son became irate as he spied the then eighteen-year-old storing his apron and putting away tools. "Where exactly do you think you're going?" Mosconi recalled him saying. "You're not going to any ball game. There are some other things I want you to do before you leave."

So quite predictably unpleasantness ensued: the two argued, Willie said the boss's son threw a punch, he ducked, and then Willie threw his tools at the junior Beinfield. "He was a big son of a bitch, over six feet and about 220 pounds," said Willie. There was no use fighting him, so Willie made a quick exit. According to a profile by Mort Luby, former publisher of *Billiards Digest,* "Willie [then] shuffled sadly home, wondering how he would survive. He had seventy-five cents in his pocket."

And here we come to the key to the story, and it shows up over and over again in profiles and interviews. As Luby would note, Willie's gloom was broken when he spied a sign advertising a billiard tournament. "He had played infrequently since his auspicious childhood debut, but the first prize was $75, and Willie was sorely in need of cash." The sign was in the window of Frankie Mason's poolhall at Seventh and Morris; the tournament lasted two weeks, and of course Willie won it. "That's how it got started really," Willie would say. And so his historic tournament career was underway.

This shows up over and over again in profiles of Willie Mosconi and in his interviews. The official story has it that Willie was working hard at a straight job, that the boss's son threw a fit, that Willie spied the sign in a poolhall window after having been unjustly fired. Journalist Maury White wrote in 1981 that "one day he saw a notice that $75 could be won at a billiards tournament. He won it and was off and running on what proved to be his lifetime occupation." Kenneth Shouler, in an undated article from Mosconi's private collection, reported that "on the way home one day after an argument with his foreman, he spotted a sign reading BILLIARDS TOURNAMENT. He liked the prospect of playing for money and entered, winning and pocketed $75. His pro career was underway."

In his own memoirs Willie reported that he dutifully ran home to ask permission from his father before entering the tournament. And then he returned to the sport. In no time his game returned to terrifying levels, and he quickly humiliated all the gamblers and the roadmen who passed through Frankie Mason's. The tournaments brought him back to pool, and the money he got from smaller individual contests in the poolhall allowed him to support his family.

• • •

Now this story of Willie Mosconi's origins is truthful in its way: No doubt Willie was dutifully working at a proper job, and it's indisputably certain that his family had fallen on hard times. No one questions that Mosconi must have been playing in local tournaments and probably winning them in short order. But the story of the beginning of Willie Mosconi's professional career does not tell all the literal facts of the matter nor, arguably, even the most important ones. Rather, this official version conveys a certain *idea* of who Willie Mosconi was. It also tells the story of a sport he would come to represent. In this way it is a creation myth that reinforces grand virtues of hard work, dignity, and sacrifice while simultaneously reminding one of the risks of wantonness.

Just compare the facts that get stressed in the official story with those that get conveniently glossed over or ignored completely. In these differences one finds hints of that same Culture War dichotomy, of those same contradictions that had come to define America's post–World War I Prohibition experience. For when America sank into the misery of the Great Depression and bad things happened to the Mosconi clan, it wasn't a straight shot to a straight job for the future king of pocket billiards. Neither did he immediately return to tournament play, or first go to exhibitions, or do all the other things to which proper players ascribe.

As with all the true greats, Willie began as a gambler. This is a fact that he would always gloss over (like the Prohibitionists, he spent much of his life railing against the hustlers and the poolroom filth), but it's a fact. Moreover, a careful reading of years and years of newspaper interviews reveals that his famous job at Beinfield's Upholsterers likely lasted only a couple of months and that he had been gambling for pots (and really big ones) years before he ever took it. This was not the dignified story that Willie Mosconi and the powers of pocket billiards would advance about their noble sport, but it is reality.

Consider this: Willie spoke of walking gloomily home after having been fired and then spying that sign for a pocket billiards tournament;

hence the beginning of his professional career. It's clear that Willie must have gotten fired from Beinfield's on October 7, 1931, because that is the date of a World Series game he mentions in his memoirs. That would have meant that Willie was then eighteen years old. Now on a few occasions he also noted that he held that famous job at Beinfield's "only briefly"—perhaps for just two months.

But on numerous occasions Willie also said that he was making money playing pool by age sixteen. That would have been 1929, when the Depression hit, and his father was sick, and the family poolroom had closed. That means that for two years, from the age of sixteen until the age of eighteen, he was gambling—*and only gambling*—to support his family. There was no straight job stretching cloth over furniture, no school, no pool tournaments. He was gambling before he ever took the job at Beinfield's and before he ever played in a single tournament. It's also absolutely clear that for two years after getting fired he supported himself and his family almost exclusively by wagering.

One can also find clues to the utter seriousness of Willie's gambling. In some interviews he spoke of making "hundreds of dollars." But again, this could not have been from tournament play, or exhibitions, or from his work at Beinfield's. It's also unlikely that he would have had so much cash himself, not during the Depression at least, so he may even have found himself a financial backer. Such backers are known as stakehorses in the pool world. Willie may never have mentioned having one because they're something typically associated with hustlers.

And regarding his job at Beinfield's, in almost every interview in which he detailed the story, Mosconi stressed the irrationality of Beinfield's son, of how he was forced to defend himself when the boss's son became irate and threw a first punch. But a reading of very early interviews reveals a different reality. Willie concedes that it was he, and not Beinfield, who went on the attack. It was Beinfield's son who was forced to defend himself. And while it might seem counterintuitive that a man with a family in such dire straights would so cavalierly allow himself to get fired from his job—especially during those horrible dark days of the Great Depression—it's not so strange if one considers that

Willie was likely wagering and winning hundreds of dollars playing pool. Under such circumstances, who needs a straight job?

This last point also underscores a central trait of Willie Mosconi's contradictory character: He may have started life as a precocious, adorable child, but what he would become was a hotheaded and often grim adult. Those who remember say Willie was a man on a short fuse, a man nervous and easily aggravated. Perhaps it was all that early attention that made him so. Perhaps it was the impatience that often accompanies greatness. But what's clear is that he spoke fast, he worked fast, he was fast to judge others, and he was quick to anger.

Willie would never deny that he had gambled—how could he? But he rarely termed it that way, and he certainly never acknowledged that in such lowly pursuits did his lofty career begin. In a 1947 article from the *Toronto Star-Weekly*, for instance, Willie said that as his reputation grew in Philadelphia he "was able to command from $2 to $10 for matches." Not from *wagering* on matches mind you, just *for* them. And in *Willie's Game,* written with Stanley Cohen, son Bill Mosconi Jr. recalled that his father "hated gambling and always discouraged it. I think he even convinced himself that when he was young and supported his family by playing for money he was not really gambling. The way he looked at it was that instead of a sponsor putting up the purse, he and his opponent put up the purse between them. He never felt that he was gambling when he bet on himself."

In contradiction to what was often written about him, or what industry leaders would have us believe, Mosconi did not come to pocket billiards because it was *fun*. It was never a pastime. Rather, what drew Mosconi was hardscrabble mean necessity. In 1929 the Prohibition years were giving way to the Depression, and suddenly the Mosconi family needed the money. That's the cold hard fact of it. "I always had access to a table, but it wasn't until my mother and father became sick that I took it seriously," he told one reporter. "That's the reason I'm in the game. I'm not a poolhall guy. I never hung around them in my life."

•   •   •

All of this is significant because later, as America's number-one ambassador for pocket billiards, Willie would lustily rail against Minnesota Fats (whom he would describe as a phony and a liar), just as he would blast all the other shoddy gamblers who would tear down the sport. He was a pool player who spent a lifetime attacking the tawdriness of poolrooms, the lowlife denizens therein, the hustlers, and the thieves. He was the living embodiment of what pocket billiards *should* be.

And that indisputable fact makes this one final thought all the more jarring: judging from Willie's comments and the comments of those who knew him best, it appears that the man America remembers as its greatest-ever pool player did not much love the sport—and maybe didn't even like it all that much. Speaking to a reporter from the *Atlantic City Sunday Press*, he said that pool "was a means to make a living. It wasn't fun. It was my business." Speaking about pocket billiards to a reporter with the *Arkansas Democrat*, he opined: "I still think it's a stupid game." These sentiments litter the record of Willie Mosconi's life.

Clearly, Willie was not among players like Minnesota Fats and others who found the poolroom life particularly enchanting or romantic. He had grown up around a poolhall; the game was part of him, certainly, but it was not any part to which he ascribed much value.[27] Keep in mind that Willie's father, the poolroom owner, incongruously had bought into that stigma so often attached to poolrooms. He told Willie he wanted something different for him, *something better*. "[My father] didn't want me to have any part of billiards," recalled Mosconi. "He wanted . . . something a little classier."[28] And so when Willie finally

---

[27] Speaking in 1979, hustler Wimpy Lassiter told *Sports Illustrated* of the romance of poolhalls: "Long time ago, I used to stand there and peek over the latticework into that cool-looking darkness of old City Billiards. . . . It seemed as though the place had a special sort of smell to it that you could breathe. Like old green-felt tables and brass spittoons and those dark, polished woods. Then a bluish haze of smoke and sweet pool chalk and, strongest of all, a kind of manliness. All through me, I could feel something else, I don't know what, but it seemed like a fine, lazy tension in the air."

[28] Willie would pass on a very similar message to his own son. Once asked by the boy why he never taught him how to play pool, Willie responded: "I want you to get an education and associate with a better class of people." As quoted in Willie's autobiography, Willie's son also recalled his father saying: "I don't want you hanging around poolhalls."

began to play, really *was made to play*, pool ceased being a game. It became work.

Willie had internalized his father's negative judgments about that life, about poolrooms, and about the men who frequented them. To the extent that he valued pool at all, it was not the result of its undisciplined players but rather the disciplined nature of the game itself. Willie Mosconi as a boy and as a man forever fought for control over his own fiery temper. Above all he valued the self-mastery that in some ways defines the sport. Men cannot exert complete control over anything in life. Prohibition had proven that. But even still, men will try. And what Willie Mosconi would control most were those ivory balls clicking one against the other. He did this like no other player before or since. The scoundrels and the speakeasies did not make pocket billiards beautiful; the subordination did.

Chapter 8

CREATION MYTH

I was born growed up.

— Minnesota Fats

Now Rudolf Wanderone didn't exactly tell it straight either. "Actually, I did hustle Ralph Greenleaf one time," he said. Or: "I won so much gelt . . . it looked like I was smuggling coconuts in my pockets." Players uptown and down emptied their wallets to him, tin-cup national champs were helpless, Wanderone played craps on the Brooklyn Bridge and poker with the Longshoremen. The lies were grandiose, gigantic, and they piled upward, upward, *upward*—like the Tower of Babel. Like Mosconi, Wanderone hid the truth. But he did even more. He created it shiny and new. He was a gambler and a hell-raiser from way back. He was, very proudly, everything that Willie Mosconi was not. Wanderone was the other side of the Roaring Twenties.

"Broadway in 1926 was the most exciting place on earth, especially for a 13-year-old man," Wanderone said in his memoirs, written with Tom Fox. "I tell you, I never was a boy. Times Square in those days was fantastic. There were more poolrooms than hot dog stands and the tomatoes running on the loose were beautiful beyond compare. The first days I forgot about pool and just stood around belting out the hot dogs and eyeballing the dolls.

"In those days I made my pocket money beating the suckers and mooches who came in looking for a mark and sometimes I played

51

businessmen, like manufacturers and executives from the Garment District, or young song writers or actors. I played way under my speed, know what I mean, and let them beat me a few. Then I'd really stick 'em up."

Wanderone claimed to have beaten a bookmaker for big money and demolished Cowboy Weston, the former national nine-ball champ, in a much ballyhooed exhibition. He said he tapped out "ole Sauerkraut clean down to his overalls." And Wanderone may have done some of these things, too. He certainly gambled and hustled and victimized the stupid. But here, too, Wanderone has invented himself through stories. He has slyly included all that which stresses his untamed greatness and craftily neglected those details that do not. Wanderone would have us know that he was a conman and scoundrel. In utter contrast to Mosconi, it was that part of his personaility of which he was most proud.

But to a certain extent, Wanderone's story also comports with America's general conception of pocket billiards. Like Mosconi, the man who would become Minnesota Fats also came to embody the entire sport. So Wanderone's story must also must be seen as a creation myth, a story of symbols—but a competing one. Wanderone never speaks of tournaments, but of hustling. He does not speak of responsibility, but its opposite. Look to what Fats says, and look to what he leaves out. Look to what Wanderone *invents* (for largely he was a product of invention) to more clearly understand the sport's place in American culture.

•　•　•

Wanderone began the decade making the mile-long walks between home and school, upper Manhattan's Public School 132, on Wadsworth Street near Broadway, huffing and puffing from his big three-story tenement. He passed by the Catholic church where his blue-eyed mom went to Mass. It was a mostly Scandanavian neighborhood then, working class, with plenty of open saloons operating before the Volstead Act[29]—and several secret ones after it. Rudolf's father loved the barroom life, and he often held forth for hours drinking and telling jokes with his Swiss cronies. Rudolf's mother was likely none too pleased about this carousing, as she often complained of her husband's laziness, her son's laziness, and the laziness of men in general. Fats said she sometimes sicced the parish priest on the neighborhood layabouts, of which there were certainly plenty.

By 1926 young Rudolf Jr. had decided that he would no longer require the benefits of education. The long, cold walk between his home at 403 West 148th Street and PS 132 had become troublesome to him. He was just thirteen by then but already wild and (so he said) somewhat adept with a pool cue. He made outlandish claims about this period. "I played the Kaiser when he was on the lamb in Switzerland," he said. "I played Atlantic City before there was any beach." All of it was said in the service of self-aggrandizement. But it's certainly true young Rudolf Wanderone was certainly playing plenty of pool and probably gambling in neighborhood rooms like Heights Recreation or Cranfields, up on 146th and Broadway, where Babe Ruth sometimes would appear.

He learned by watching, and for tutors he had all the greats: men like Andrew St. Jean, from Lowell, Massachusetts, but famous also in the New York rooms. He probably picked up some of his prowess with banks from St. Jean. Wanderone also would have witnessed Ralph Greenleaf, the great and almighty, shooting trick shots on Broadway. Greenleaf was the greatest pool player anyone then had ever seen and he got paid $2,000 per week just for knocking in wing shots beneath giant mirrors at the Palace Theater.[30]

Eventually Wanderone took the name Fats (he was, after all, a fat child), and sometimes he went by Double Smart Fats,[31] or even Triple Smart Fats. His first car was a Stutz Bearcat, and then he moved on to a Caddy—both bought and paid for with illicit gambling proceeds.

---

[29] Passed on October 28, 1919, the Volstead Act prohibited the manufacture, sale, and transportation of beverages containing more than one half of one percent alcohol per volume. Congress adopted the Volstead Act (officially known as the National Prohibition Enforcement Act) shortly after the ratification of the Eighteenth Amendment—and over the veto of President Woodrow Wilson.

[30] Accompanied by his lovely wife, Princess Nai Tai Tai, the Oriental Nightingale.

[31] According to legend, Wanderone received his first nickname courtesy of Titanic Thompson, the famous golf hustler and card shark. The two became friends during those early New York years.

He claimed to have beaten former nine-ball champ Cowboy Weston during an early exhibition at Heights Recreation (probably during a jubilee celebration of the invention of the automobile) and scored off a Coney Island hustler by the name of Smart Henry. He counted as friends the famous golf hustler Titanic Thompson, odds-maker Jimmy "The Greek" Castras, and Arthur Rothstein, who helped rig the 1919 World Series.

Wanderone said he cut his teeth hustling, gambling, and sharking suckers. During those early years he *never* spoke of playing tournaments. He said he hated those trophy-winning stiffs in tuxedos. "I ain't going to play in no coat, Willie!" he'd say. "Eight, ten, twelve, fifteen jack offs playing in tuxedos. . . . I mean, ain't that ridiculous?" But here, too, the very first journalistic evidence tells otherwise.

In 1931, for instance, the *New York Times* reported that Wanderone competed in an important billiards tournament sponsored by the Greater New York Room Owner's Association and held at Dwyer's Broadway. "In the uptown division Ed Widtman conquered Rudolf Wanderone, 50–13, in forty innings," read the five-paragraph piece that appeared February 27. Later, on March 3, Wanderone again makes a very public appearance: This time the *Times* reported he defeated a player by the name of Vaino Korhonen, 50–15, in fourteen innings. Again, it was during a citywide tournament—but this time Wanderone was playing at the prestigious Penger & Gibson poolroom.

Now stop a moment and contemplate this. Rudolf Wanderone, the *hustler* Rudolf Wanderone, was competing in tournaments in February and March of 1931. That means that Wanderone was competing in high-profile tournaments—tournaments covered in the *New York Times* no less—at least *half a year* before Willie Mosconi played in that first modest event at Frankie Mason's. Wanderone was playing serious tournaments by March of 1931, Mosconi in October.

But these men did not tell these separate stories about themselves because these stories did not comport with their separate visions of pocket billiards. Mosconi said he started as a tournament player, but there's clear evidence that really he began as a gambler. Wanderone said he started as a gambler, and yet he had his very beginnings as a tournament player. He was in fact so prominent a tournament player that no less than Chicago's *Billiards Magazine* listed Wanderone in 1932 as one of the most prominent in America. The venerable pool magazine was not in the habit of bestowing this distinction upon two-bit hustlers.

And by contrast the magazine in 1932 makes no mention of Mosconi at all. None whatsoever. The *New York Times* was writing about Fats, and the billiards press was writing about Fats, and Mosconi, the then-*gambler* Willie Mosconi, was nowhere to be seen. "Willie didn't come into prominence until 1933, when he finished second for the national title," said promoter Ursitti. "Nobody ever heard of Willie Mosconi in 1932, but they heard of Rudolf Wanderone."

•   •   •

So he comes up the steps, striding across wood floors looking fat and well fed but no doubt with desperation behind a carefree façade. The Depression then beat down upon the nation; men were broke, families were starving—and maybe Rudolf Wanderone was, too. Sometimes he lived at home, sometimes not. He had foraged through the poolhalls of Manhattan and Brooklyn, and then, when the easy pickings played out and when his name started appearing in the newspapers and the pool magazines, he took to the road. And so here he comes, he's arrived in Philadelphia, and at his side is that other back room player of shady repute, Babyface Alton Whitlow, and together they scan the room.

Suckers, suckers everywhere, they must think.

If they were starving, they never let on. If they were one loss away from homelessness, they never said.

Wanderone has no known skill at anything but cards, craps, and pocket billiards. He has never held a job, and so, exactly and precisely like Willie Mosconi, he has sought refuge in poolhalls. But unlike Willie, Wanderone embraced this life with gusto. Unlike Willie, Wanderone never cared about looking like a lowlife scoundrel but rather being mistaken for a penniless bum. During those days when joblessness defined America, Wanderone summed up his life's meaning with a flash of green, a nervous twitch, a W. C. Fields taunt, an unquenchable thirst for larceny. Hustling in small rooms and big, moving, moving, moving brother, Wanderone *reinvented* himself. Carrying Babyface Whitlow's cue not out of deference but because they probably only had the one between them, Fats made his scratch the best way he could. And he did so with *style*.

So now Rudolf Walter Wanderone has come to Philadelphia flashing his $250 cash money, calling it a fortune, and yet pledging to make it double. *"Who wants some of . . . this?"* he taunts.

It's a siren call, as true as one ever hears in a second-floor poolroom. "I say I'll play anyone, anyone at all. . . ."

And who is there to hear this call but a man about Wanderone's age, a man about Wanderone's height, a man looking more irritated with every passing moment. He's there behind the counter, he's the houseman, and Wanderone has cast his larcenous eye upon him.

"Hey, there, *you*, buddy. Why don't you play me some one-hole, *c'mon*."

Wanderone would appeal to the houseman's vanity and his arrogance and taunt him into a game, because that is how the hustle worked.

C'mon, Buddy, he says.

He has taken the houseman for a chump.

Let's go!

And so finally the houseman screws together his cue. He steps out from behind the counter. If he smiled that day, it would have been utterly without warmth. Rudolf Walter Wanderone that day may have miscalculated.

"Let's see what you got," says the houseman. "I'm Willie Mosconi. Let's play some pool."

Chapter 9

FATS VERSUS WILLIE, ROUND 1

> You play him, and if you can beat him, do it.
> — Poolroom owner Frankie Mason to Willie Mosconi

Hustlers traffic in impatience, ignorance, greed, and ego. Their tools are personal charm, an understanding of odds, an innate sense of human psychology, and an ability to deceive. Hustlers can victimize better players, or they can victimize lesser ones. They can victimize members of the general public. The most low-down of the hustling tribe can even cannibalize his own financial backers.

Hustlers employ a myriad of different techniques, but most represent simple variations on two broad strategies. The first is simply to "play on the lemon," which means to mask one's true ability by purposefully making position errors, scratching, or missing balls. A player on the lemon might typically win but only just barely. Or he might win only slightly more games than the other fellow. Or the hustler might win only when the stakes have grown to his liking.[32] A man on the lemon creates the comforting illusion that he isn't stealing another man's money. And if played with subtlety—that is, if played with good

---

[32] Hustlers may be attracted to pool more than other sports because pool seems made for the lemon. A fairly skilled player can even fake bad luck and cause seemingly well-hit balls to pop out of pockets.

humor and flattery—the hustler's victim might keep losing for days over the course of multiple sessions.[33]

The second broad strategy is "sharking," and this is when a hustler behaves in disruptive or disconcerting ways to throw his opponent off. This can be as subtle as removing one's handkerchief while an opponent is shooting. It can be as overt as making physical threats. Sometimes the player getting sharked doesn't even realize he's getting sharked. Take, for example, those sometimes very funny hustlers who disarm their opponents with nonstop jokes and pratfalls.

Now when New York Fats met Willie Mosconi for the first time in Philadelphia it appears that Fats combined both of these techniques into a single ploy. Called "The Big Hoorah,"[34] the hustle allowed Fats to use all of his athletic and psychological skills, while at the same time it did not require Fats to depend too heavily on those attributes always in short supply with him: namely patience and humility. Under ordinary circumstances the ploy might have given him a good chance of success. Of course, playing Willie Mosconi does not constitute ordinary circumstances.

In a nutshell, this is how the "Big Hoorah" is supposed to work: The hustler walks into the poolroom, maybe with a confederate, and starts knocking balls around. All the while the hustler brags about his supposed skill and daring, but *loudly*, "Look at this shot! Lookee here!" he might say. Or: "Here it goes! Here it goes! Here it goes—*beautiful*." The more obnoxious, the more ridiculous, the flakier, the better. The key is to not play well, not even close to well—again, to play on the lemon— but all the while to affect a vulgar swagger that verges on the imbecilic. This sort of sharking Fats was perfect for.

---

[33] Like the very charming Jersey Red. Red (whose real name was Jack Breit) would speak about regularly taking an attorney's money in Houston every day for a year or more. Red said he couldn't help but make friends with the guy—hell, they were playing all the time—and Red finally confessed to the attorney that he was a hustler and could beat him at will. The attorney responded that he had already figured as much, but he enjoyed Red's company so much that he didn't mind losing.

[34] Fats did not use this name for this technique. Rather that name is attributed to Don Willis and Wimpy Lassiter, two of the most feared hustlers ever. For more on the Big Hoorah, see Appendix II of Hustler Days.

Typically the hustler's relentless crowing combined with his seeming ineptitude will lure in a mark. And typically this mark will be some sort of local poolroom hero who would be utterly helpless against a professional. If the hustler has done his work, the local's own pride will drive up the wager, while his ire will unbalance his shot making. Hence, the Big Hoorah is the perfect combination of sharking and hustling. The hustle also rewards an itinerant player like Fats, who then had neither the desire nor the patience to stick around any single room for long. Flit in. Piss off the helpless locals. Take their money. Clear out.

The disadvantage is also clear: not every local is helpless.

Philadelphia during the 1930s was the top city in the nation for pocket billiards. Former national champion Andrew Ponzi[35] made his home there. And then there was George Kelly, a national-class player, and Jimmy Caras,[36] another future world champion. Even the great Ralph Greenleaf spent some of those years in Philly, mostly in Allinger's but also sometimes over at Frankie Mason's. Greatness attracted greatness to the City of Brotherly Love, so when hustlers came looking to hook their fish there, they'd be wise not to cast their lines too far. The Philadelphians of the 1930s and 1940s played pool at terrifying levels.

●   ●   ●

Wanderone would have been specifically aware of Mosconi's reputation as an intimidating straight-pool player. But Wanderone also knew that Willie was the houseman, the guardian of the till, and that he would have to get through him if he was going to really score that day at Frankie Mason. At Wanderone's side, remember, was the chain

---

[35] Real name: Andrew D'Alessandro.

[36] During his career, Caras won the world pocket-billiards championship five times. He was born in Scranton, Pennsylvania, the son of Spiro Caravasilis, who owned several poolhalls. He legally shortened his name to Caras in 1943.

smoking Babyface Alton Whitlow, another hustler of growing renown. With their gold bracelets, their wide ties, and their cocked fedoras, they were roadmen of the most dandified sort. Straightaway they got to a table, and they began playing back and forth, and Fats starts flashing his turd-sized wad of cash, and he starts bragging about his ability to pocket balls and probably also his ability to lay women.

If they were playing one-pocket, Fats certainly wouldn't have been showing everything he had. He'd run twos and threes, certainly but never fours and fives. He also would have been passing on those crazy-ass banks. He sure-as-shit wasn't hitting three-railers or running out. And all the while Fats would have been working Willie's nerves like a boxer on the heavy bag, crowing about each and every damn shot, bragging about obvious luck, making Willie ache with his nonstop stupid prattle. For good measure Fats also turned his taunts to the back room card players, Willie's old Italian cronies that sat beneath the bluish white haze of cigar smoke. *Save me a seat!* Fats said. He'd be back there to take their money just as soon as he won a few pool games.

That is, if someone at Frankie Mason's had the nuts to play him.

Willie did not jump at the opportunity to play Fats. Fats wouldn't shut up, couldn't shut up—*C'mon, Mr. Straight Pool; c'mon, Mosco-o-o-o-ni, let's go*—but Mosconi at first remained unmoved. It's not that the man remembered as America's finest-ever pool player didn't figure to beat Fats, although at that early age he might not have been absolutely certain. It also wasn't that Fats had not sufficiently sparked his ire. Rather what was probably the case was that Willie did not have enough to cover the stake.[37] Wanderone came in flashing his big wad, cursing and babbling and taunting, and it was all so very humiliating. But Willie needed someone to back him up.

---

[37] Willie vaguely recalled in his memoirs that the match occurred in 1949—but here his memory probably fails him. He has said in another interview that the matchup was in the 1930s, and that's more likely. Remember: By 1949 Mosconi had quite publicly sealed his reputation as one of the world's most spectacular pool players. Moreover, Mosconi in the 1940s would not have been seeking guidance from Frankie Mason about whom to play and whom not to.

Fats knew this, and Babyface knew this, and they knew that Willie would want to play but couldn't afford it. But they also knew that Mosconi had a supporter and a very well-heeled one. That supporter was Frankie Mason himself, the owner of the poolroom, and one must consider him the target of Fats's hustle that day just as much as Mosconi was.

"Why don't you play this guy and shut him up?" Frankie Mason said finally. "You play him, and if you can beat him, do it."

And this is precisely what Fats was waiting to hear.

And so that's how it began: Fats and Babyface barging into Frankie Mason's, crowing and boasting and making a spectacle of themselves, and Willie getting pissed, and Frankie Mason presiding over the first great matchup of the would-be hustler king and the greatest player on earth. Fats figured to get the advantage by insisting on one-pocket, that game that Willie always considered a hustler's gimmick. Fats understood the angles; Willie, not so much. The wager was set at $50 per game. Willie and Fats would play five games in all.

•   •   •

The rules of one-pocket are simple; the game, deceptively difficult. Each player has assigned to him a separate corner pocket near the far rail. During the course of the game the players can only shoot into that preselected pocket; that is, one player tries to get balls into the right-hand corner pocket, while the other tries to get them into the left-hand corner pocket. To win, the player must sink any eight balls—the majority of balls in the rack—into his or her preselected pocket.

And that's it.

But here's the thing: If a good player gets good position and gets hot, he can sink eight balls but fast. Bang. Bang. Bang. *Bang*. It's like oil leaking from an engine block, like quarters falling from your pants' pocket. The game goes twenty, thirty, forty minutes—with each player shooting safeties, leaving the cue ball stuck up on the far rail or awkward against the stack or buried down near an opponent's pocket—and then one bad move, one bad safety, one errant cue ball, and then it's *eight-ball corner, nine-ball corner, three-ball corner, five-ball corner,* on and on, until it's all over, and the unwary or the unlucky are opening their wallets.

Fats was an aggressive one-pocket player, a top player in his youth, and sometimes sank five or six in quick succession. He was also an expert banker and would go for the eight-and-out victories—bang, bang, bang, bang, *bang*—and beat players by not giving them an opportunity to shoot. He could play defense, too; he understood the strange patterns of one-pocket, and he loved them. He could go three rails sometimes. Fats during the 1930s and '40s was not a man to be trifled with at this game.

Mosconi, for his part, was also an aggressive player. but he did not have Fats's understanding of the sometimes counterintuitive patterns of one-pocket. Neither did he respect it and so did not spend much time studying it with any seriousness. And while Willie did all things well, it may have been true that he did not then bank as expertly as Wanderone. For Willie, cue-ball control was paramount. And he was matchless at it. Literally. At the top of his game, no other player in the world could control the white ball like Willie Mosconi could. It was as if he picked it up with his hand and placed it on the table exactly as he wanted. And of course, Willie was an expert shot maker.

•   •   •

It could get drafty and cold inside Frankie Mason's, and there was that near-permanent smell of pool chalk and acrid cigars and that smell too of old men and of old wooden floors. The tables were mostly ten footers, but there were also the pocketless tables for the sweet game, for three-cushion.[38] The tables stood in a line, each next to its brother, just like

---

[38] Three-cushion billiards is that variety of the sport played on a pocketless table with three balls. Each player has a cue ball. The object of the game is to use the cue to strike the two other balls on the table and three rails. Each of these "billiards" counts for one point. Wanderone's expertise in this game probably contributed to his well-known facility for making bank shots.

soldiers for morning reveille. Around one table old men gathered. Pulling their hardwood chairs across hardwood floors, screeching and scraping all the while, they murmured anxiously, and they placed their bets.

And then, oh sweet Jesus, it began, and the murmuring ended, just like that, it ceased. It was like the silencing of crickets at the sudden burst of light. Men stared in astonishment as Fatty stroked, but softly, and they watched as whitey magically went coasting into the stack. Some of the balls spread out to the rail nearest Fats's pocket, and then the cue ball landed down by Willie's pocket, useless and dead. It was a perfect defensive break. And that's when the sharking started. *C'mon, Willie!* he would have said. *Do something with* that, *Mr. Straight Pool!*

The railbirds had fallen silent, but Fats was making a terrible racket. *Hooo, Sonny Boy. Have you ever seen such a thing?*

Willie takes his shot. It works out well enough. And then Fatty takes his. Willie shoots. Fatty shoots. It goes back and forth for a while, and then somewhere in there, Fatty makes a mistake. He makes one ball, then two and three. But then he shoots safe, and he leaves too much. And that's when Willie falls upon table, falls upon it with eyes blazing like a wild animal. Willie Mosconi always played with hatred, the absolute and pure form, and that hatred became all the more acute that day in Frankie Mason's poolroom. Willie Mosconi did not simply wish to beat Fats. He did not simply wish to take his money.

What you gonna do, Mosconi?

So here it comes. Here it comes.

Bang, bang, bang, bang. Bang.

The balls fall in a torrent, and the room and the men and the whole world outside vanish away. Fatty's jabbering and cursing seem like a distant thing. And Willie keeps dropping balls one after another. *Pay me, goddamnit,* he would have said. *Pay me!* And then Fats and Willie played again, and Willie won again. In between, Mosconi would snipe at the sweaters, telling them to keep it the hell down. Fatty kept racking. Willie kept running balls.

Pay me, he said.

Pay me.

Now, it must be said that no one remembers the scores. No one remembers which balls fell first and which fell second. And accounts vary as to who actually won.

In his own memoirs and in countless interviews, Fats insisted he came out on top. He "whacked out" Willie but good, said Fats. "He couldn't beat a drum," he said. "I played him a hundred times, and I beat him a hundred times." But that's not all. Willie Mosconi, said Fats, proved himself at Frankie Mason's to be the biggest joke the world has ever known. "He was always scared of me. He can't beat me for money."

Mosconi said they played five games and that he won all five. He said Fatty may have come looking for a quick score but what he got was broke. "I beat him five straight times for fifty bucks a game, and I had to lend him train fare to get back to New York," Willie said. "Fats was just another one of dozens of pool hustlers around the country who made their living off unsuspecting marks." He said he never beat anybody good. "He was, in a word, a con man, but he was as good a con man as I'd ever known. He knew all the angles when money was at stake."

And so here we find a flashpoint, a flint-and-steel moment to spark the conflagration decades later. Mosconi said he won. Fats said it was bullshit. Most must agree that Mosconi's story was the more credible simply because most agree that Mosconi was the more credible player. But what's indisputably certain here is that both men then were intimidating players, both had spent those tough years honing their respective skills, and that the first great Fats & Willie Show, just like the second, represents just as much a conflict of style as it does a conflict of ability.[39]

During those years Fats beat men by sharking and taunting and playing on the lemon. He worked hard to perfect those tricks of his trade. Willie learned during those years about shape and cue-ball control. His ability to win grew in direct proportion to his hardening disdain for Fats and for all men like him.

The months and the years passed, and the high-stakes money challenges piled up, and his antipathy for gamblers etched a jagged groove further into Willie's already rough personality. These men were a loud-mouthed, wretched lot. The desire to beat them grew inside Willie like a black cancer. The prospect of defeat at their hands was an intolerable one, too humiliating to contemplate. And so maybe this too helps explain the man who just then was emerging as an uncompromising competitor.

Maybe he owed the sharks that much, at least.

---

[39] There are conflicting reports as to whether they confronted one another on other occasions during those early years. Fats said they did; Mosconi never mentioned it.

Chapter 10

JAWING THE YELLOW BALL

> Rudolf, who had trailed throughout the game, was
> apparently ready to call it a lost afternoon and
> congratulate young Mosconi on a handsome debut
> to big time billiards.
>
> — The *Chicago Tribune*'s Charles Bartlett on Willie
> Mosconi's first world tournament appearance

Not just anybody can play in a world tournament. You can't just show up, raise your hand, and say, "Pick me, sir!" You can't even pay an entrance fee. Back in the 1930s, when the Billiard Association of America governed pool, there were two routes in—just two, and both involved victories over unspeakable opposition.

Route one: place in the money during a previous national or world tournament. Do that, and the BAA typically seeded you automatically for the next event. During the 1930s this meant that men like the mindlessly slow Frank Taberski got in or maybe Kansas City's Bennie Allen. Of course, Ralph Greenleaf was there, always, and also George Kelly and Andrew Ponzi, both of Philly.

Then, of course, there was that second route, the route that everybody who made it in had to take at some point, the route that Willie Mosconi followed in 1933. The Billiard Association of America then sanctioned a series of qualifying matches in different regions of the country. It was a way to find new talent, promote the sport, and drum up enthusiasm. The BAA would have them in the Northeast, the Midwest, the West, and the South. But of course one couldn't just show up and play in one of these either. One couldn't even pay an entrance fee and get in. To compete in a qualifying tournament, a player had to have the sponsorship of a respectable room. The BAA wanted no riffraff. And then once sponsored that player would have to defeat all comers at the local level, then all comers in a sectional tournament, and then finish strong in the national event.

In 1933, just as *King Kong* premiered in Hollywood and construction began on San Francisco's Golden Gate Bridge and Charles Lindbergh was preparing to fly across the south Atlantic, the BAA began preparing for the world's tournament in Chicago. William Joseph Mosconi had at that time come in neither first nor second in any world or national event. Willie Mosconi had never even played in a regional event or been selected as a room representative. He had seen Greenleaf play two years before, seen him make mincemeat of the competition during the world meet that year in Philly,[40] and had watched world-class play in Allinger's. But Willie Mosconi had never gotten his own ticket punched for the Big Show.

Happily, however, for Willie, 1933 was also the year that Eddie Brown died of the same disease that had killed magician Harry Houdini seven years earlier: peritonitis. Eddie was just twenty-four years old, one of Philly's great hotshot young players, and the pride and hope of Fox Billiard Academy owner Izzie Goodman, who had sponsored him in that year's divisional event. "But the poor guy died just a week or two before the tournament was to start," said Mosconi. "Eddie suddenly fell ill. He had an appendectomy; Izzie had already paid the entry fee, so he asked me if I would take Eddie's place."

Willie said the divisional was supposed to be a freebie for Andrew St. Jean, a hotshot player from Massachusetts. The so-called Lowell Kid had come in second to Ralph Greenleaf during the 1928 national

---

[40] Greenleaf won the 1931 world tournament, held November 30 to December 23 at Allinger's. Second place fell to George Kelly, and third went to Erwin Rudolf. According to billiards historian Charles Ursitti, it was a twelve-man round-robin field.

championship and was occasionally on Coca-Cola's payroll as a professional exhibition player. One of the other room owners had imported St. Jean in for the divisional event, ringer style, with the expectation that he would mop up the local talent. But it didn't happen that way. St. Jean was a gambler, a hustler, and a drunk—the sort of player that Willie abhorred—and Willie plowed straight through him. Willie also plowed through every other player; in fact, he plowed through them twice because it was a double round-robin event, and he didn't suffer a single loss. For this startling effort he pocketed $75.

Next came the sectionals. Willie remembers being nervous as hell. "None of the eight players had ever heard of the brassy little Italian kid," *Billiards Digest* founder Mort Luby wrote about that seminal tournament. "And when Mosconi announced that he did not own a cue of his own, they were convinced that his [earlier] victory over St. Jean was a fluke." That year's event was at the Strand Academy, one of New York's best poolhalls.[41] Willie didn't have much money. He didn't own a suit. But in his opening match against Onoforio Lauri he ran seventy balls in less than six minutes. As in the divisional event, the young Turk again plowed through everyone, *everyone.*

And so finally came the Big Show, the national tournament. Mosconi had used part of his $250 winnings from the sectional event to buy himself more dignified clothing. He took an overnight train to Minneapolis, where the nationals were scheduled to begin October 30. He remembers it as being cold as hell. He would face nine of the greatest players in the country before newspapermen and big crowds. If he won he'd get $450, plus a percentage of the receipts, and—most important of all—sudden national acclaim.[42]

---

[41] It was located below the Strand Theater in the middle of the downtown theater district. It was also the site of Greenleaf's 1928 challenge-match victory over St. Jean.

[42] According to the October 26, 1933, edition of the *Minneapolis Star,* tournament participants included Walter Franklin of Kansas City; George Kelly and Willie Mosconi of Philadelphia; Charles Seaback of Astoria, New York; Arthur Church of New York; Harry Wood of Duluth; Eddie Sauers of Oakland, California; Charles Summerell of Little Rock, Arkansas; and Marcel Camp of Detroit, who had recently won the northern sectional title.

As he had during the previous two rounds, Willie Mosconi started out by plowing through the opposition. An early barrage of eighty-five gave him the high-run record for almost the entire tournament.[43] He played fast, and he played mean, and he found he could win without paying much mind to the opponent, to the defensive possibilities, or even the lay of the table. He simply outgunned anyone who stepped up against him. By the end of the two weeks he found himself locked in a three-way tie for first.

But if this was a winning strategy during the beginning of the national event, it would begin to fail Willie Mosconi by the end of it. He had found he could simply overwhelm the two-bit hustlers at Frankie Mason's, and he could probably overwhelm guys like Arthur Church and Sylvester Schliesman, too. Those were players in the national tournament now lost to history. But against former national champion George Kelly in the playoffs, Willie would have to show more finesse, more caution.

He would have to show more brains.

According to the *Minneapolis Star* Mosconi just about had Kelly whupped on November 14 and stood at the cusp of winning that year's national tournament.[44] "Mosconi registered one run of 25 and took a commanding lead which he gradually increased to the 90 mark," the newspaper reported. But then Willie left an opening in a battle of scratches, and Kelly fought his way back with a run of thirty-three.

Mosconi then proceeded to blow two more chances and once let the object ball jump from the pocket by inexcusably applying too much force. And that's when it ended. "Kelly took advantage to run out the match," the paper reported. The final score: Kelly 125, Mosconi 97. Willie's defeat came in twenty-eight innings.

While Kelly ended up winning the national title,[45] Mosconi's second-place finish nonetheless earned him the right to join him in that year's

---

[43] Only George Kelly's run of 125 against Charles Seaback would best it, and that didn't come until the very last regular game of the two-week event.

[44] Willie already had eliminated Seaback 125 to 72 in twenty-one innings.

world competition in Chicago. If there was any consolation, then that was it. Willie also got another $450 for his performance in Minneapolis and figured that he had earned $750 so far. Not bad, considering many of his friends were waiting in food lines. The nineteen-year-old sent much of his money back home to his father, who used it for seed money to open a bar. Willie also spent some of it to purchase a custom-made cue from the famous Herman Ranbow, who operated from the basement of Brunswick Billiards in Chicago.[46]

•   •   •

Willie said Bensinger's Adams-Wabash Recreation was a class place. He remembered velvet curtains, burnished brown wood, immaculate tables, and oil paintings. A wrought-iron cage brought the Young Turk from the first floor to the second. It would be the venue for that year's world tournament, and it would host an intimidating field. Greenleaf was there, of course, plus Ponzi, Frank Taberski and Pasquale Natalie. As in New York, Willie Mosconi was the youngest in the field.

The *Chicago Daily Tribune* put the total prize fund at $6,500, including $1,000 for the champion and a diamond medal. The competition would begin December 4, go eighteen playing days, and typically feature two games each afternoon, and one each night. Joseph M. Ferguson, a New Yorker, served as referee. The games went to 125; the format was single round-robin; the table size a tournament-standard 5 by 10.

"The world's tournament, the first of its type to be held in Chicago in five years, is one of those events that goes on for days and days, for its schedule of 45 games, and will not be concluded until Dec. 21," reported *The Tribune's* Charles Bartlett. He noted the main attraction

---

[45] This earned him $550 in prize winnings and gate receipts, plus a diamond medal emblem.

[46] Before then, Mosconi had always used house cues. Of course, a busted-up cue right off the wall wouldn't do in world competition. He was just nineteen, but even still, a man had to have standards. In his memoirs Willie recalled his new cue as a nineteen-ouncer (his preferred weight) and fifty-seven inches in length. The shaft was a bit thinner than most to accommodate Willie's smallish hands. Ranbow had it ready for him in time for the warm-ups.

would be Greenleaf, a man who had run out a championship game in two innings, had gone through twenty-one world tournament games without a single loss, had run 126 balls in a 125-point match. Greenleaf, Bartlett reported, had "won the world's title so many times it has ceased to be amusing."

As it turned out, however, Greenleaf had the most disastrous showing of his career. He was a well-known drunk and apparently had gotten deeply into the sauce during the 1933 event. But how could he help it? Greenleaf then was in the midst of an attempted divorce: his wife, Emelia Ruth Parker, actually served him with papers in the tournament room, actually marched in before the other players. To make matters worse Prohibition was just then coming to an end. The zero hour was midnight, December 4, a Monday, which was precisely one day into the world championship. Shiploads of foreign liquor had been steaming across the Atlantic. By noon on Tuesday Greenleaf had an entire nation with whom to share a drink.

It was a testament to Greenleaf's towering skill that he could remain standing, much less compete. Greenleaf had an hour and a half in which to drink before the afternoon matches. He could drink for a full seven hours before the evening ones.

Yes, he lost seven times during that 1933 title event.

But playing against the world's best pool players, Greenleaf also *won* twice.

"Greenleaf had no enemies except the bottle, and the more fame that was thrust upon him, the more refuge he sought in the grape," wrote *Billiards Digest* columnist George Fels in a 1993 column about the great champion. "As long as he kept his drinking suitably low-profile, Greenleaf wore his success well. It was only demon rum that could be counted on to bring the man down with consistency."

On December 11 referee Ferguson called a forfeit on Greenleaf because he was making a fool of himself. The *Tribune*'s Charles Bartlett wrote that for much of the afternoon the "magpie fire had been audible to the journalists fortunate enough to be seated in Ralph's corner." Who knows what Ralph was ranting about, but by the twelfth inning

Ferguson had had enough and called the match on behalf of Jimmy Caras. Greenleaf continued to fail for the remainder of the tournament, sinking finally to a 2–7 record. Willie Mosconi delivered the coup de grace during a humiliating 125–55 rout December 18.

Mosconi sliced similarly through the other competitors, dazzling spectators and journalists alike. He began Chicago an unknown, an underdog, and a long shot. By the middle of the event, journalists were calling him a young sensation. The march began December 6, when Mosconi won his very first match 125–81. He was playing Bennie Allen of Kansas City and ran a sixty-four in the second inning. It stood as the long run for much of the tournament. The *Tribune*'s Charles Bartlett said the nineteen-year-old "pranced at the table." On December 8 Willie won again, this time beating Frank Taberski in twenty-nine innings.[47] The inexorable snail lost the lag, then sat back and watched unhappily as the young Philadelphian ran a twenty-one in the ninth, and then a twenty-six in the thirteenth. On December 12 Mosconi beat Jimmy Caras 125–95 in twenty-five innings.[48]

But as it turned out the key match happened for Willie before the tournament had really gotten underway. He didn't then realize the importance of it, he didn't understand what happened until much later, but had it turned out differently, it would have been one of the most significant matches in the history of pocket billiards. The outcome of that game hinged on one ball, one *damn* ball, and Willie missed it. It was the most important missed ball of Willie's career, and it went astray before Willie's career was underway.

---

[47] The final score was Mosconi 125, Taberski 115.

[48] This, according to the *Chicago Daily Tribune*:

"Two young men, one of whom has been allowed to play with the big boys last year and another who was in the world show for the first time, packed the house in the evening. In less than two hours, the younger, 19-year-old Willie Mosconi of Philadelphia, disposed of 22-year-old Jimmy Caras of Wilmington, Del., Greek, 125 to 95 in 25 innings."

"After 18 innings, Mosconi led only 55 to 29, but he got going in the next frame with a run of 14 to lead 69 to 44, and Caras came closer only once in the 34th, when he pulled up within four points."

The date was December 5. Willie was playing former champion Erwin Rudolf. He had the game wrapped up, was leading 124–83. The *Chicago Daily Tribune*'s Charles Bartlett, an eyewitness, describes the scene.[49]

"A yellow-hued billiard ball with the numeral 1 stamped upon it lay within a foot of one of the leather-shouldered pockets of the playing table. Five feet down the rail gleamed a cue ball. It appeared to be a simple matter for one so talented as nineteen-year-old Willie Mosconi of Philadelphia to propel the white sphere against the yellow cousin and send No. 1 into the pocket. This movement would bring a 125–83 victory over Erwin Rudolf of Cleveland in the second game of the 1933 world's pocket billiards championship tournament."

Bartlett said the gathered railbirds wriggled quietly in their overcoats. Mosconi applied a final dab of chalk to the end of his cue. Erwin Rudolf had been trailing all afternoon and was ready to throw in the towel. It would be a handsome debut for Mosconi.

But then, Bartlett continued: "THE BALL REFUSES TO FALL."

"Maybe it was Willie's cue. Maybe it was the eternal perversity of billiard balls. But whatever it was, the lemon colored No. 1 ball, after having received its impetus from the cue ball, struck both corners of the pocket and then trickled back onto the cloth of the table." He wrote that Rudolf did not simply step to the table but rather bolted for it. "Mosconi may have been confident that he would not run the required forty-two for victory, but Rudolf thought otherwise. The final score was Erwin Rudolf 125, Willie Mosconi 124."

Had Willie sunk the one-ball during his second match of the 1933 world tournament, he would have won that game. That victory, in turn, would have given him the margin for the tournament-best record of 7–2 at the conclusion of the regular matches on December 21. But as it turned out the world event ended up in a four-way tie

---

[49] The headline was "Rudolf Runs 42 to Snatch Cue Victory: Rally beats Mosconi, 125–124." The story appeared on the front of the sports section on December 6, 1933.

between Mosconi, Ponzi, Caras, and Kelly, all of whom finished with records of 6–3.

During the playoff Willie came in fourth and out of the money. Had he sunk that yellow ball, had he not rushed it in, had he not hacked away at it impetuously, he would have not only been crowned world champ, but Mosconi would have been the only player ever to have won on his first outing. He also would have entered that extremely exclusive cadre of men to have won a world straight-pool title before age twenty-one. Greenleaf did it in 1919, at age twenty. Mosconi also was twenty when the yellow ball got away from him.

"Willie admitted that he was a young, cocky kid," promoter Charles Ursitti said of that errant one ball. "He fired that ball, he never forgets it his whole life, he fires the one in the upper right-hand pocket, and it jaws. Rudolf bolts out of his chair and runs forty-two and out. That game could have made Willie the first player to win the title in his first attempt. There are so many things hinging on that one ball, so many, and Willie never forgot it. Even the great Ralph Greenleaf didn't win on his first attempt."

Willie nonetheless acquitted himself more than admirably: the press then took to describing him as a young sensation; he beat just about every national and world-class player thrown against him; his key losses came about mostly because of his own mental errors, not because he was outclassed at this top level of play. Perhaps it's also fitting that Mosconi delivered the final humiliating blow to Greenleaf; that he sent the sleek-haired champion packing back to New York with that final rout in his ninth game. The great Greenleaf would have many more victories in his future—he still played better drunk than most world champions played sober—but Mosconi's appearance in 1933 presaged his doom. Despite the humiliating showing that year, Greenleaf was still then considered the best player living, the best player who *ever* lived.

But now there was Willie Mosconi on the scene.

Chapter 11

WIDE WORLD OF SPORTS

> Spanning the globe to bring you the constant variety
> of sport. . . .
> — *Wide World of Sports* signature line, broadcast every
> Saturday at 5:00 p.m. Eastern, 4:30 on Sundays

While ABC dealt with Hal Cayton of the Big Fights team on a fairly regular basis, those who remember said it was specifically Jim Jacobs who served as the partnership's friendly public face. Big, ruddy, and healthy, Jacobs was as beloved as any who sells professional sports for a living. And not only that, but he also had a ridiculously bright bald head. "He was a really great guy, really great people," recalled one long-time associate. "I started dealing with him in the 1960s, dealt with him for years, and I knew him to be a tremendous athlete and a real up-front guy."

Jacobs was a former national handball champion, a man who dominated the sport during the 1950s. This was a fact that somehow made him impossibly even more likable. Also, his Big Fights partnership had signed such big names as Wildredo Benitez, Edwin Rosario (considered pound for pound one of the best fighters ever), and Mike Tyson. He had amassed a big, beautiful, impressive film collection of old fights. And so to the very hail-fellow Jim Jacobs, a man with long-standing relations with the network brass, the responsibility fell to lobby for the Fats & Willie Show. This only made sense.

Did you see them go after each other? he would have said. *Could you believe it?* It would have begun with the agitated phone calls to ABC's Roone Arledge, and maybe also to Coordinating Producer Dennis Lewin. Jacobs, then forty-seven, would have explained the money-making potential of Fats and Willie. Jacobs also would have presumptuously explained how he believed the program should air and when Fats & Willie should play. He certainly shared the numbers.

And finally, Jacobs would have insisted, *insisted*, on ABC's *Wide World of Sports*. He had regular and long dealings with Arledge, the show's creator, and he knew that Mosconi's trick-shot exhibitions had done fairly well for the program. He probably remembered that *Wide World* had sent Jim McKay and a sixteen-mm film crew to the famous hustler jamborees in Johnston City during the early 1960s. The program was a big part of the reason that Fats the Motormouth had become so pain-in-the-ass famous.

"That's what *Wide World of Sports* was created to do," said one long-time producer.

The first organizational meeting was over at ABC's Fifty-sixth Street offices. Network VP John Martin was there, as were Producers Chet Forte and Lewin. Arledge himself may have stuck his head in on occasion.

Promoter Charles Ursitti said it came together perfectly: Fats, Willie, the likable Jim Jacobs. "Everything jelled right," he said. "If you had to pick the magic formula, we had the ingredients for it. We had the greatest player in the world. Mosconi was the best. This is just factually true. We had Jacobs with a formal affiliation with ABC. The timing was right; the players were right; the ingredients were right. God was on our side. And we knew from the beginning it would be *Wide World of Sports*. It was perfect."

•   •   •

The iconic sports program began during that faraway time before the Internet and before cable, when there was no such thing as ESPN or ESPN2. On the air since 1961, it had become famous for its depiction of Chinese Ping-Pong, Japanese baseball, and European track and field. *Wide World of Sports* aired Russian weight lifting, barrel rolling, figure skating, and foreign mustachioed men in toboggans. It would run any sport, from any nation, no matter how bizarre—just as long as there was money to be made and a story to be told. "It was the biggest thing in sports television—*period*," said former coordinating producer Dennis Lewin.

He said that a well-hyped sports program from those days could outdraw just about everything from the postcable era. And he said *Wide World* was the Big Daddy of them all, the show to beat all sports shows. *Wide World* on occasion would draw 20 percent or more of the entire American population. Contrast that with postcable-age programming that might attract just 7 percent and still be considered a smash hit.

"If you got a big rating then [prior to cable], you'd have millions and millions and millions of people watching—much more than you have watching now," Lewin said during a 2006 interview. "That's the kind of buzz you'd get, that's what *Wide World of Sports* was all about. From the early '70s to almost the mid-'80s, it completely dominated weekend sport television. It was a huge big deal at the time. It was a different animal."

Why did *Wide World* stand out, even among other sports programs? What did *Wide World* have to sell? In a memo to ABC brass, creator Roone Arledge delivered the two-word answer: "Show business." The network's mission was not to bring sports to the viewer but to bring the viewer to sports—no matter how far afield, no matter how foreign. ABC would translate, transmit, capture, and propagate enthusiasm for games intrinsically foreign to American audiences. Only with the tools of show business could sports programmers ever hope to succeed, he explained.

ABC should use "every production technique that has been learned in producing variety shows, in covering political conventions, in shooting travel and adventure series," Arledge wrote to network bosses shortly after coming to ABC in 1960. He wanted cameras mounted in jeeps, on mike booms, on risers of helicopters—anything necessary. With rights purchased for $50,000, the show began by airing amateur track and field—but what it really was selling was drama.

"Our first job, of course, was to get the rights to broadcast these events," Arledge[50] recalled about those early days. "So I sent Chuck Howard, who was then a recently hired production assistant, and who eventually became our vice president for program production, over to my previous network's microfilm library to look up the dates of the events we were interested in. With this information in hand, I then took several foreign trips to secure the rights to things like the British Open, the Japanese All-Star Game, Le Mans, and the US/USSR Track and Field Competition."

The famous opening sequence, "the thrill of victory and the agony of defeat" bit featuring the colossal wipeout of Slovenian ski jumper Vinko Bogataj, provided a meaningful target for the show's producers. It was the raison d'etre for the entire enterprise: no matter what the sport, drama was drama, and victory and defeat transcended culture and language.

"I thought that if we're going to do an anthology program that spanned the globe, that presented the thrill of victory and the agony of defeat as common to sports competition, we needed to express that in a way that would make people watch the show regardless of what sport we're going to televise," said Arledge. "This philosophy led directly to what became *Wide World's* general creative concept: the idea that there are values and emotions inherent in all sports, and if you, the audience, tune in and give us a chance, we'll prove it to you."

•　　•　　•

---

[50] *Life* magazine in 1990 listed Arledge among its "100 Most Important Americans of the 20th Century."

Show business as much as sports would define the Fats & Willie Show. Think Evel Knievel jumping the Snake River Canyon; think the Harlem Globetrotters facing the Washington Generals. Think *the world's greatest hustler facing the world's greatest pool champion.* What Jim Jacobs and Hal Cayton and Charlie Ursitti were selling was a *story.* With enough hype, enough promotion, enough pizzazz, kids would skip their homework for it.

They decided to call their spectacular Fats and Willie competition "The Great Pool Shoot-Out." It would be money in the bank.

Chapter 12

RALPH AND WILLIE

They did all these exhibitions: on top of a car where a
platform was built, on top of a bus. They did things like
that. Brunswick would have a way with sports heroes,
they would clamp on to them.

— Brunswick historian Joe Newell

Shortly after Willie Mosconi demolished Ralph Greenleaf during the
1933 world championship, Brunswick Billiards hired the twenty-year-
old upstart as a foil to the former champion for a 112-day road tour.
For years it was Greenleaf whom the company trotted out as the main
attraction for its Brunswick's Better Billiards Program. He was a huge
draw, a star. But Greenleaf's drinking then had reached epic levels, his
wife had tried to divorce him, his title was gone and his image tar-
nished. That he now had to team up with Willie Mosconi, the man
who on December 17 had caused him to miss "more called balls than
he had in any previous tournament held in the last decade," must have
seemed like torture.

It was as if the pool gods were punishing him.

Greenleaf and Mosconi shared train berths and lodging, but they
never became friends. Greenleaf never offered instructions, never became to Mosconi a father figure. Instead, the man some remember as
the sport's greatest champion did all he could to strangle Mosconi
with his soft sidearm shots, with broken clusters and perfect position

play. Greenleaf weaved silent patterns on the table even as he weaved staggering around it. He tottered while Willie pranced.

"We traveled together for almost four months, but during all that time Ralph never took me aside to offer any instruction," said Mosconi. "It didn't matter to him that these were just exhibition games; that there was no money at stake, no title to be won. He didn't care that we were, in a sense, part of the same team, working for the same employer. He wanted to beat me every game, and by as big a score as possible. . . . He was a fierce and friendless competitor."

Although pool lore abounds with tales of famous pool-playing teams (Wimpy Lassiter and Don Willis, Jersey Red and Boston Shorty),[51] there was never a partnership like Greenleaf and Mosconi. To this day the cognoscenti argue over which was the greater champion—not which was the best player then playing but which was the best who *ever played*. Partnering Greenleaf with Mosconi was like partnering Ty Cobb with Babe Ruth, Michael Jordan with Wilt Chamberlain. And while neither was then at the top of his game (on the best of days, Greenleaf's drunkenness was simply out of control), it still must have been something to behold.

Not much is known about the Mosconi & Greenleaf Show—at least, not much beyond what Willie himself said of it. Although Brunswick[52] made plenty of references to the Better Billiards Program in its catalogues, Willie doesn't begin to appear in them until the 1940s.[53] Neither is the 1934 tour mentioned in *Billiards Magazine*, then the main industry rag. Pool historians Mike Shamos, Charles Ursitti, and Joe Newell can find no independent reference to Mosconi's participation in 1934.

What we know for certain is that Brunswick pumped hundreds of

---

[51] See *Hustler Days*.

[52] Moreover, Brunswick Billiards, which has suffered fire and flood over the years (and has done a notoriously bad job of maintaining historical records), had no information about the 1934 program.

[53] Until then, the company would promote Greenleaf, three-cushion star Willie Hoppe, Jimmy Caras, and others.

thousands of dollars into promotional events. We also know that Mosconi had a long-standing relationship with the company. "They kept these guys around and used their names as a PR thing," said Newell, an expert on Brunswick. And we know that Mosconi often recalled the events of that year: that Brunswick Promotions Director Clyde Storer approached him with a $150-per-week offer, that he accepted, that his first assignment was that 112-day tour with Ralph Greenleaf, whom he had just humiliated in a world competition.

Willie would speak of the tour from time to time in interviews, mentions it in his 1965 book *Winning Pocket Billiards,* and devotes several pages to the exhibition tour in his memoirs, written with Stanley Cohen. There he explained that Brunswick then kept twenty-one topflight players in its stable and that when he accepted Storer's offer he became the youngest. Willie said the players were divided up, seven each into three geographical regions, East, Midwest, and Pacific. And while he didn't mention particular cities, one assumes he and Greenleaf kept close to the East Coast. He said they seldom stayed more than a night or two in any given city and that he always kept $100 stashed in his watch pocket in case he got stranded.

All told, Mosconi and Greenleaf played 107 games, and Greenleaf won most of them, even though he was drunk pretty much all the time. But of the fifty games that Mosconi claimed he won, most came during the final weeks of the tour. That is, Mosconi improved as he went along; he got slammed by Greenleaf during the first two months but came roaring back at the end. For this, Willie credited his own powers of observation: "I watched him like a hawk," he said. Remember, before 1934 Willie wasn't much more than a witless kid (albeit a preternaturally talented one) and a child who would never, *ever* finesse a ball when he could slam it instead. He was so young that in Minneapolis he actually had to deny to the media that he had run away from home. In New York he brashly told one reporter that his elders had nothing to teach him. Given the breaks, he said, he could beat anyone alive.

But on the road with Greenleaf, getting killed by a drunk day in and day out, Willie realized how wrong he had been. He said he couldn't even have kept Greenleaf off the booze if he'd wanted to. He said that Greenleaf seemed to have friends everywhere. They'd bring liquor to Ralph in his hotel room, and he never went anywhere without a flask. This was the man who once trounced about the lobby of New York's luxurious President's Hotel in nothing but his pajamas. He once purchased an entire wardrobe from a bell captain after his wife jettisoned his clothing from the upper-floor window of the Walton Hotel.

And yet more than half the time Willie couldn't beat him.

"I don't know how he did it," said Willie, who acknowledged that even on such a booze-soaked tour Greenleaf still displayed the softest touch he'd ever seen. "Even on long shots he seemed to be able to feel a ball right into the pocket, to shoot it just hard enough without banging away. It was like watching a virtuoso playing the violin, just beautiful. . . . And Greenleaf played position like no one else; there was no other player in his league. He would sometimes play whole racks without having to make a long shot."

• • •

So they played 112 days. Ralph won most, but Willie also won some. And at the end of it Willie was approached by a promoter, a man by the name of Sylvester Livingston, who then also had regular dealings with Brunswick. Livingston offered Willie a piece of another tour, one under which the future champion would get 75 percent of the proceeds. But in this one Willie would be on his own. There would be no Greenleaf to face, just whoever was the local hotshot. Livingston said Willie would have to cover his own expenses.

And hence began another stage of Willie's life: He spent the next eight years, tough ones, on the road for the promoter Sylvester Livingston. He faced local sharks on broken-down, crater-pocked tables, often before hostile crowds. He could neither win too quickly nor bore the crowd by taking too long. And then each night he would trudge back to a dingy motel room where he'd wash his clothes in the sink. "I sometimes played as many as four exhibitions a day in four different towns," said Mosconi. "That meant you spent more times on the highway than you did playing. . . . It was a tough, grinding life."

More than twenty thousand miles each year, that's how much Mosconi figured he logged for Sylvester Livingston. But because the promoter already had a legal arrangement with Brunswick, the touring never posed any sort of business conflict for Willie. Willie also continued competing in national and world tournaments—at least, when there were world tournaments. The nation was still deep into the ruinous Depression (in 1933 nearly one in four Americans went jobless, and many more were underemployed), and so Brunswick, ever cautious, elected to suspend full-blown world competitions temporarily.

It's not that the popularity of the game had dwindled. In fact, poolhalls during the Depression became the gathering place of choice for America's out-of-work men. Brunswick itself noted this phenomenon, as did sociologist Ned Polsky in his *Hustlers, Beats and Others*. But Brunswick understood that the men then loitering in poolhalls had only dust in their pockets, not the cash needed to support an intricate multicity competition. Plus, table sales were down. So Brunswick, a hard-hit company but one that weathered the Depression as well as any, decided to play it safe. Renting tournament space, paying travel expenses, creating a prize fund, doing all the innumerable things that go into a world competition: none of that came cheap.

In two of the years without full-blown tournaments, the Billiard Association of America mounted less expensive two-player challenge matches.[54] They came in 1934 and 1936. Mosconi was not invited to participate in either one. During the other years Mosconi came up short but not by much. And he always said he could have won had he exercised a bit more caution. "I began to understand frustration," he

---

[54] According to information provided by Charles Ursitti, Andrew Ponzi won in 1934 by besting Erwin Rudolf 750–607 at the Capital Bowling & Billiards Academy on Broadway in New York. In '36, Rudolf again placed second in a challenge match—this time to Jimmy Caras, 750–743 in Philadelphia.

said in his memoirs.[55] In 1939 the BAA didn't even bother with the inconvenience of a challenge match. And so it was exactly then, with support falling from Brunswick and the economy still foundering, that Mosconi decided to retire again from the sport. He cancelled his contract, stopped touring for Livingston, packed his bags and moved to Hollywood.

What can be pieced together about this brief hiatus comes to us through family records and through Willie's own recollections. Mosconi wrote in his memoirs that he had no plan, none whatsoever, when he quit pool. He chose Hollywood only because he had a cousin living there and because California was warmer than Philly. ("Might as well starve where it was warm," he said.) But honest work came no easier in California, and so Willie found himself inexorably drawn back to the game. How else was he going to survive? Like it or not, pool was all he knew. Livingston, who was probably desperate himself, approached Willie about another tour with Greenleaf. And as has been the story of his life so far, Willie turned to pool not out of love for the game but out of self-preservation. He didn't count the number of games he won (or the number he lost) because he did not care. Returning to pool, then, probably felt like a retreat.

One other note.

While on the road with Greenleaf, either in Georgia or South Carolina, the two pool aces flipped their car. Mosconi never mentioned the incident, not in his memoirs or his instructional book or in subsequent interviews, but his son William heard the story. His father was on the road with Greenleaf, the car flipped, and Willie Mosconi broke his neck. He ended up in traction for weeks or maybe months. "They hit one of those wild pigs on the road, and they flipped the car over," said

---

[55] In 1935, for instance, Mosconi won his sectionals but then placed behind George Kelly and Jimmy Caras in the nationals. Caras also won that year's forty-five-game world competition, which was conducted over purple-clothed tables at the Pennsylvania Hotel, just across the street from where Madison Square Garden now stands. The year 1937 marked a resurgence for Greenleaf, who won both the national and world events that year, plus a challenge match with Irving Crane in December. In 1938 Jimmy Caras won the nationals and the world event. A dozen of the nation's top players competed in each event.

Mosconi's son. It's unclear whether Ralph was driving, or Willie, or whether they had been drinking.

• • •

Now, it's important to mention here that Livingston, Mosconi, and Greenleaf would not have embarked on this new tour without at least the tacit approval of Brunswick Billiards. For much of the last century (and part of the century before that) the company's invisible hand moved just about anything having to do with pocket billiards. Remember, the venerable company sponsored that promotional gimmick, known as the Better Billiards Program, that put Greenleaf and Mosconi on the road together and over the years had pumped millions of dollars into other marketing efforts. But what's perhaps even more startling is that not only did Brunswick sponsor the Billiard Association of America, which was then the official sanctioning body of pool, but actually *controlled* it. Mosconi said the Better Billiards Program tour never conflicted with the BAA championships because the BAA was, quite literally, a company subsidiary. Besides operating as promotions director for the pool company, Clyde Storer also served as president of the BAA. Besides organizing exhibition tour stops for Mosconi, Livingston also helped organize future world championships on behalf of Brunswick and the BAA.

In its official history Brunswick itself acknowledges that its dominant business position allowed it to "direct" official tournaments for nearly one hundred years, from the 1880s until the 1970s. At one point the company even owned the copyright on the official rules and record book. It wasn't pool in America unless Brunswick said it was. And players didn't likely get into world tournaments without the company's consent. In *The Encyclopedia of Sports* Clement Trainer called it the "billiard trust" and said the hold that a small number of manufacturers had on the sport was sometimes perceived with something less than affection. "With tactics today that would induce coronaries in the Department of Justice, they ruled the game with an iron hand," wrote

Trainer. "They donated the 'championship' emblem, and only contests played with their equipment were recognized as being for the 'championship.' Matches had to be sanctioned."

Why is all this significant? Because the pool establishment—the people who made money off pool tables, the people who organized the professional tournaments—were all the same. In some ways Mosconi and Greenleaf and all the gods of that era became indentured servants to Brunswick: for their tournament earnings, for their tour money, for their prestige. All the paychecks—whether through Storer's exhibitions, or those operated by Livingston, or through the challenge matches and the tournament round-robins—all of them flowed from Papa Brunswick. "Brunswick kept the clean-cut players around, to use their names; it was a PR thing," said Newell. "They did all these exhibitions. On top of a car where a platform was built, on top of a bus. They did things like that. Brunswick would have a way with sports heroes; they would clamp on to them. And they invested in all these tournaments. They invested millions to keep the sport in the public's eye."

So when one thinks of the American pocket billiards during this early heyday, one must think of it in these terms: Brunswick equals Billiard Association of America equals Willie Mosconi and Ralph Greenleaf. Willie didn't make pool his life's calling because he loved it (because, in fact, he did not) or because of his fascination with the poolroom lifestyle (which he held in complete contempt). It was the offer of easy money that first brought Mosconi to the sport and it was the offer of a regular paycheck from Brunswick that kept him there.

Pool historian Mike Shamos likened Brunswick's hold over pool at that time to that of the Mafia. "You could not buck Brunswick; it was death to do so," he said. "It was total, dictatorial control. . . . If you messed with Brunswick, you didn't get invited to the next tournament; even the sectional tournaments were invitational. So there was no chance that an up-and-coming rising star could [succeed] on ability alone. They had to get invited by Brunswick, and Brunswick controlled all the organizations."

This is a point to be returned to later, but suffice to say there is no room in the equation for gamblers and hustlers, for those whose pursuit of the sporting life more truthfully defined pool. Brunswick's main interest was to expand the market, to sell tables to Mom and Dad, to brother and sis. That family-friendly strategy also became the BAA's strategy and Clyde Storer's and, by extension, the lifelong work of Willie Mosconi.

At the beginning of the century, the company sold tables as fast as the company produced them from eight distinct factories. It had offices in twenty-seven cities, plus five dealer rooms in Canada and even more in London, Paris, Buenos Aires, Honolulu, and Mexico City. Journalist Rick Kogan, writing in *Brunswick, the Story of an American Company*, notes that at one time Brunswick owned more than a thousand acres of timberland near Lake Superior and was the world's largest user of hardwood. The company owned a sawmill, a lumber camp, boarding houses, repair shops, a small railroad, steamboats, and slate quarries. It produced four hundred thousand cues each year, and could produce six hundred thousand more if need be. The company created more pool tables during the 1920s than all American piano manufacturers created pianos. "At one time the company controlled 75 percent of raw material and 85 percent of the market," said Newell, the company expert. "They were the *instigator* of billiards in our country."

To promote these interests, and to expand upon them, the company engaged in a long, determined effort to define the culture of the sport. They would sell tables to the middle class by making billiards respectable for the middle class. Old *Saturday Evening Post* advertisements show men in suits playing pocket billiards at home with their wives. A kindly grandmother looks on. The conservative *Christian Herald* magazine printed illustrations of various YMCA buildings where "billiards, the gentlemen's game, is played regularly."[56] Brunswick promoted this half-fiction that pool was family-fun entertainment, not a lure to the streets. "How Present-Day Parents Keep the Hat-Rack Filled," reads one old advertisement. And: "$5 Brings a Brunswick Home Billiard Table (along with a monthly payment of $2.50)."

Seen through this lens of culture, a $2.50-per-month payment for a Brunswick table can be interpreted as a tithing. It was the industry leaders who changed the official name of the sport from pool to pocket billiards so the sport did not seem so closely aligned with the hustling element. It was the industry leaders who insisted that tournament players wore impractical tuxedos during competition, as if they were heading to the opera and not instead bending over chalky tables. Brunswick for years had been in the business of creating a truth not only about their company but about the game itself. And in men like Willie Mosconi, it even created gods to define that truth.

So where does a man like Minnesota Fats fit into this pantheon? The short answer is that he does not.

---

[56] This was cited by John Grissim, in his book *Billiards*. He also noted that on November 8, 1924, the magazine withdrew future billiard advertising and posted the following announcement on its editorial page: "In correspondence that developed over the billiard advertising, it was evident that a number of our readers felt that the carrying of this advertising was equivalent to an endorsement by the *Christian Herald* of the public billiard hall. This was not true. The *Christian Herald* is, and has been, unalterably opposed to the public billiard hall as most of them have been operated. In fact our attitude was one of creating such competition for these halls so they would be forced to clean house or get out of business. While there were only approximately 50 people who wrote us on the matter, they were so unanimous in their failure to agree with us that we feel it represents a real volume of sentiment of the readers of the *Christian Herald*."

Chapter 13

THE TRICKSTER
1978

> Trickster is at one and the same time creator and de-
> stroyer, giver and negator, he who dupes others and who
> is always duped himself. . . . He knows neither good nor
> evil yet he is responsible for both. He possesses no val-
> ues, moral or social . . . yet through his actions all val-
> ues come into being.
>
> — Anthropologist Paul Radin

What a stir they created. What a commotion. Dowell, Illinois, population four hundred, home of the famous Veterans Inn, where the old
fogies drank beer. And then there was nearby Du Quoin, population
five thousand, with the Evening Star and the declining St. Nicholas
Hotel with Joe Scoffic's kitchen-table poker games.[57] Nothing much
happened in Dowell, and nothing much happened in Du Quoin—
leastwise not since they barred the airmen from Scotts Field and all the
mines closed down. But now these TV men had blown in; *they were all
over* . . . and they were asking questions.

"Who's the most famous person in town?" High schooler Cecil
Williams gets practically accosted walking along the tracks of the Illinois

---

[57] See *Hustler Days*.

Central Gulf Railroad. The New Yorkers shove a microphone in his face. Flustered, Cecil can't figure the proper answer.

"How much does Fats eat? I mean, really?" They ask this one over at the house on the outskirts of Dowell, the one Fats shares with his wife Evelyn. His mortgage-paying mother-in-law says Fats eats plenty. "Wish we could make him stop."

Dowell, Illinois—just five miles south of Du Quoin, fifteen miles west of Benton, and right smack in the center of that patch of Illinois known as Little Egypt—became the landing spot for ABC Sports, which sent down its film crew in the winter of 1978. Up and down Missouri Street tore the black, yellow, and white ABC van; up and down Union Avenue, interviewing Dowellonians (Or is it Dowelle-cites? The New Yorkers never knew.), muscling into cafes, setting their sixteen-mm cameras a-whirring atop metal tripods.

The crew was putting together a setup piece for The Great Pool Shoot-Out, now scheduled for Feb. 14, and to be aired eleven days later. Roone Arledge and Producer Dennis Lewin had sent down a crew to Dowell, Fats's adopted hometown, and Du Quoin, where Fats did his shopping. The locals even remembered Howard Cosell making an appearance.

This is what the film crew learned in 1978, when they appeared in Little Egypt like outer-space aliens:

- Fats beat the shah of Iran before there was ever any Iran.
- Fats clobbered the kaiser in World War I and humiliated the führer in World War II.
- Fats flew to every city in the world twice and went down with the ship three times.
- Fats shot craps atop the Brooklyn Bridge.
- Fats swam the ocean with Moby Dick. This, however, was when Moby Dick was a guppy.

And these are the people that Minnesota Fats beat playing pool for money:

- Andrew Ponzi

- Jimmy Caras
- Ralph Greenleaf
- Wimpy Lassiter
- A man named Cowboy Weston
- *The eyeballers*
- Anybody with *da gelt*
- Willie Mosconi—repeatedly

The film crew knew all this to be true because Fats claimed it to be true. The film crew also knew this to be true because Fats said he never, ever lied when it came to money ("I kept winning and winning until I thought I'd have to call an armored car to get out," he would say) and because some of the locals, *some of them,* actually agreed that Fats had done these things.

At the Veteran's Inn, right next to the movie theater and Ogolini's Bakery over on Union Avenue, the pool hustler strutted about like a well-fed rooster. The Veterans Inn was a BYOB joint, and although Fatty didn't drink himself, he wasn't shy about getting on the phone double-quick to bark crosstown orders for brown-bag cocktails. A film crew had come to capture Fatty in action. "I want a fifth of whiskey," he'd say, and "Bring some beer." He instructed John Ogolini, his old friend on the other end of the line, to go get wife Evelyn and tell her to bring sandwiches. "There will be a big tip in it for you if you're quick." A photographer snaps his picture. It's snowing outside.

And then Fats holds forth, speaking grandly for the cameras: "And I'm not talking fun games, you understand," he says. "I'll play for money, marbles, or chalk! Put your money down, and I'll play!" Fats reminds everyone about the kaiser, and the führer, and about Moby Dick. Fats reminds them about the piles of cash he'd won from all those in power. He says he can make long bank shots whenever he pleases, and that he can run eight and out at will, and that he always succeeds when everyone bets on him to fail.

"But can you beat the champ?" they ask Minnesota Fats, insistent. "Can you beat Willie Mosconi?"

•   •   •

Some Americans, many of them in fact, actually *believed* Fats could win. Not that he would win, not that he was a sure thing or the favorite—but that he *could*. Fatty, after all, was wily. He was a hustler. The best ever, according to his own claims. And wasn't pocket billiards a game of hustlers? Wasn't it possible that Minnesota Fats could spring some devious trap? As soon as ABC started running the promos and the advertising began, so too did this speculation: Fats had something up his sleeve, some secret deception—and he would produce this deception at just the right moment (rope-a-dope style) and surprise the world. In schoolyards and country clubs, men and boys asked aloud the same tantalizing question: could Minnesota Fats succeed?

It wasn't the answer to this question but the question itself—the way it was posed and the fact that every male between the ages of seven and seventy posed it—that explains what happened next. The Great Pool Shoot-Out gained a currency in the United States that none of the organizers could ever have predicted, a currency outstripping most other sporting events during that year or any other. Willie Mosconi versus Minnesota Fats. Minnesota Fats versus Willie Mosconi. The trickster challenging the great champion. Big Fights and Promoter Charles Ursitti had unwittingly come up with a potentially explosive combination.

Ursitti recalls getting invited to a birthday party for Joe DiMaggio. Ursitti was a nobody, an unknown, and his invitation came about only by virtue of Ursitti's relationship with ABC. But when DiMaggio said he *knew* the promoter, said he was *aware* of his work, it was then that Ursitti began to realize the value of the question. "I mustered up the courage and went up to him," recalled Ursitti of that first meeting with the baseball legend. At that moment Ursitti had hoped only to snag DiMaggio's autograph. "But then he takes me aside and says,

'Can I ask you something?' And I'm thinking *Holeeee Shit.* He's there, and there's [a bunch of players from] the Bronx Bombers. And I say 'You're a legend and a hero, and I grew up watching you' . . . and DiMaggio says to me, 'I know exactly who you are, and I want to know if Willie wins.'"

Ursitti had never met DiMaggio, had no relationship whatsoever with him, and yet here he was, conferring with the sports icon about a match between two *pool players.* DiMaggio had placed a wager and wanted to know whether he should press. The possibility that Willie Mosconi could get outplayed, that the world's greatest champion could lose to a two-bit hustler, somehow had entered DiMaggio's mind.

Fats, after all, was *tricky.*

•   •   •

In the days before the Great Shoot-Out, that same question, *Can Fats win? Can he beat Willie Mosconi?* floated over Little Egypt like that winter's first snow. There, in that patch of southern Illinois that Fats called home, the men and boys had heard the stories, and some (not all, but some) had seen Fats in action. So they thought they knew what he could do. Did they need to believe? Was it a craving? Former Dowell mayor Luciano Lencini, a grown-up man who acknowledged that "about eighty percent of what Fats said was bullshit," would nonetheless never bet against Fats. Nor would he advise others to do so. It was like the hesitation of a shaky agnostic before the prospect of cursing God. Best just to leave it be. "Hell, I seen him throw down a damn $1,000 bill and say, 'Let's go,'" said Luciano, marveling. "A damn $1,000 bill! The man never worked a day in his life, and he had a $1,000 bill."

Brad Holford, whose parents had become a favorite of Fats by virtue of the fact that they owned the local Kentucky Fried Chicken franchise, used to squire Fats all around southern Illinois. Mostly it was so the old hustler could play exhibitions, but sometimes Fats would gamble, too. Holford said he had seen him win thousands of dollars, *thousands*—and do so easily. "There was this guy in St. Louis, and he beat the guy out of like $8,000 or $9,000," recalled Holford. "He just killed him. By the end of the game, the guy couldn't make a ball, and Fats had everybody laughing. He won that bunch of money, and I witnessed it all. . . ."

And so Holford said there was some truth in everything Fats said. "Absolutely, I thought he could win. I knew he could play because I had seen him play. . . . I didn't think he'd walk away with it, but I thought he'd win."

One after another Fats spewed his lies, always in the form of buckshot one-liners, always insisting on the Truth of his Greatness with unwavering certainty. He told the stories on the sidelines of tournaments, disrupting play, and he told them when the newspaper men came to call, and he told them to magazine writers and the TV journalists. They have been described as tall tales, although folktales would have been closer to the mark, as folktales are what get associated with trickster figures like Brer Rabbit. And that is exactly how the American public perceived Minnesota Fats in 1978, when he insisted that every word that came out of his mouth was 100 percent on the square.

"He and that Howard Cosell, they came into that tavern, and he'd give them that song and dance," said Luciano Lencini, the mayor, laughing and stomping his feet as he recalled the deceit. "Fats drew them in that day. He was a wicked pool hustler and a natural entertainer. Hell, I watched him sucker in Howard Cosell himself. I watched it. The ABC crew believed him. But I will tell you this: Fats could do what he said when it came to hustling."

And so when one of the ABC men asked the question, when he put it to him—Fats did not hesitate. He never hesitated. "Sonny boy," he said, "there's about as much chance of me losing to Willie Mosconi as an airplane crashing into my house!" As always, Fats spoke with utter and absolute confidence. His answer came from a place deep within him, like a growl.

As ABC edited the sequence later, a plane would actually go crashing into an old rickety house. Editors crosscut stock 1930s silent-era footage into their interview with Fats, an old biplane dropping from the sky—and *ka-POW!*—a house collapses. Dennis Lewin, the ABC coordinating producer, recalls his own skepticism regarding Fats's outlandish claims. Plus Roone Arledge, the head of ABC Sports, knew Willie Mosconi personally, had watched him play, and understood that he was the greatest champion in the history of pocket billiards.

But even so, the ABC producers themselves couldn't be too sure.

Chapter 14

THE PROPHET

Tense? Sure, I'm tense. I've never met a good competitor who isn't high strung.

—Willie Mosconi, speaking to *Bowlers
Journal* writer Rocky Wolfe in 1941

Zero. Zero. Zero. Zero.

Eleven zeroes in all: that's what the score table showed for William Joseph Mosconi. It's March 19, 1938. It's New York City. Willie slides the cue ball up against the end rail, and pockets *nothing*. Or he nestles the cue ball behind the stack and again pockets *nothing*. Sometimes Mosconi sends one ball down the hole or maybe two but not enough to score . . . because Mosconi also has scratched.

Repeatedly.

Zero. . . . Zero. . . . Zero. . . . Zero.

That night the *New York Times* tallied eleven innings of nothing for Mosconi. Pitted against fellow Philadelphian Andrew Ponzi, he turned in a performance that to the untutored would have seemed bungling and imprecise. As always Mosconi sprinted about the table, lithe, nimble, and confident. The bleachers at New York's Capitol Bowling and Billiard Academy were full, the Depression-era crowd expectant.

But while Mosconi scratched, made nothing, or sunk so few balls as to stay in the red for eleven innings, one could nonetheless detect a new ingredient in his game. It wasn't until the fifteenth that he raised his per-inning average higher than a one. The *New York Times* called his performance "erratic." And yet Mosconi played that day with defiance, focus, and—most important of all—brains. He pushed whitey against the rail, he took an intentional scratch, with little enthusiam he played *backwards*.

And then slowly, slowly, pecking at the stack, driving a ball or two away but leaving nothing, Mosconi dug himself out.

Like Minnesota Fats, Mosconi could sit still only with great difficulty. But in 1938 he managed to subdue his fiery nature long enough to win. In that long match with Andrew Ponzi (it went twenty-eight innings), Mosconi finally came up with two points in the twelfth; then thirteen in the thirteenth, thirteen in the fourteenth, sixteen in the fifteenth, and thirty-six in the sixteenth. He played not with patience, never with patience, but with something approaching it. In that year's world championship, in what would become a defining match of the world championship, he beat Andrew Ponzi using *defense*.

Final score: Mosconi 125, Ponzi 118.

The Capitol Bowling and Billiard Academy in New York hosted the tournament; Joseph Ferguson, again served as ref. With his victory Willie tied with the two other tournament leaders, Ponzi and Jimmy Caras of Delaware, each with 9–3 records. As it was the last regular match of the tournament, Willie's performance also sent the meet into a playoff, which Willie would lose. And it had been Willie's last real go, his last shot at a world title before his self-imposed exile to California. Willie's day had not yet arrived, not yet: but that showing hinted that his day was not far off.

Afterwards the *Times*'s Louis Effrat said Willie's style of play was not without guile. He said Mosconi took advantage of his opponents' errors and then overpowered them with terrifying long runs. Mosconi also recognized the change: "In addition to position play, I was always a good defensive player—[but only] after I got started, not right away," he said during an interview with *Billiards Digest* decades later. "By playing with these greats, I picked up their knowledge and combined it. If they put me down at the end of the table with a long shot, that didn't bother me."

Charles Ursitti said that there was improvement not just in Mosconi's defense but also in his position play. Mosconi the great offensive player had become even more *offensive,* said Ursitti. Consider this: A review of Mosconi's world-tournament high runs prior to 1938[58] reveal nothing higher than a ninety-eight. After 1938 he would run hundreds, not on rare occasions but *every few days.* In 1940 and 1941 he ran 125 and out once every dozen games or so. "Willie didn't have a lot of patience and only played safe when he had to," said Ursitti. "That was his style, even as an older player. . . . But [after '38] he played more like a veteran. His position play became even more accurate. Nothing was missing."

The world championship of 1940 did not feature Mosconi. Although back from his self-imposed exile in California, and certainly eligible, he nonetheless got passed over for the invitation-only event for the likes of Caras, Ponzi, Rudolf, and Crane.[59] Willie also recalls getting married just before this tournament—but here his memory clearly has failed him. What's more likely is that he then made the acquaintance of his future wife, Anna Lucy Harrison, who was then about twenty-two years old and five years Willie's junior. But they did not then marry.

Little is known about the relationship other than it was no doubt tumultuous. Anna had run away from her Michigan home at age fourteen or fifteen, and she was the youngest of her family. She met Willie at the King Edward Hotel, a fifteen-floor luxury establishment on West Forty-fourth in New York. It's unclear whether Anna worked as a singer there or as a waitress. Separate records indicate she had been

---

[58] Here's another billiards note from 1938: Before the onset of hostilities between the Allies and the Nazis, an industrial chemist in Germany discovered a way to cast liquid phenolic resin into various shapes, including the shape of billiard balls. At that time, celluloid composition balls were in general use. The scientist that year contacted an English subsidiary of the Albany Billiard Ball Company with an offer to turn over his secret in exchange for help gaining safe passage for him and his family. The balls appeared on U.S. tables after World War II and are the sort most universally used today. This historic footnote comes to us courtesy of John Grissim's 1979 book *Billiards.* Grissim cites as the original source historian William Hendricks.

[59] Ponzi won.

on her own in New York for at least three years. She was also brunette, leggy, and sexy but with a dignified bearing that reminded the casual observer of Joan Crawford. And as she was a great lover of the high life—"a party girl" is how her sister described her—she must have seemed like sweet nectar indeed to the brooding and intense Mosconi. "She was a slender-figured woman," recalled Bill Mosconi, Willie's son. "She was kind of tall and fair-skinned. She was pretty."

Willie wrote very little about his first wife in his memoirs and said almost nothing about her to his children after the divorce. But it's clear that Anna and Willie were a new couple in November 1940, when the Billiard Association of America embarked on its next big world championship, and that Anna was pregnant with Willie's child during the six-month-long competition.

With regard to the tournament, it got its start in New York, in rooms like Julian's, not far from the King Edward where Willie met Anna, and also at McGirr's Academy and Doyle's.[60] Other matches played out in Newark, Philadelphia, Boston, Scranton, and Syracuse.[61] Anna may have traveled with Willie then—she may even have been in the crowd November 12 when Willie beat Onofrio Lauri twice at McGirr's. Willie ran 125 during his first game that day, during his very first inning at the table even. In the second game he went ninety-nine and out. And these victories came not on today's 4½ by 9s but on the

---

[60] One of the most famous features of the poolroom was the beautiful girl known as Kristie, who was purported to be the owner's daughter. She had terribly long legs, she was blonde, and she was gorgeous. Women were not permitted in the poolroom in those days, but the high-living Kristie got some sort of special dispensation on account of her purported family relationship. It is unclear what became of her.

[61] The rooms mentioned in *New York Times* accounts—Julian's Fourteenth Street Academy, McGirr's Academy, and Doyle's—were among the most famous in pool history. They've all since shut their doors.

[62] Asked by a *Billiards Digest* interviewer during the early 1980s about comments made by some younger players that the smaller 4½ by 9 tables are more difficult than the larger 5 by 10s, Mosconi responded, "How do they know? Did they play on the big tables? That's an asinine statement. The tables today are much easier. On the 5 by 10, you had to play defense because the shots were harder to make. If you put a guy on the end rail, he's not going to play that ball so easy. The shot was tough. On a 4½ by 9 you move everything up. A long shot is like a short one on a 5 by 10. That, plus the fact you had to play position on a 5 by 10. Half the guys today just bust the balls all over the table and then pick 'em off. These are nine-ball players talking today, not the people who really know."

much more difficult 5 by 10s. "A long shot on a 4½ by 9 is like a short one on a 5 by 10," Mosconi would say.[62]

On November 25 he smashed Ponzi with another 125-ball long run. On February 10 he did it again, this time in Newark against George Kelly. (He also beat Kelly twice that day.) Now consider this: Through almost the entirety of the tournament—through November, December, January, February, and March—Andrew Ponzi, the *then-world champion* Andrew Ponzi, had only managed a single high run of 120. And it wasn't as if Ponzi was suffering a bad tournament. Throughout it he led almost all other players. But even so, just one run of 120. With few exceptions, nobody else had done any better. But Mosconi—then twenty-eight years old, just then starting to turn gray, playing fast and playing angry—by the approximate midpoint of the world tournament he had run 125-and-out *five times.*[63] Not by the end of the tournament but by its *midpoint.* Also, with a record of 84–22, Willie held a full fifteen-game lead over his closest rival.

He wasn't just beating his opponents. He was burying them.

The *Times* reported more run-outs in March and April. "Mosconi shot [a] perfect game in the world pocket billiard champion series when he beat Onofrio Lauri, 125 to 0, at McGirr's last night," the paper reported April 22. "With an unfinished run of 125, Mosconi won the opener, 125–0, in two innings," the paper reported March 12. And when he wasn't running 125s and out, the paper reported he was running eighties, nineties, and hundreds . . . and then out.

Although Anna may not have understood the significance, sports fans surely did. And not just the cognoscenti: anybody who read the *New York Times* would have known that Willie Mosconi, that hither-to-then little-known player Willie Mosconi, was putting together in 1941 something historic. Runs of 125 and out were relatively rare achievements in all the years before Mosconi. Greenleaf managed it on occasion, as did Ponzi, but never with such utter ease and frequency. Never with such flair. Billiard writer George Fels said Mosconi would

---

[63] One run went 126.

bury his opponents with long runs, with one hundred after one hundred after one hundred. Historian Ursitti said Mosconi's level of play in 1941 must be seen in the same light as DiMaggio's fifty-six-game hitting streak, which coincidentally occurred in that same year, or with Bob Beamon's twenty-nine-foot long jump in 1968.

"Every eleventh game he ran out with 125s, 126, or 127," said Ursitti. "Does this sound normal? Does this sound human? And remember, he's not playing just anybody. He's playing world-class players. He's playing Ponzi and Rudolf and George Kelly." Upon his double victory over Jimmy Caras in December, the *Times* described Mosconi's lead as "commanding." After he scored his hundredth win, in February at McGirr's, the *Times* characterized it as nearly insurmountable. On April 7, a full three weeks before the official end, he beat Onofrio Lauri 125–102 and clinched the title outright. The last New York match came May 1; the tournament ended for good the next day in Philly, Willie's hometown.

Although Jimmy Caras did well on the final day,[64] neither his performance nor that of Andrew Ponzi, Joe Procita, Onofrio Lauri, Erwin Rudolf, George Kelly, or Johnny Irish—none of the competitors that year—came close to rivaling Mosconi. At the end he held a full thirty-game lead over the man in second place. On fifty occasions, nearly one fourth of all his games played, Mosconi ran one hundred or more. Nobody now could question his dominance of the sport.

Here are the final standings:

	Wins	Losses
Mosconi	176	48
Ponzi	144	80
Caras	125	99
Procita	117	107
Lauri	109	115
Rudolf	99	125
Kelly	85	139
Irish	41	183

•　　•　　•

If the entire nation did not follow the 1941 world tournament, then at least anyone who read the sports sections did. The *Times* published more than one hundred reports from Scranton, New York, Philadelphia, and Boston. Other papers followed suit. But even that start-to-finish coverage wasn't enough for some fans: New Yorker Arnold Weller complained that the *Times* articles weren't nearly *long* enough. "I say the pocket billiard event, held in New York and followed with interest by thousands of New Yorkers, is certainly deserving of more journalist attention than it has been receiving up to now," he griped in a January 29, 1941, letter.[65] As measured in newspaper coverage, the interest in pool during those years far outstripped interest in the sport during the latter half of the twentieth century or during the beginning of the twenty-first. Pool historian Shamos said that rather than running two stories a year about pool, the *Times* then typically ran two stories a *day*.

Now it's also true that the game had reached its peak of popularity just before Mosconi first appeared on the national stage in 1933, and it's also true that its popularity had been declining since. But that doesn't mean the game in 1941 was anything but explosively successful. "If you said 'Greenleaf' in the 1930s, people knew who you were talking about," said Shamos. If it was not then as popular as football or basketball, it was nearly so. Its coverage in the media roughly equaled that of professional boxing. Its stars were bona fide celebrities.

As *Times* reader Weller noted in 1941, when Ralph Greenleaf or three-cushion ace Willie Hoppe took center stage, people wanted to know about it. Weller wrote that thousands of fans followed their exploits, but hundreds of thousands or even millions was probably closer

---

[64] Jimmy Caras managed a 126-ball run in one of the final games that day.

[65] And the stolid *Times* actually agreed. Despite having published at least one article, every day, for six months—and having published them sometimes prominently on the front page of the sports section, along with stat boxes—the editors acknowledged in print they would have done a better job if not for the tournament's late-night, deadline-busting format.

to the mark. Mosconi's celebrity was nearly instantaneous. He was colorful, passionate, *fast,* handsome. His star had been rising for some time, from that first Chicago appearance in 1933 and through his third- and fourth-place finishes during the latter part of the decade. But now he had exploded nova fashion in the nation's largest cities. Back in the day, Mosconi recalls drawing more spectators than the Chicago Bears would draw to a football game.

And so it is here and then that he began to achieve the status of national phenomenon, that Willie Mosconi became something greater than a mere player. With the backing of Brunswick Billiards, Willie was becoming a goodwill ambassador and a prophet. By then the company had added Willie to its Better Billiard Program, which featured leading players in coast-to-coast exhibitions. Advertisements in *Billiard and Bowling News* during the 1940s featured Willie along with other professionals like Hoppe and Greenleaf.[66] As Willie's fame rose, so did his ability to spread his message about pool, a game that he did not always love but one for which he always had faith. From his increasingly high vantage point, Willie argued for the *potential* goodness of pool, its *potential* wholesomeness . . . despite what the hustlers and sharpers would make of it.

• • •

It's not that Willie believed pool was inherently good or wholesome. In fact it may have been that Willie believed the opposite. But like that of any prophet, Willie spread the word that when pursued properly and with discipline it was an endeavor that could transcend the worldly muck. Directly or indirectly, he promoted the notion that those who play his game should be clean-cut, should eschew gambling and vulgar language, should refrain from excessive drinking. He felt that only in this way could pool truly flourish. Of course, this was also Brunswick's view,[67] but Willie did not simply ape it; he truly believed it. And he further colored this vision with his own grim notions of sacrifice and self-control.

Candace Fritch, his daughter, said her father wasn't a moralist, per se (he wasn't a regular churchgoer, for instance), although he did have very black-and-white notions when it came to pocket billiards. He worked hard to achieve excellence. He sacrificed. And she said that her father saw the poolroom riffraff as a sorry, boastful lot. Neither did he suffer the company of fools, said Candace. "It had to do with being able to recognize quality—he recognized quality in everything," she said. "He knew what hard work was, he knew what a champion was, and for someone to say he was a champion without the hard work galled him."

Shamos, the historian, said Mosconi had nothing but disdain for those who would tarnish the game's image. "He really did feel it, sincerely. Mosconi aspired to perfection. Remember that for the top players this was their profession. It was the same for a doctor or a lawyer. Lawyers don't like other lawyers who associate with criminals or engage in criminal behavior. They look down on shysters. And doctors look down on quacks because it reflects poorly on their life's choice. It wasn't that Mosconi was scared of getting beat by hustlers; it's that he didn't like the foulness associated with them."

Like life in general, Willie believed the poolroom could be divided into those two great camps: those who worked hard, flew straight and maintained some dominion over their baser instincts; and those who did not. And like salvation in general, Mosconi believed the salvation of pool lay in making right choices. This moral reckoning of Willie's was recognized by all those closest to him. But like any prophet his relationship to the Good News was also a tortured one. Remember, not so long ago Willie Mosconi also had gambled on pool. Remember, when

---

[66] Others included Hoppe, Greenleaf, Jimmy Caras, and Carl Peterson.

[67] In its all-out marketing blitz to promote the wholesomeness of pocket billiards, Brunswick actually managed to get pool tables in churches. "One of their greatest successes was getting churches to install pool tables," said Mike Shamos, the billiards historian. "[The thinking was] if you put the table in the basement of a church, you can put those rowdies somewhere where you could see them.

"It was close to saying, 'Let's hire prostitutes—at least we can watch them screw in the church. It was close to that, and yet Brunswick made it work. . . . Brunswick did an amazing job selling billiards as a family-recreation thing."

his mother was dying and his father was sick and his family faced starvation, it was gambling he turned to. And like most moral messages, there was an element of *exclusion* to what Willie said. It was as if poolroom heaven would be reserved only for the select few. "Foulness he could not abide," said Shamos.

And yet foulness for many years had paid the bills.

After gaining that grand soapbox after 1941, after becoming a national figure, Willie would deny having ever hustled (which he distinguished from gambling), and he spoke relatively little about his gambling days. But he would not deny those days outright. Rather Willie set himself apart in his stories; he made himself the protagonist in a play wherein the wicked got their comeuppance. And if one listens closely one detects the moral: that the true gamblers, the morally weak, get a dose of their own medicine when confronted by the righteous. This would be the fate he would wish upon them all. "I was never a hustler," he told one reporter. "But when the hustlers came to town, they would have to play me because I was the youngest. And they wouldn't get to play again."

Willie never, ever embraced this lifestyle. He loathed it. But Willie also understood the allure. And he must have known at some unconscious level that the desperation that drove him to gamble also sharpened his survival skills and, through them, inexorably, his killer instinct. As biographer Stanley Cohen would observe: "Any opponent, at any stage of a game, was deemed a threat he could not abide." This emotion is called hate . . . and it was an important weapon for Willie Mosconi. It was, in fact, his most important weapon. Like the relationship of all prophets to human frailty, Willie's was fraught with ambiguity.

Chapter 15

WAGERS MADE WITH SUCKERS

The women all want to dance—I dance all night,
every night.
— Rudolf Walter Wanderone, a.k.a. Minnesota Fats

For Rudolf Walter Wanderone the truth, always, was a slippery thing. But what's certain is that the man who one day would redefine pocket billiards had been on the road, hustling pool and lying about it, since at least as long as Willie Mosconi had been playing in professional tournaments. Willie toured the fancy rooms of New York and Chicago. Wanderone feasted upon the down-and-out in Brooklyn, Hoboken, and Philly. Willie slipped into his $27.50 dress suit[68] in 1933. Wanderone supposedly was relieving three-cushion ace Arthur Thurnblad[69] of great wads of cash in California. Reliable evidence suggests Wanderone ranged as far west as Los Angeles, as far south as Arkansas and Oklahoma, and spent a winter in a D.C. suburb, where he confronted future world champion Luther Lassiter.[70]

Wanderone often claimed that he was the best in the world at the following pursuits (listed here in no particular order):

---

[68] That's how much Willie paid for his first dress suit—$27.50, money he made in 1933 by his top finishes in regional and national competitions.

[69] National three-cushion champion Thurnblad nonetheless was never known for his skill at pocket billiards.

[70] See *Hustler Days*.

- Playing pool

- Eating

- Sleeping

- Staying awake

- Shooting pistols

- Rifle marksmanship

- Talking

These things also are true about Rudolf Wanderone:

- He played one-pocket exceedingly well (which Mosconi called a hustlers' gimmick) and could also play bank pool.

- Wanderone attributed his prowess at these games to his ability to shoot rail-first shots, which he further attributed to his ability to play three-cushion billiards.

- While not flawless, he possessed a stroke that was nonetheless fluid and beautiful. Some said Wanderone's stroke was prettier than Mosconi's.

- Wanderone stood nearly upright as he shot, a habit made necessary by his rapidly expanding midsection.

- By the 1940s Wanderone was not merely heavy or overweight—he was fat. His breaths came in great gasping chugs; he had thick fingers like the pink legs of little babies; he groaned as he scaled the stairs at Cranfield's or Allinger's.

- Rudolf Wanderone was a petty thief, a habitual liar, and lazy; he gambled at dice and cards. Wanderone hardly ever drank alcohol, although he would enthusiastically eat whole chickens (and even turkeys) without help.

- He enjoyed the company of women and despite his growing waistline enjoyed some success with them.

•   •   •

Here's a story about Wanderone: While in California during the late 1930s, he apparently seduced and left pregnant a teenage girl by the name of Dorothy Hawkins. Wanderone was then about twenty-five, Hawkins no older than fifteen. Wanderone was spending his nights in Los Angeles's Central Avenue dance halls, also frequented by the fast-living Dorothy, and that's where they presumably met. They became an item, they had sex, she got pregnant. Nine months later Dorothy Hawkins gave birth to a girl and named her Jamesetta. Jamesetta grew up to become the famous rhythm-and-blues singer now known to the world as Etta James.

Of course, Wanderone never publicly owned up to any son or daughter and certainly never to Etta James. The man who would become Minnesota Fats traipsed through life sexually irresponsible and sexually irrepressible. He was a scoundrel and a cheat, a man whose life course did not allow for such mature acknowledgments. But in her autobiography Etta James said she was told of the identify of her hustler father by several of her mother's close friends, including Willie Best, the famous actor best known for his shuffling porter roles in Marx Brothers and Shirley Temple films.[71] Best was almost precisely Fats's age, and the two remained for a while inseparable. "Willie and Fats were thick as thieves, [and] Fats had a taste for colored girls," James wrote in her memoirs. "'Girl,' Willie said to me one time, 'you look just like your papa. You're the spitting image of Minnesota Fats." James said that her mother also talked about Fats.

Both Wanderone (as Minnesota Fats) and Jamesetta (as Etta James) would become world-class entertainers. In photographs both look startlingly alike, with their wide faces, their tiny tulip mouths, their small but piercing eyes. James's oldest son Donto also bears an eerie

---

[71] Best became a well-known face in Hollywood films, even while he got stuck playing the stereotypical roles then offered African-American men. During his early films, he sometimes received on-screen credit only as "Sleep 'n' Eat." Bob Hope referred to Willie Best as one of the finest talents he had ever worked with.

resemblance. And what's more, evidence suggests that Wanderone also sired a second daughter. A Wanderone associate said he maintained a cordial and private relationship with the second woman and went so far as to visit her in New York on occasion.

Just like the monkey trickster of tribal folktales, Rudolf Wanderone flitted through life lying and seducing. He was Harold Hill from *The Music Man*, Brer Rabbit, and Annise the Spider all rolled into one. He was, in short, the sort of amoral creature from which mothers should hide their daughters. As Mosconi attempted to play the role of father and mother to the drunken Ralph Greenleaf, as he tried to keep one of the sport's greatest champions and the sport itself respectable, Wanderone was seducing teenage girls. As Mosconi wowed the world in a tuxedo, Wanderone was spilling chop suey on himself and playing his Big Hoorah.

•　　•　　•

Mosconi's clean-cut performance in the world tournament of 1940 and 1941 was one of the most stunning in the history of pocket billiards, a performance forever linked to the man—and yet even that defining championship became trickster fodder for Rudolf Walter Wanderone. "He recognized an opportunity when one presented itself and knew how to capitalize on it," Willie said in his memoirs.

The man who would become Minnesota Fats followed the tournament through the newspapers and on occasion watched live from the cheap seats. He also had become familiar over the years with the relative ability of each of the players. He knew, for instance, when Greenleaf was hitting the sauce or when Ponzi or Caras had fallen into stroke and which players played a good defensive game and which could be counted on to fold under pressure. With this knowledge Wanderone created a betting system, and then with this betting system he searched out less knowledgeable gamblers.

There's a word for such gamblers. They're known as suckers.

Wanderone placed 156 bets in all, presumably all set during the beginning months of the tournament. He won 154 of them.

"I determined the odds and then did business with anybody who had the scratch," Wanderone crowed years later. "It really wasn't such a difficult proposition . . . because back then all tables were a standard 5 by 10, so all things were equal at all times. After awhile my study was so thorough and complete that no one on earth knew as much about the players as I did. I charted the players like horses."

Wanderone made loads of cash from the enterprise, more in fact than Willie won during the entire event. With the tournament still far from over, Wanderone then took his cash and his green LaSalle on the road. He ended up in southern Illinois, where he played cards at the St. Nicholas Hotel and where he held forth at the Veterans Inn. With money from wagering with suckers on Willie's first world championship, Minnesota Fats set his stake in Little Egypt.

And before Willie's world tournament was over, Minnesota Fats would be deep in love.

Chapter 16

HERMES AND KRISHNA

Now, when he had finished what he had in mind and
when ten moons had risen in the sky, Zeus led his noto-
rious child into the light. Maia gave birth to a wily boy,
flattering and cunning, a robber and a cattle thief, a
bringer of dreams, awake all night, waiting by the gates
of the city—Hermes, who was soon to earn himself
quite a reputation among the gods, who do not die.

As the sun rose on the fourth day of the month, lady
Maia bore him; by noon he played the lyre and by
evening he had stolen the cattle of Apollo, who shoots
from afar.

      — *The Homeric Hymn to Hermes*

People have always conferred great powers on the trickster. Ulysses was
one. There was the Greek god Hermes and the Norse god Loki. Slaves
told of Brer Rabbit and Native Americans spoke of Coyote and Raven.
For generation upon generation, in myriad different cultures, throughout written history (and during those times before written words),
stories were told: wily trickster sets himself against the powers that be;
sometimes he wins, sometimes he loses; he always brings about important change or reveals important truths. Tricksters are, as the
Washington Post's Michael Dirda calls them, "the Gods of mischief

. . . the Gods of artistic and cultural renewal." Their stories resonate on the most basic of levels.

Lewis Hyde, in his 1998 *Trickster Makes This World,* argues that early relationships between predator and prey, between hunter and food, gave birth to the trickster tale. The stories typically describe prey escaping in some tricky way or predators using deceit to capture food. The stories connect to the natural order of things, but they also speak to humanity's spiritual and aesthetic aspirations. They describe power relationships, including relationships with the sacred.

What makes a trickster? In stories of Loki and the Raven and Krishna, what patterns do we find? For one, the trickster is driven by lust and a voracious appetite. One Native American story has trickster Coyote getting himself in trouble by breaking a promise and eating a magic cow. A story from the Veda tradition has Krishna stealing the household butter—smearing his face and hands with the creamy stuff—and then lying to mother Yasoda about his misdeeds. "The trickster is often imagined as a sort of 'hungry god,'" writes Hyde.

Another trait, and a related one, is his facility for deceit. Vishnu lies to Yasoda about the butter. The Greek god Hermes, a day after being born, steals cows from the great Apollo and then lies about his misdeeds. Moreover, the trickster displays no anxiety in lying: he tells big, bold, beautiful lies. The trickster's deceptions can be ornate and entertaining. Hyde says the trickster "tells his lies with creative abandon, charm, playfulness, and by that, affirms the pleasures of fabulation." If someone tries to trap the trickster, says Hyde, then the "trickster can counter with a series of deceptions and slip the trap."

Also, the trickster typically does not have a "way"—that is, in stories he seems always to lack some innate skill with which to succeed in this world. But the trickster can copy others and by so doing deceive them. In this way, the trickster can be a boundary crosser, a figure rooted in different worlds, or, said another way, a figure rooted in no place at all. Hyde says that every group has its dividing line, and that's where one finds the trickster. He's the happy-go-lucky wanderer, the aimless traveler; he has neither home nor destination. Hyde says appetite drives the trickster's wanderings.

"In America, one likely candidate for the protagonist of a reborn trickster myth is the confidence man," Hyde writes in *Trickster Makes This World*. "Some have even argued that the confidence man is a covert American hero. We enjoy it when he comes to town, even if a few people get their bank accounts drained, because he embodies things that are actually true about America but cannot be openly declared."

Sociologist Charles Lemert, another leading expert on the trickster archetype, said that pocket billiards, at least to the untutored, seems to have an element of magic about it. There are the strange angles and colors and the counterintuitive path of masséd balls. It seems to appeal to that part of the brain that finds wonder in sleight of hand and stage magic.[72] So it's also fertile ground for the trickster, said Lemert. "Pocket billiards plays on a different kind of deception—it involves the ringer and the hustler and all that is part of culture," said the sociologist. "And the trickster is ubiquitous in every culture—and particularly prominent where the hope of transformation is not very realistic."

Rudolf Wanderone made more money gambling on Mosconi's 1941 world championship than Mosconi made by winning it. This is only possible because those most interested in pool were enthusiastically interested in accepting wagers. That is, wagering was at least as much a part of the pocket-billiards culture as Mosconi's dignified world tournaments. Wanderone flitted from Los Angeles to Oklahoma to Philadelphia gambling, lying, and fucking—and he made a comfortable living doing so. He was New York Fats to some, Chicago Fats to others. He was, in this modern world, the wandering trickster who built success by divorcing himself from the truth. But in so doing he exposed something also true. Like Mosconi, Wanderone came to symbolize what we think of when we think of

---

[72] There are examples of billiards enthusiasts who also fancy themselves amateur magicians, including the author of this book. Another is Robert Byrne, the man behind the sport's most popular instructional books.

pocket billiards. But Wanderone would symbolize a *different* pocket billiards.

Remember, in 1940 Brunswick was pool. The industry leader controlled the tournaments, and it controlled the stars, and through its marketing it propagated the "proper" image of pool as good, wholesome fun. Mosconi, too, was a part of this effort. He devoted his life to establishing pool as legitimate. "But then Fats comes along and plays it out the other way," said sociologist Charles Lemert. "The trickster-artist is the one who starts the revolution, he challenges the borders of whatever is, the cultural spheres of the community, and he calls attention to them in new ways."

Wanderone was a fine pocket-billiards player, a skilled professional who easily fleeced farmers and sailors. But Wanderone never possessed the skill of pool's most celebrated champions. He could ape it, certainly; like all tricksters he could claim the prowess of others as his own. "I played them all, and I beat them all!" he would crow. But this was a lie. Wanderone never competed in Mosconi's world-tournaments level, never competed against Ponzi and Greenleaf and Joe "Meatman" Balsis in structured competition, and maybe it was because he lacked the skill to do so. But this was not true of all hustlers. An example was John "Rags" Fitzpatrick,[73] remembered as perhaps the finest one-pocket player ever. He was only an infrequent participant in tournaments and curiously absent from most pool histories. He died in 1960. And there were doubtless others. But it was impossible for any to emerge onto the world stage without at least the tacit approval of Brunswick.

"If you messed with Brunswick, you didn't get invited to the next tournament, and even the sectional tournaments were invitational," said pool historian Shamos. "And [Brunswick] was only interested in somebody who could display reasonably well in tournaments. If he was going to be a drunk like Greenleaf, he had to control himself. They

---

[73] See the players appendix in the updated version of *Hustler Days*.

also wanted somebody who was under their control, somebody who was going to get most of their money from Brunswick-related activities. If it were some hustler who was regularly pocketing three times the tournament prize, they wouldn't have any control over them and so [Brunswick] wasn't interested in them."

Brunswick may have controlled the sport, but the company could not control the hustlers, and it did not control Rudolf Walter Wanderone. And so he came to define the sport on their behalf, just as Mosconi would define it for the industry. Wanderone was the trickster who set himself against the powers that be and would set himself apart from the popular morality. He was the hustlers' champion, a man who used the example of his life to challenge the gods of his sport.

Worlds, culture, and life are born of creation myths. This is where we always find the amoral trickster, and when it comes to pocket billiards, this is where we find the man who would become Minnesota Fats. His mission was to recreate the sport for the coming modern age: post-sexual revolution, post-Vietnam, post-innocence, the amoral age when gambling and fucking and *hustling* will be okay.

Chapter 17

THE BEST TRICK YET

Everytime a newspaper reporter interviews me, he'll say: "Minnesota, where did you grow up?" They all ask the same question and I always give them the same answer. "I was born growed up," I say. And that's the way it was. I never was a kid. . . .

I've been shooting pool since I was four years old. No con. By the time I was six I was playing for stakes. My first sucker was a neighborhood kid in Washington Heights. I spotted him coming out of a candy store with an enormous bag of gumdrops. He was about five years older than me, but I shot him straight pool and I won every last one of those gumdrops. He went home crying. When I was ten, I started playing for cash.

— Minnesota Fats, *The Bank Shot*
and Other Great Robberies

In 1941, supposedly as the result of a car accident, Rudolf Wanderone and his road partner Jimmy "The Greek" Castras found themselves stranded in a remote section of southern Illinois known as Little Egypt. The story went that Wanderone had lost control of his green LaSalle while driving to Hot Springs, crashed into some mailboxes, and then somehow managed to steer his way back to a repair shop in the tiny town of Du Quoin.

Now there is much evidence that this entire story is horseshit. What's much more likely is that Rudolf Wanderone and Jimmy Castras, city boys both, came deliberately to Little Egypt to fleece the locals. The convenient car accident gave them an excuse to loiter for days around the local pool tables. Fats, remember, had a pocket full of cash from side betting on Mosconi's world championship. Castras was then little known but likewise highly ill regarded. They were conmen pure and simple.

But whether he *accidentally* ended up in Little Egypt, whether it was *fate* that brought him there, what's certainly true is that his life's journey—and that of modern pocket billiards—became indelibly marked as a result. Here Wanderone would find acclaim, celebrity, and love. Here he would help create some of the most celebrated pool tournaments in American history. Here Howard Cosell and ABC would find Rudolf Wanderone in advance of the Great Shoot-Out, the most-watched pool competition in American history. Little Egypt, specifically the towns of Du Quoin and Dowell, marked not just a stopping-off point for Rudolf Wanderone on his way to Hot Springs but also a stopping-off point on the grand journey that was his life.

Wanderone craved attention as much as he seemed to crave losing at dice, and here, in Little Egypt, he would find it. He became the veritable big fish in the proverbial small pond—and in 1941, when the two city boys came crashing through in their money-green LaSalle, what a pond they found! There were farmers here, yes. Little Egypt was rural and provincial, certainly. But in 1941 those towns of Du Quoin, Dowell, and West Frankfurt had become outposts for wanton lawlessness. Home to Scotts Airfield (which three years earlier had been designated the general headquarters for the air forces of the U.S. Army) and scores of mines, but very far away from the authority of big-city police departments, Little Egypt was famous for its paid-off deputies, its open gambling, and its fun times. There were whorehouses, too. By some accounts there were six in Du Quoin alone. "If you wanted liquor, you could get it; if you wanted women, there were women," one old-timer fondly recalled. "On a Saturday night, the sidewalks were so crowded you walked in the street."

More hell-raisers came from northern Illinois or from nearby Indiana and Missouri. Grifters on the road made pit stops. Finding high-dollar poker games was no problem for Wanderone and The Greek. Hell, half the time Titanic Thompson was dealing cards in the kitchen of the St. Nicholas Hotel, where they both took rooms.[74] The hustlers got lunch at the Beanery, which had pool tables out back, and they wolfed down sizzling-hot steaks at the Evening Star, which was that nightclub on the outskirts of Du Quoin.

And it was also at the Evening Star that Wanderone made the acquaintance of a sexy five-foot-seven brunette by the name of Evelyn Inez Grass. It was March 7, the day after Willie Mosconi dissected Onofrio Lauri, 125–106, and then lost to him 125–96 in Scranton, Pennsylvania. Wanderone recalled that he and Castras were famished and looking for chow and that Evening Star owner Joe Scoffic sent him over to the restaurant with the promise of a delicious meal, a great floor show, and the company of a beautiful hostess.

"Me and Jimmy the Greek got in the LaSalle and drove over to the Evening Star, and just as we're walking in the front door, I pulled out a $100 bill and stuck it in my handkerchief pocket," recalled Wanderone. "Now who is standing just inside the front door but the tomato called Evelyn Inez, who happened to be the hostess and head waitress. She was beautiful beyond compare, a gorgeous doll without a flaw. She was a tall, dark-eyed brunette who . . . had just the right padding in all the right places. And legs? Listen, Betty Grable never had legs like Evelyn Inez."

Like Anna Harrison, Mosconi's wife, Evelyn Inez was also a great lover of the high life. She was five years Wanderone's junior, just as

---

[74] The St. Nicholas was owned by Joe Scoffic. Such luminaries as Titanic Thompson and Hubert Cokes would join in the poker games. For more details, see *Hustler Days*.

Anna Harrison was five years Mosconi's junior. The local boys called Evelyn the Gingham Girl (for all the denim she wore), but Fats simply called her "the most fabulous-looking tomato of all time." He started courting her at very nearly the same time that Mosconi started dating Anna Harrison. Both women were then twenty-two years old.

Further parallels: Mosconi met Harrison at the King Edward's Hotel, where she may have worked as a lounge singer or waitress. Wanderone met Evelyn Inez Grass at the Evening Star, which definitely had lounge singing, and where Evelyn waited tables and worked as hostess. Mosconi likely was at the King Edward's during a stop in the multicity world's pool tournament. Wanderone also was on the road playing pool, but in his case he was hustling.

Fats would later come to call her Eva-Line. She lived just on the outskirts of nearby Dowell with her mother, Orbie. He invited Evelyn to dinner, and to ice cream, and to sleep with him . . . although it's unclear in what order. He was like a damned octopus, she said. "He had his hands all over me." Evelyn remembered Fats as a charming man and rakish, and Lord—cocky wasn't even the word for it. He was a man she could have fun with, and Evelyn was never shy about wanting to have fun.

This is the story of how they got married:

One day he collapsed in a sobbing heap on the floor of Evelyn's house. He just fell onto his knees, blubbering. He wanted to take Evelyn back to New York with him, to go with him to the unexpected funeral of his sister. He was just all busted up about it. He said he'd never felt a pain like it. "Evelyn Inez, you must accompany this poor boy to New York—if you don't, he'll never get there," said Orbie. So then and there Evelyn and Fats became road partners. They hardly knew each other, but she went with him all the way to Washington Heights. It was just the two of them together in Fats's big green LaSalle.

One must assume that Fats and Evelyn knew each other a great deal better by the time they returned to Little Egypt. Not surprisingly, Fats soon got it into his head that he wanted to go on the road again with

Evelyn, but this time on a gambling trip to Chicago. Orbie objected, although she did not exactly forbid it. She simply said that Fats had to marry her first. And Fats, perhaps in a rare moment of clarity, perhaps in a fit of utter madness, agreed.

The young couple eloped across the border to Cape Girardeau, Missouri, where the JPs don't require blood tests. They said their "I Dos," they kissed in the upstairs court. They shared an ice-cream soda (as they often did during their brief courtship), and then the deed was done. The date: May 7, 1941, precisely five days after Willie Mosconi won his first world championship.

A few more observations: There was no honeymoon, but Rudy and Evelyn did go on the road soon afterward. First stop was Chicago and then later Norfolk, Virginia. But eventually they did return to Little Egypt and took up residence in the childhood ranch-style home that Evelyn had always shared with her mother. It was far, far away from the lights of Brooklyn Heights, and it was surrounded by cornfields, but the man who would become Minnesota Fats was quite content to live there as long as he didn't have to pay the rent.

This would foreshadow the living arrangements at the very end of his life, when Wanderone lived nearly rent free at a fine hotel in downtown Nashville and then completely rent free at the home of another wife, on the outskirts of Nashville. So perhaps "lifelong mooch" is another way to accurately describe the trickster, Minnesota Fats.

Be that as it may, just note this: When Fats collapsed in Evelyn's home, blubbering and wailing during the winter of 1941, it was for him a unique and unprecedented display of vulnerability. Wanderone never acknowledged the superiority of any adversary, never admitted to any weakness, except maybe to craps. Look through all that was written about Fats, all that was ever said about him, all that he said about himself, and see that it's true. So when he fell apart in the home of Evelyn Inez Grass, saying he *needed* her to partner with him on the road, he ensnared the beautiful Gingham Girl with the trick of honesty, the trick of meekness.

From a man who admitted to nothing but absolute and utter fear-lessness, it was perhaps his best hustle yet. With it he captured the heart of the most beautiful girl in Little Egypt.

Chapter 18

DUTY AND RESPONSIBILITY

I was really sick of life in general and the billiard game
in particular.

— Willie Mosconi speaking to
Billiards Digest founder Mort Luby Jr.

PHILADELPHIA, Nov. 7 (AP)—Erwin Rudolf, veteran
Cleveland cue expert, won the world's pocket billiards champi-
onship for the fifth time tonight by defeating Irving Crane,
Livonia, NY, 125–65, in nineteen innings. . . .

"In championship play-off matches today Rudolf won from
Mosconi, Mosconi beat Crane, and Crane defeated Rudolf.
Then, on the basis of points scored, Rudolf and Crane played
another match for the crown. . . .

"Rudolf succeeds Willie Mosconi, Philadelphia, as champion. . . ."

Willie was livid, raging, yelling. The eager and startled newsmen at
Town Hall wolfishly anticipated violence, notebooks at the ready.
Willie quite publicly had threatened the tournament organizer! He
might actually attack Byron Schoeman! The newsmen watched with
fascination as the now ex-champion raged and cursed and stomped
about. These rules, he was saying, were *bullshit!*

Never mind that they had actually agreed to them.

"Willie had a terrible temper," recalled Schoeman, speaking to the *Bowlers Journal* way back in the summer of 1962. "He used to beat himself by blowing off steam at the wrong time. I doubt if he would have become such a great champion without that temper, however. He finally learned to control it."

But not in the winter of 1941, not when Willie lost his crown in a three-way tie . . . on *points*. He had led throughout much of the tournament. He had the high runs. But after two weeks with Irving Crane, Rudolf, Ponzi, Kelly, Caras, Greenleaf, Procita, Lauri, and the up-and-coming Cranfield, Willie got ushered out of the play-off because of the *point spread.*

This is what happened: The Billiard Association of America had selected Town Hall as the venue for their world tournament, but they could not use the space indefinitely. It was a popular meeting and event venue in downtown, and the BAA had it reserved only through the first week of November, which could be a problem if the tournament ended in a three-way tie. A two-way tie can be settled with a single play-off game. But three players determining a winner can turn into an unending game of rock-paper-scissors; that is, with three players each can win and lose play-off games in equal measure and so leave the relative standings undisturbed.

And in the winter of 1941, as Willie defended his title for the first time, that's precisely what happened. At the end of two weeks Crane, Rudolf, and Mosconi were tied with 8–3 records. They then played a single play-off round in which Mosconi beat Crane, Crane beat Rudolf, and Rudolf beat Mosconi. Now they were tied at 9–4.

The BAA did not want to transfer the finals from the posh Town Hall, and they didn't want to continue playing tiebreakers. Tournament organizer Schoeman said part of the rationale was that the longer the play-offs continued, the more likely it was that someone would suggest it was fixed. The solution was the tiebreaker agreement presented by Schoeman to Crane, Rudolf, and Mosconi and which read as follows:

"In case there is another three-way first place tie in games won and lost after the playoff, the two players having the largest total of points will meet for the championship of the world. Parenthetically, the player having the lowest total number of points in the playoff—and if the playoff results in a three-way first place tie again in games won and lost—is eliminated from the championship final."

The three played again, they tied again, and Willie Mosconi, the highest-scoring player in the tournament[75] ended up getting eliminated on the ball count during the playoff. He had the same win-loss record as Crane and Rudolf but still lost the title without what he thought was a legitimate chance to defend it. Eyewitnesses said Willie threatened to wrap his cuestick around Schoeman's neck. It's not an exaggeration that the newsmen, their hats tipped back on their heads, hoped for and expected violence. His face had gone red, he was sputtering, he stomped about Town Hall before storming out altogether.

In his memoirs Willie downplayed his nearly violent rage over the loss, which he described as an unfortunate learning experience. He said it taught him to never show mercy and that, even when he was ahead in the ball count, it was important to keep piling up points. For ever afterward Mosconi would say that when it came to playing pool, it wasn't enough to get the knife in.

He also had to *twist it.*

Rudolf ended up winning the title in a final 125–65 playoff against Crane. The game went nineteen innings.

• • •

Little William, the champion's firstborn child and only son, was born at the City Hospital of New York on August 4, 1941—almost precisely three months after Mosconi won his first world title and three months

---

[75] According to the *New York Times*, Mosconi scored 1,259 points during the two-week tournament, while Rudolf scored 1,212, and Crane scored 1,214.

before he lost it again. The very sexy Anna Harrison, then twenty-three years old and presumably living with Willie in midtown Manhattan (although some evidence suggests Willie still resided in Philly),[76] endured a labor lasting two-and-a-half hours. She gave birth to William at 9:20 that morning. Four months later the Japanese bombed Pearl Harbor.

Willie's life was changing, changing like never before. Fats said he was *born* grown-up; Fats said that ever since he was a child he acted and seemed like a full-on adult. In some ways nothing can be further from the truth. Mosconi, however, was earning money for his old man at age seven, was gambling and playing tournaments for his family as a sixteen-year-old, and had become the sole wage earner at eighteen. And Mosconi said he never even *liked* it. He said he was *sick* of it; he was just a kid; he just wanted to play stickball. But Willie could not escape his native talent. His ability to pocket balls sealed his fate, whether he would have it that way or not. He played pool out of his sense of duty, out of *responsibility.* . . .

And now this: a family.

Not long after William's birth, the Japanese dropped bombs on Pearl Harbor, and a massive explosion on the USS *Arizona* killed 1,104 men—burned them up, really; and drowned them—Willie and Anna and little William migrated to Leslie, Michigan, which was close to the Goodyear[77] plant in Jackson and close to where Anna's mom and dad lived. Mosconi took a factory job, and a more awful one can hardly be imagined. Grinding wheels, operating a lathe, and sweating cannot be anything but torture for a man of Mosconi's talent. It was like Rembrandt roofing houses. "It was the dullest, most tedious job I ever had," he said, truthfully.

But the job also had its benefits. It gave him a deferment from the war. It let him stay close to his son and make love to his sexy, half-crazy

---

[76] Her address, listed on William's birth certificate, was listed as 355 West Fifty-second Street, New York. Newspaper accounts put Willie's home in Philadelphia.

[77] According to information provided by Brunswick Billiards, Charles Goodyear helped revolutionize pocket billiards with his invention of vulcanized rubber. As a result, table cushions would never be the same.

wife Anna. And ironically enough, it *freed* him from pocket billiards, a game he never loved despite the irresistible force-of-nature quality of his talent.

Remember: for Fats and his sorry lot, pool was all about freedom—freedom from rules, freedom from feminized society, and freedom from the moral duty to do what's right. Fats might knock up a teenage girl and then go about his business. He might come bulldozing into a tiny town, lie and cheat his way to a thicker pocket book; he might get admonished by the clucking womenfolk, but he would persevere. This was not Willie's way. Notions of freedom and responsibilty would get all scrambled up in his brain, making him strive and smolder and suffer, sometimes doing what's right, sometimes not. But he was always *aware* of the right course, always felt its oppressive presense.

Like all men, Willie *wanted* freedom. Who dreamed of a life making widgets? Who wanted to get tied down? But from the time Willie was seven, from the time he was the child prodigy supporting his dad and his sick mom, Willie Mosconi did what he was supposed to do. He dropped out of school and took up gambling—not because of a slothful nature, not like Fats for whom all of life was a celebration, but rather to support his family. A sense of duty led him then, just as a sense of duty gave him the *freedom* to stay home with Anna and little William, at least for a little while, in 1941 and 1942.

Willie worked day shifts, night shifts, split shifts, ten-hour days, sometimes seven-day weeks. Further exacerbating the mindlessness was the realization that just a year earlier he drew down $10,000 playing pool. *$10,000!* Thinking about it was maddening. And now he spent his hours behind a lathe. "And for me, the long hours and the monotony of the work were [also] aggravated by the fact that I was unaccustomed to a regular work schedule," recalled Willie. "I had not held a conventional job since I was a teenager, and it was not easy to make the adjustment. But . . . with a young baby at home, even the long hours were preferable to being away at an army camp."

He hardly ever picked up a cue. He may have missed the money but not the playing. His relationship with Anna veered wildly—at first frosty, then maybe plate-throwing tantrums, then frosty again. Mosconi worked hard, he was ill tempered and incommunicative, and the former nightclub worker Anna Harrison more than likely had envisioned a far different life with him. She was, after all, a party girl. And now she was spending her days cooped up in Leslie, Michigan, in a tiny bungalow changing diapers.

On November 19, 1942, Willie made an honest woman of Anna, the mother of his son, and then two weeks after saying his vows before a JP, he drove off to Detroit for a new world tournament. It did not matter that he did not love pool. It did not even matter that he probably didn't love Anna. The world championship was at stake, and Willie believed quite firmly that he was the world's greatest. If Mosconi understood anything about life, he understood this: that people faced duties and responsibilities that they could choose to embrace or that they could choose to ignore.

Willie's duty was to prove that he was the greatest, but it was also his responsibility to provide for his family. Both weighed on him heavily. And so each morning he left Anna and Little William behind in the bungalow, and each night he came home edgy and nervous. He was married just two weeks, and already his destiny had begun to pull him in two. Love of pool didn't enter into the calculation, nor for that matter did love of Anna. For Willie, it was all about duty and responsibility.

•   •   •

By November 30, 1942, a year into the war, America also had become consumed with grand notions of duty. Men were getting blown to smithereens overseas, women took up the slack at home, factories like Willie's operated double-time. The Billiard Association of America responded by ratcheting it down a notch. There would still be competitions but not like before, no longer the ambitious multi-city spectacles seen in Philly and New York and Syracuse. It's not that the association didn't have available to them world-class players (many top pros were too old for the draft), it's just that mounting such extravagant events seemed tacky, given the dogging stigma attached to the sport and the nation's hardships in general. So it was decided: the year's event would be held only in Detroit, and afterwards, for the duration of the war, there would only be challenge matches. The association also announced early that the winner of the 1942 event should expect war bonds, not cash.

Controlling everything—who played, where, and when, the association in this case catered the November event specifically to Willie's needs. They put on the show in Detroit, close to Willie's home base, because Willie was the only competitor then with a full-time job. "Goodyear gave me a week off, I squeezed in a few hours of practice, and I was as ready as I was going to be when the tournament opened," he recalled. Only former world titlists were invited, so that meant that Greenleaf and Ponzi were there but also Irving Crane,[78] who had bested Erwin Rudolf six months previously, and Jimmy Caras.

The 1942 event went as might be expected. It began with Ralph Greenleaf throwing a terrific tantrum and ended with Willie Mosconi's regaining his crown. Willie recalled that Andrew Ponzi—"The Old Ponzola," Willie called him—began needling the haughty Greenleaf about his supposed lack of decorum. Now dignity, which Ralph could sometimes possess, was also just a hair's width away from pomposity, which Ralph *always* possessed. And so, quite predictably, the great champion lost his mind. Willie said he roared and stomped about, his concentration wasted, his fate sealed.

On the evening of December 4, a Friday, Willie beat Greenleaf 125–97 in nineteen innings. Earlier that day he demolished Crane (who then held the title) 125–26 in just six. "Mosconi, producer of most of the tournament's long clusters, ran 84 minus a scratch in the fourth inning and then closed out the match . . . with an unfinished

---

[78] The BAA no doubt saw Mosconi as the future of the sport but also the up-and-coming Crane, a man who one day would become another thorn in Willie's side. At twenty-nine, Crane was relatively young (he was the same age as both Willie and Fats, each having also been born in pool's great year, 1913) and now with his May 9 victory over Rudolf, Crane became the official champion. The May 9 victory was the first of many for the lanky but dignified Livonia, New York, native.

string of 44," the *Los Angeles Times* reported. The next day Willie clinched the title with his 125–32 victory over Erwin Rudolf. He posed for the photographers, accepted his $1,500 in war bonds, and then drove back to Jackson, where his lathe was waiting.

•   •   •

The next two years were a time of transition for Willie. His daughter Candace was born in November of 1943, almost exactly a year after his world title, but by then he was no longer world champion and no longer working at the Goodyear Plant. He probably wasn't spending much quality time at home, either. A lifetime of long absences was underway. "He was gone all the time," recalled Bill Mosconi, his son. "It was very difficult."

In April of 1943, with Bill less than a year old and Anna pregnant with Candace, Willie drove out to Kansas City, where he got beat by Ponzi in a challenge match. Then he toured army bases in the south. After that, he came back but immediately almost lost his finger on his left hand in an accident at the Goodyear Plant. As a result he changed jobs, but the one he took was a hundred miles away, in Toledo, Ohio. This would have been about the time that Candace was born.

The solitary travels would become a mark of Willie's life—either as an exhibition player or with his constant ranging from city to city for tournaments, or later, during the TV age, when he flew to Los Angeles for the Ed Sullivan or Johnny Carson shows. The travel also marked his family. Daughter Candace said it plain: "I felt like an orphan." In March of 1943, with his daughter just four months old, Willie left his family again—this time he made the drive out to Kansas City, where he would win his third world championship.

And then, not longer afterward, he quit his second wartime job and went on the road full time. He was nearly thirty-one years old, he was sick of the factory work, sick of Michigan, sick of Anna. No matter that by quitting his second job he also became immediately eligible for the draft. "Who needs this," he thought, "I'd rather be in the army."

Willie didn't get inducted right away and so went on tour alone, traveling the nation, entertaining troops, offering instruction, performing trick shots. In January he went on a four-city tour with Ralph Greenleaf, whose best days were long behind him. Willie won the world title for the fourth time.

He said he enjoyed it more than the factory work, but he was also lost out there. Over and over again, through the entirety of a life, Willie Mosconi said he despised the loneliness. It was like he forever wore a mask, lost, traveling day in and day out, alone among strangers. "And now gentlemen, Willie Mosconi, the pocket-billiards champion of the *world!*" Applause. Hoots. An autograph. "How ya' doing, folks," he'd say in his Philly accent, a bare hint of Italian shining beneath like an exposed penny. "Who'd like to see some *pool?*" he'd say. "Here it goes, folks, here it goes—six balls at once."

He could not stay home. He hated staying away. "I was really sick of life in general and the billiard game in particular," he said of those days. In March his government finally sent for him: he was to report to Fort Dix, New Jersey. At the time he weighed 148 pounds, had grey hair, three dependents, and was listed as married. He became an "entertainment specialist" for Uncle Sam. His stint as a GI lasted seven months only.

When he got home, his family wouldn't be waiting.

Chapter 19

THE FATS & WILLIE SHOW

My father spent a lot of time on the road, he was always gone, and one of the big things I remember at my childhood, I always remember what a big deal it was when he came home.

> — Bill Mosconi, speaking about
> his father, the world champion

My dad came from a very hard family. His family was loving, but, I dunno, maybe it was a generational thing. He did the best he could.

He was put in a situation that very few people would have been prepared for.

> — Candace Fritch, speaking about
> her father, the world champion

Just as Willie Mosconi began traveling the nation, little Minnesota Fats began traveling the world. In Persia, which is what they used to call Iran, little Minnesota Fats held an audience with the mighty shah. Even in the faraway East the prowess of little Fatty had become the object of great wonder. As an infant Fatty was known to have run scores of balls without a single miss; he was a gurgling baby child who had no use for chalk or for straight sticks. He could best great champions, even with balls made of cement.

In a great palace, the little boy with the fat cheeks stood before a solemn maharajah, a tall turban balanced atop his regal brow. Beautiful big-bosomed harem girls curled like cats on thick pillows. The great sultan had a 10-foot-by-5-foot table for pocket billiards, intricate in detail, gold in-laid. And Fatty, just a little thing, just barely big enough to see over the side, had come to rob him.

"You may be a powerful sultan, but you've never seen the likes of me," *said the fat-cheeked boy. "For marbles, money, or chalk, I'll play you!"*

And so the sultan set the wager (it was many thousands of dollars) and fit the balls into the triangle. The little fat-cheeked boy broke open the balls with a quick stroke and then sank each ball in turn. When the balls had all vanished from the table, the sultan arranged them again in the trian-gle, and the boy again sank each in turn. He did this over and over until finally the sultan cried for mercy.

"I cannot beat you," he said. "Here, take my money, and do not return!"

The little fat boy impetuously gathered up stacks of bills and gold ingots and kissed three of the harem girls and then vanished from the land of Persia.

A truer story was never told because Minnesota Fats never, ever lied.

In the stories told by Willie Mosconi it was the morally impover-ished who get their comeuppance. Always Cue Ball Eddie coming through Frankie Mason's, or the pair of larcenous pros in Kansas City, or Minnesota Fats himself. In Willie's telling each rues the day they thought to steal his money. And despite Willie's constant travels, there always seemed to be some tortured connection with home in his sto-ries. It was always the hustling riffraff who *came to him*—either as he held forth in his hometown, caring for his family (and not hanging out too much in the poolroom) or sometimes when he ventured into a foreign room—but always for a tournament, and always, like Ulysses, searching for a way home.

In the 1930s it was Benny Allen's and Walter Franklin's turn. They had secretly gimmicked the pockets to trip up the champion. But the effect for them was disastrous. "Allen missed the first shot and I went 125 and out. This went on for three days. Franklin is ribbing Benny

Allen after the afternoon game the second day. I said, 'What are you laughing at, you might not get a ball either.'" Another time it was Fats carrying the poolcase for Babyface Alton Whitlow. "I beat him five times in a row," Willie would always insist. "I had to lend him train fare back to New York." And sometimes it was State Street Willie or the Big Sausage. "Hustlers devise games only *they* can play," he'd say.

With Fats, by contrast, it was those of power and authority who get their due. Wanderone fleeced the sultans or the kaiser or generals or the shah of Persia. And unlike Mosconi, that paragon of stability, Fats flitted from place to place. The wandering trickster would *parachute* into Germany. He would *smuggle* himself into Persia. Fats grandly proclaimed that he robbed a murderer's row of self-important tournament players, men like Ponzi or Greenleaf or even Willie Mosconi himself. *I played him a hundred times, and I beat him a hundred times!* Of course, Mosconi told mostly true stories, and Wanderone told mostly made-up ones—but even so, even in the lies of Minnesota Fats we learn something new about ourselves.

"I knew Conrad Hilton when he was looking for work.

"I've been playing Atlantic City since the turn of the century. I was here when there wasn't any beach.

"A tuxedo? I was driving Duesenbergs in '33, when so many millionaires were jumping out of windows, you could walk down the street and catch them with nets.

"I played the kaiser when he was on the lam."

"Practice? Practice is for suckers, junior. This guy used to go out and play tournaments 365 days a year and still go home and practice eight hours a day. While he was practicing, I was making money."

In the self-invented folktale that was Fats's life he always stood at center stage, like a circus ringmaster, and always he confronted the powers that be. In words and deeds he opposed forces of stability, which were really those of decency, respectability, and responsibility. It's the common fascination with such antiheroes that helps explain the enduring power of Fats, both as symbol and as man, and the public's fascination with pool hustlers generally. If Mosconi was characterized by responsibility and respectability, Fats was driven by their opposites. If in his fables he sometimes was admonished, Fats nonetheless persevered. The pool hustler broke rules, he ate to excess, businessmen were wise to store their wallets, mothers to hide their daughters. By boasting about impossible victories and never-ending winnings—*by lying*, he really whispered something secretly desired by any who would listen.

• • •

After getting married, Fats and Evelyn hit the road. They went to Atlantic City, New York, Philly, and Chicago—any place with pool, cards, horses, and dice. However, it was in Norfolk, Virginia, home to the entire Atlantic fleet, where Fats found true happiness . . . at least for a while. The action there was the stuff of legend. In the history of America there was no greater mecca for poolroom vice than Norfolk during the 1940s. The seamen got taken by the chumps, who got eaten alive by the shortstops, who lost their money to the big boys, who were devoured by the likes of Fats, Luther Lassiter, and Rags Fitzpatrick. Billiards hustler Danny McGoorty said the bums would yelp, "You win; here's your $10" when you stumbled over them in the gutter. George Rood, another old-timer, said that *everybody* was in Norfolk— and everybody had money.

"I went to one downtown poolhall. There couldn't have been more than seven or eight tables, and they charged us time on the table according to how much we won. I remember they charged me $200," recalled Rood, still marveling decades later. "That's $200. $200! For one session! I was shocked. And all that money got redistributed. Everybody had it." Boozing, whoring—but most of all gambling—it went on nonstop, every day, with wagers placed both rapid-fire quick and big, big, *big*. Tens floated like ones. Hundreds floated like tens. The poolroom economy had gotten upside down: craps, pool, blackjack . . . *nonstop*.

If the 1920s are remembered as the finest days for pool, then the 1940s, in Norfolk, must be remembered as the finest for *hustling*. If Fats is remembered as a true hustler, a true gambler, then Norfolk during the 1940s was the place and time of his purification. The city was a giant moonshine still, boiling and steaming and dripping out vice in the true form. They were great days indeed, in some ways the greatest of Fats's life, but of course they could not last. Fats and Wimpy Lassiter partnered for awhile,[79] but then both went bust. Lassiter was said to have won hundreds of thousands of dollars but then got ratted out to the IRS. He lost it all. With Fats it was the craps table. He couldn't keep his hands off the dice, he had a lecher's craving for them, and they would be his undoing.

Not long after the war's end, Fatty and Evelyn fled back to Dowell, broke. Orbie, Evelyn's mother, welcomed them back into her home—although perhaps "welcome" is too strong a word. Fats remained jobless, became fatter on Orbie's fried chicken, and only occasionally ventured out on the road to pick up a pool game. For twelve long years he remained in hibernation there among the cornfields with his beautiful wife and her tiresome mother, living a bucolic and sedentary life, collecting dogs and cats.

After all, home is where the heart is.

•   •   •

Bill Mosconi, Willie's son, said his mother just took off. He was three, maybe four years old when it happened. Candace was just one. Bill vaguely remembers an elderly couple—*were they his foster parents? The landlords?*—and he's seen references somewhere to a "boarding house." For the life of him, though, he can't remember what his mother

[79] Ed Tarkington, a friend of Wimpy's, said during an interview in 1999 that "Minnesota Fats went on the road with Wimpy. Every time they had somebody to play, Fats wanted Wimpy to do the playing. He'd go in the back and play the cards and lose all the money he had won. When he got on the road, Minnesota Fats owed him $500, and he never paid him. Wimpy won all the money, and Fats lost it all playing cards. He was lazy. He didn't want to play."

looked like, or what she wore, or the smell of her perfume, or even whether she ever loved him. They were kids, living in Michigan with their mom while their dad was in the army . . . and then she was just *gone.* "Isn't that amazing?" he says. "It's a complete blank." Bill says his mother may have moved to another house in town but maybe not. She may have left money for his upkeep but maybe not.

Bill Mosconi knows this one thing: from that moment on Anna Harrison was never again a part of his life or that of his younger sister Candace. They didn't speak to their mother, they didn't see her, and with only one exception she never paid them a visit. Anna Harrison tried to explain it all later, but Bill Mosconi said he didn't want to hear.

"We were in a foster home, and I remember vaguely there was an elderly couple that was there, taking care of us," said Bill, remembering some of it, having been told about other parts. "I think what happened is that she was there for a bit, and then she disappeared, and these people didn't know what to do, so they went to the Red Cross, who got in touch with the army, who then contacted my father. . . . I think she was working, maybe in a defense plant, and we were with foster parents because my father was unavailable. Then she disappeared, and nobody knew where she went. Nobody knew what to do. So these people got in touch with the army. They said my mother had taken off."

Corporal William Mosconi got an early "dependency section III" discharge to go deal with the family crisis. He took his Victory Medal, took his walking papers, took his $142.83, and then made the ten-hour drive from Camden, New Jersey, to Jackson. He unhappily bundled the children off to Barrington, New Jersey, where his father owned a three-story house. The bar he had helped his father buy was practically across the street. "My aunt and her family lived on the second floor, and my grandfather and one or two of his brothers lived on the first floor—and that's where we lived for a couple of years," Bill recalled.

He also said he played a lot of baseball, goofed off with his cousins generally, and enjoyed himself. It was an okay life, and it seemed normal despite his father's long absences and his mother's total absence. "When we lived in Barrington, it was a great way to grow up. Maybe they felt sorry for us because of our situation. But we were always playing ball in this big lot across the street. I didn't feel abandoned—maybe we were naïve—but we had a pretty happy childhood."

Although the kids were not then aware of it, Willie's absences were not entirely attributable to road trips. In 1947, when little Bill was six and Candace was four, Willie inexplicably moved to Kansas City. Here he stayed for two years, mostly doing exhibitions in the city but also traveling to Chicago and beyond. Little Candy he left living with Billy at his father's house, but this situation lasted only for a year or so, as it was all men there: male cousins, uncles, her grandfather, more male cousins. With the exception of a single aunt, there was not one other female presence in this two-story house of baseball players and boxers. Willie apparently had some concern about the living arrangements, so he separated his children. Bill stayed at his father's house, but Candy was sent to live with separate cousins about a mile away.

She lived there for several years, isolated from both her brother and her father. Perhaps it's not surprising then that she expresses much less satisfaction with their nontraditional childhood.

"There was a sense of abandonment, ours wasn't a close relationship," she said. Candace said that she soon began to understand that her father was not like other fathers, and that other people, strangers even, had a very different idea of who he was and how they lived.

"This was part of the confusion of a child," she said. "You grow up with a very famous person, and you have to coordinate that with reality. I came to understand fame a lot. Fame is somebody else's story put on somebody's head. When somebody talks about famous people, a lot of times they really don't know them. They grasp a different thing. It's a fragment of that life. It's not total. It's just part of the picture.

"I mean, they got the scores right. They got the profession right. But people looked up at my father like he was a god. It was a worshipful kind of thing. And when you grow up with a famous person, you don't see that. He's not a god—he's human. You can see their harmful qualities, and you have to step back from that. . . .

"And if you have a kid that's growing up in a family that's disconnected through travel and stuff like that, then there is a longing to be like all the other kids. Everybody says, 'Your dad is famous.' I would have loved to have a normal family, I thought. I didn't understand that they're looking at me like that, saying, 'You're so lucky.'"

Chapter 20

FATS'S NO. 1 HELPER
1978

He didn't care who won or lost. He was like, "Hell, I am
Minnesota Fats." He was more interested in entertaining people. He loved the fact that people didn't know
who Mosconi was but knew who he was.

— Du Quoin resident Brad Holford

Brad Holford's parents owned the Kentucky Fried Chicken, which was
Fats's favorite restaurant, and so that's how the two became friends. The
old pool hustler came in every day to eat chicken, sometimes two of
'em (it was like he'd never tasted one before), and then, suddenly, somehow, the fifteen-year-old had become Fats's number-one helper. "Can I
come, Fats?" he'd say. "Take me, Fats!" The sandy-haired high school kid
drove around with Fats to the exhibitions. He carried his stuff. When
he got his driver's license, he became Minnesota Fats's chauffeur.

Now there's no evidence, none whatsoever, that Fats had ever won
a tournament. Not a world tournament, not a national-class one, not
even one at the neighborhood tavern. But this fact never occurred to
Brad. All he knew was that Fats was the most famous person he'd ever
met, that he was the most famous pool player in the whole world, and
that he had been the guest of Johnny Carson. As far as Brad was concerned, Fats was the best pool player who had ever lived. "He was not
an ordinary person," said Holford.

And so Brad was proud to be Fats's friend, and he brooked little doubt that he would beat Willie Mosconi, and he about fainted when Fats invited him and his family to go to New York City to witness first-hand the drubbing he would hand out at The Great Shoot-out. Brad was a freshman at Du Quoin High School. He remembered he had to miss classes that Friday, plus a football game, but he didn't care. Charles Ursitti, the promoter, picked his family up at the airport.

"To me it was a huge trip," said Brad. "That was the first big trip I took with Fats, and I got to meet Howard Cosell. We got in a day late because we got snowed in at St. Louis, and we came down to the Wal-dorf-Astoria, and there Cosell was, down in the lobby. We came in right in the main big lobby, and there was a bunch of tables off to one side, and Howard Cosell was down there. Fats was there talking to him for about ten minutes, and he introduced us."

"Now I didn't know who Willie Mosconi was, except for Fats talking about him. But Mosconi came over, and he introduced himself. The Mosconis: they were supernice. He came up to me specifically. I didn't ask for autographs, and maybe he did it to irritate Fats—but he came up to me specifically, and he gave me an autograph. Like I said, Mosconi hated Fats."

It was also during that trip that Holford was startled to learn that Fats apparently had a second daughter—and not Etta James, the fa-mous blues singer. Fats apparently met this second daughter's mother at a carnival. Holford didn't catch the daughter's name, didn't know how old she was exactly, or where she lived. But Holford said this woman, whom Minnesota Fats accepted as his daughter, appeared un-expectedly at the New York hotel after they arrived.

He described the woman as at that time approaching middle age and with reddish hair. She claimed that she was married to a banker and that Fats had helped her out on occasion by sending money. The description was vaguely confirmed by promoter Charles Ursitti, who also claims to have been introduced on more than one occasion to a "stocky" woman whom Fats identified as his daughter.[80]

"She showed up at the Waldorf when we showed up," said Holford. "It was the first day we were there. We never heard word one about Fats having any children, but this woman came walking up, with her arms stretched out, saying 'Daddy!' She started hugging him. That was the first we heard of Fats having a daughter. The next day she spent the whole day with us. She took me and my mom and all of us out to the Statue of Liberty. She took us to Chinatown, and she took us to Little Italy."

Holford couldn't remember the name of the mysterious red-haired daughter, but neither did he ever forget the encounter. "Evelyn knew about her, and I don't think there was a problem," said Brad, who speculated that she was in occasional contact with Fats's wife. Holford even has a picture of this mystery woman sitting there with her banker husband at the New York City restaurant. The tables are pulled together. She's wearing fur. The picture was taken on that day before The Great Pool Shoot-Out, after a long day with the woman in New York City. She looked just like Fats," he said.[81]

---

[80] He said this woman was not Etta James.

[81] Theresa Bell, his second wife, denies that Fats fathered any children, although she also said she had no knowledge of Holford's story until the author asked about it. She also said that Fats personally denied that Etta James was his daughter and that Evelyn Wanderone, his first wife, had said that Fats was infertile. But even if Fats was firing blanks during his married years, that doesn't speak to the possibility that Fats could have sired children before getting married, which presumably is when the children would have been born.

Irving Crane, known as the Deacon, was one player who consistently gave Willie Mosconi fits during high-stakes tournament play. Mosconi's championship runs were seldom interrupted, but when they were—it was often the slow-playing, defensive Crane who did the interrupting.
Photo © Billiards Digest

Babyface Alton Whitlow was with Fats the day he first met Willie Mosconi in a Philadelphia poolhall. Whitlow and Fats were then traveling together and Fats was said to have carried Whitlow's cue. **Photo © Billiards Digest**

Willie Mosconi joins a summit of the greatest hustlers and tournament players at the world straight-pool tournament in April, 1956 in Kinston, North Carolina—including, arguably, the world's greatest nine-ball and one-pocket players. From left to right are Irving Crane, nine-ball great Luther Lassiter, Mike Eufemia, "Cowboy" Jimmy Moore, an unidentified man, one-pocket legend John "Rags" Fitzpatrick, Erwin Rudolf, Richard Riggie, and Mosconi. Mosconi demolished the competition during the tournament.
Photo courtesy Christine Schaffer and John C. Fitzpatrick

One-pocket great Ronnie Allen, seen here shooting with the rake, sometimes went around referring to himself as Fast Eddy. Allen also once found himself opening his wallet to the real-life Minnesota Fats during a very expensive one-pocket session in Johnston City, Illinois. **Photo © *Billiards Digest***

National champion Ed Kelly also was sometimes known as Fast Eddy, and like Ronnie Allen once lost a great deal of money playing Minnesota Fats. Kelly recalls that Fats was a master of managing other players during gambling sessions. **Photo © *Billiards Digest***

Ralph Greenleaf, seen here appropriately wearing a crown, is the only other player in American history whose legacy comes close to matching that of Willie Mosconi. Some say Mosconi was America's best ever player, some say it was Greenleaf. Seen here from left, it's Andrew Ponzi, Joe Diehl, Greenleaf, and Bennie Allen.
Photo © *Billiards Digest*

Promoter and historian Charles Ursitti was one of the leading forces behind The Great Shoot-Out.
Photo courtesy of the author

Willie Mosconi won his first major title in 1941, and then continued winning them through the 1950s. He played fast, and with grim determination. **Photo courtesy Mosconi Estate**

Mosconi lags for the break with Jackie Gleason. Gleason portrayed Minnesota Fats in the 1961 film The Hustler, which also starred Paul Newman. Mosconi served as a technical advisor for the film and coached Newman, who portrayed a hustler by the name of Fast Eddy. Gleason was an expert pool player and needed no instruction. **Photo © *Billiards Digest***

Howard Cosell stands with Mosconi during a televised competition. Mosconi is wearing a tuxedo, which was very much his style when playing what he considered the gentleman's sport.
Photo © Billiards Digest

A brooding Mosconi surveys the table during one of his later exhibition matches.
Photo © Billiards Digest

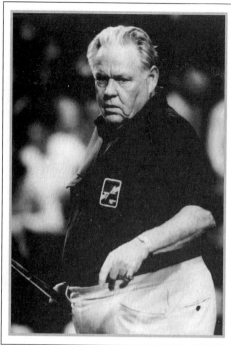

Rudolf Wanderone, AKA Minnesota Fats, stalks the table during one of his televised matches. Like Mosconi, Fats played fast. But Fats had more of an upright stance than Mosconi. **Photo © *Billiards Digest***

Fats stands outside the country home in Dowell, Illinois he shared for decades with his wife Evelyn. The house was surrounded for the most part by fields of corn. He lived a life in southern Illinois far different from the one he knew growing up in New York City. **Photo © *Billiards Digest***

Fats, left, and Mosconi lag for the break. Both men removed their suit jackets shortly after this photo was taken. Whether or not to wear them—Mosconi wanted them, Fats wanted to play in his shirtsleeves—became the subject of a heated argument watched by millions. **Photo © *Billiards Digest***

Mosconi, right, looks ready to storm out of the competition. Cosell is trying to calm down Fats, who had been needling the great champion.
Photo © *Billiards Digest*

Howard Cosell interviews Minnesota Fats after the first Great Shoot-Out with Willie Mosconi. Fats and Mosconi were roughly the same height and age.
Photo © *Billiards Digest*

The former Flora Marchini, seen here at her New Jersey home in 2006, married Willie Mosconi in 1953. She was 28 and working as a telephone operator when she met the world champion and then went on to create a stable and loving home for his children. **Photo courtesy of the author**

Chapter 21

PENELOPE AND ITHACA

Aren't you hungry? Don't you want something?

— Flora Mosconi

Willie then had Bill and Candy to support and a wife that had gone missing, and he had this one unassailable skill: playing pool. He may not have been there for his children emotionally. He could be a hard man and distant. He was, after all, his father's son. But Willie understood that a man must provide for his family. If he had a code and lived by it, then this was it. *A man must be responsible.* And so when he returned to pool shortly after World War II, he did so not because he loved the game or because it was fun but rather because duty demanded it.

A more striking contrast in philosophy is hard to imagine. For Fats and the boys the sport represented a release. For them, it represented freedom. For Willie it represented security, a regular paycheck . . . maybe even a burden. This sense of disciplined duty guided all his decisions and not just those about pool. It colored how he saw the world. It explained Willie Mosconi's failures and his success.

Consider his words to Bob Burnes, sports editor of the *St. Louis Globe-Democrat*, shortly after his discharge from the army. Mosconi said, "I'm in this game for all I can get out of it." When asked about the sport, Mosconi didn't talk about its greater glory, or express gratitude for the opportunities it had afforded him, or even speak of his passion for pocketing balls. Willie said pool to him represented a *paycheck*. He told Burnes that he wanted another shot at the title so he could make a quick buck. And then, he said, he wanted out.

These undiplomatic words—born both from Willie's frustration at being a single father, and his acceptance that it was a responsibility he could not shirk—would have a bearing on his life's course. Shortly after he uttered them, Brunswick Promotions Director C. P. Binner summoned Willie to Chicago. There C. P. told Willie that this was no way for a champion to speak. Willie was told that the fans and the company saw him as the future of the sport, and so his words were really, very important.

"But I've got no future," Willie protested. "I'm going to have to get something else."

"Okay. You're on contract," the promotions manager told him. "That's your security."

So that's why Willie Mosconi played pool, and that's why he stuck with Brunswick. It was his sense of responsibility, his craving for security, his desire for a regular paycheck. He remained on the Brunswick dole for the next twenty-five years, perhaps a record. On behalf of the Chicago suits, he returned to the old billiards circuit, he showed off in exhibitions, he picked up extra cash at minor events. He lived out of his car for weeks and months like a Willie Loman, but one who seldom suffered failure.

And then consider the story of Madelyn O'Day, a woman with whom Willie lived for several years. She appeared in Willie's life in 1948, when Willie was thirty-five and dealing with the growing burdens of being a single father. She apparently hailed from the West Coast and had recently been married to one of Willie's Dancing Mosconi cousins. "He just started dating her, or whatever you want to call it, and then they moved in together," said Bill, Willie's son. He was seven or eight at the time. "I remember we lived with her for about five years, and we even called her Mother. She and Father got together back here in Philadelphia, and then we moved into an apartment in Philadelphia for a year, and then they bought a home out in the suburbs."

Bill said he wasn't sure how it was that she hooked up with his father, or why or where, but he said that he got close enough to Madelyn O'Day to think of her as his very own mom. "Amazing, isn't it?" he said. Although their childhood was far from over, the very young Bill and the even younger Candy had lived briefly in the home of Anna Harrison, were jostled to foster care, lived for a while in the home of Willie's father (while their father lived separately from them in Kansas City), stayed for a while in the residences of separate cousins, and now were calling Madelyn O'Day "Mom" in the suburbs of Philadelphia.

During a two-city tour in May of 1947, Willie won the world title again. In November he won it another time. In May of 1948 he won again, and then once more in 1950—this time at Navy Pier, in Chicago. Willie won even more titles in '51 and '52. He ranged far and wide, moving, moving, moving, competing on the East Coast and on the West. He sent money home. He put food on the table for his kids. He cared about his family and felt keenly the burden of his responsibility for them.

But he was like a man lost at sea. He was always gone. Willie had hoped that Madelyn O'Day would serve as his proxy and tend to his children. (Why else, after all, would he so capriciously set up house with her?) But her patience was not limitless.

"She sent us up to bed early one night, and when we were asleep, she emptied the whole house," Bill said. "We woke up and there was no furniture. Everything was gone. The whole house was empty. How she did it, we never heard. I remember I was in the sixth grade."

So their weird twilight life began again. Bill and Candace became the ward of housekeepers.

●   ●   ●

Here's the story of Florence Marchini, the future three-times-married wife of Willie Mosconi, the famous pool player. To call her colossally important to Willie and to his children is to understate her value. She was the glue that pulled it all together. She was Penelope to Willie's Ulysses and really even more than that. If Willie spent a lifetime searching, then what he hoped to find was not a hero's glory but rather home, stability, respectability, and goodness.

In Flora Marchini he found all these things. Flora Marchini was Ithaca itself.

In late 1952, then nineteen-year-old Flora was spending her days connecting phone calls for Ma Bell in Philadelphia. One of her best friends was Mosconi's cousin, who sat next to her at the switchboard. At the time the cousin was dating a man name Mike, and Flora was dating precisely no one. The conversation probably came in the morning, sometime in January or February.

"Well, you know, I worked at the telephone company with Willie's cousin, and she asked me one day to go out on a double date," recalled Flora. "You know, I never heard of Willie Mosconi, never heard of billiards—and she wants me to go out with Willie Mosconi. She says, 'He's divorced and has two kids,' and I said, 'No, thanks! I don't want a man with kids!'"

Any prospect of a Mosconi-Marchini union could have ended there, but Willie's cousin hounded her. "I'm not asking you to marry him," she said. "C'mon. It'll be fun." Flora worried aloud that this grey-haired pool champion might take a fancy to her, that dating him could lead to complications. "I don't want a man with kids," she said. "And what if he likes me?"

So Flora and Willie and Willie's cousin and Willie's cousin's boyfriend all got together. Willie was all dressed up and handsome, his grey hair pushed back. He smelled good, too, and spoke so easily and with confidence. It was such a nice time, so pleasant. Here, thought Flora, was a real man. She knew nothing of pocket billiards. She had never heard of Willie Mosconi. But he was painfully handsome, simultaneously brooding and charming, maybe a bit on the short side, but she could get over that.

"I knew right away, I mean—*I knew,*" said Flora. "And when I got home, my brother was asleep, and I woke him up, and I said, 'Guess what? I'm going to marry Willie Mosconi.'"

Flora's brother looked up, half asleep, uncomprehending. "I didn't even know you *knew* Willie Mosconi. . . ."

Now Willie was a quick operator. On the second date—that is, the very next time he set eyes on Flora—Willie suggested they pursue a committed relationship. "He asked if I was going out with other fellas, and I said yes, but he told me, 'No, I don't want you to go with anybody else; I want you to be my girl.'" Flora asked what his intentions were, and Willie, a man accustomed to fast-living women, said his intentions were entirely honorable.

Willie, then, was at the zenith of his career. He was then the reigning world champion, a distinction he had held nearly continuously since 1944.[82] He was also traveling, traveling, traveling. It's all he *ever* did. Remember, first Willie left the kids with Anna Harrison, then later with aunts and uncles, then with Madelyn O'Day, now with random housekeepers. He did not trust women—not then, perhaps not ever—because he had never had a responsible female figure in his life. Remember, his mom had died when he was little, and his father could be a mean son of a bitch. So now he was taking up with Flora Marchini.

Their first date likely came not even weeks after the sudden departure of Madelyn O'Day. On the second date he wanted Flora as his steady girl. By the third or the fourth, he had brought her home to meet the kids. The then nineteen-year-old Flora had said she was not ready for marriage or—if she was—certainly not with a man with children. But "I think he thought I'd be a good mother for his kids, and he needed somebody for those kids," she said. And when she finally met them, she fell in love with them. They were beautiful.

•　　•　　•

The story of Willie and Flora getting married three times goes like this. The first time was before a judge in Fort Lauderdale, where he

---

[82] With only brief interruptions from Irving Crane in December 1946, and Jimmy Caras in February 1949.

was traveling for an exhibition or a tournament. They were married on February 11, 1953, three days shy of her twentieth birthday. Then this awkward fact came to light: it turns out that his divorce from Anna Harrison had never been finalized (if indeed it had ever been initialized), and so Flora and Willie had to remarry. But by then Willie was in New Mexico, and so the two took their vows again, this time on February 18, 1953, which was four days after Flora's birthday. "And then we got married again," said Flora. "I'm Catholic, and so is Willie, and so we had to get married in the church. We got married where we lived in Haddon Heights. That was the third time."

There's one other little something that should be noted about the first marriage, the second marriage, and then the third. Somewhere between them, probably between the first and the second, and certainly between the first and the third, Willie's first wife Anna Harrison made an unexpected appearance . . . and an unexpected demand. She wanted custody of Bill and Candy. They went to court.

"She showed up when he was going to remarry; I guess it was because he wanted that divorce," recalled Bill Mosconi, although he doesn't recall actually setting eyes on her then. "The judge called us into his chambers, my sister and I, and said, 'Would you like to go live with your mother or your father?' and I said, 'I don't know that lady, and I don't want to leave my father.' And so the judge says, 'That's good enough for me.' My father got custody. What I said, I said in innocence. I was a kid, and I really didn't know her."

Flora also remembers having her first conversation then with Anna Harrison. "When she called me, she said, 'You have some nerve having those children think you're their mother.' I told her I knew that I was not their mother, but I also asked her how she could leave these two beautiful children. I mean they were really beautiful kids. I told her that if I had had a son or daughter myself I would have scrubbed floors to keep them. I told her that Willie loves those children. I said he would have given you money every week to support them."

So Willie got custody of his kids, and Willie got his divorce from Anna Harrison, and Willie married Flora Marchini—although not necessarily in that order. And then Willie went back on the road. Immediately. Flora and Bill and Candy agree that it was a tough life.

"He was gone a lot for more than ten years—even when I went through high school, [Flora] raised us up through high school," said Bill. "He wasn't here. For six years he wasn't home at all, except during the summer because they didn't have air conditioning, and so he didn't play pool then.

"My opinion is that he married Flora because she would be a good mother and because he never knew his own mother. She died when he was very young. [Flora] made a home for him. It was a process of evolution, going though mistrust to complete trust. At the end of his life he said she made all our lives as good as they could be. She created a home, which we never would have had."

Chapter 22

RECORDS

He would break, and he would look at the balls, and he
would be on the next shot before the cue ball stopped.
He was unbelievably fast. He had such great control of
the cue ball. He would break off three or four from the
rack. And get those. And he would have the ball picked
out where he could get the next bunch open. So he might
take ten shots in a row from one end of the table. I remember someone saying once that he's not that good—
that he never made a tough shot in his life. But my father
said, 'I don't have to.' It's because he played such great
position. He had such control over the cue ball. He didn't
have to make a great shot. That's where the art is.

— Bill Mosconi, describing his
father's style of play

Back when he was still doing his part for the U.S. Army, and even
though he wasn't playing all that much pool, Willie Mosconi did manage this one thing: he *tied* the world record for most balls pocketed
during a single inning. Of course, Willie wanted to exceed the record—
and, in fact, believed for a moment that he had done so—but then it
turned out that the record he targeted was the wrong one.

To explain: For years the high run in straight pool was an astronomical 277. Greenleaf set it on one of those old monsters, the 5 by

10s, with nearly ten feet more playing space and pockets that looked like pinholes. Greenleaf started shooting, went up table and then down, kept whitey mostly off the rail, found his key ball, *rack!* Fourteen more balls—*rack!* Fourteen more—*rack!* On and on he went, clearing 277 before one got away.

Irving Crane came along later and added thirty-two more balls to the mark—that's another two racks—while playing an exhibition in Layton, Ohio. But that was in 1939 when Willie was taking a break from the game, so he missed the news. Now flash forward to 1945, six years later. Willie then was working as an entertainment specialist for the U.S. Army. He was mostly cleaning pools and rec rooms but in October of that year got a reprieve to play an exhibition. His opponent would be Joe Procita,[83] a native of New Jersey. The exhibition would be held in Perth Amboy, not far from Mosconi's home base of Fort Dix.

As he had done so many times in the past, Mosconi effortlessly ran up the winning margin without a single miss. That's 150 balls straight. Then Willie kept running racks, thinking to take the world's long-run record. But again, he was targeting the *wrong* record. He was targeting Greenleaf's intimidating 277, not realizing then that just behind it was Crane's even more terrible 309.

"Every ball after 250 began assuming the terrifying proportions of the devil in a child's nightmare," recalled journalist Clive Howard. "In the Perth Amboy match he was on the point of blowing up on every shot until he passed the old record, then he settled back into stride and went on to 309. The run took about an hour and half to complete."

And so Willie believed that he had taken the record and that he could now rightfully claim to have run more balls than any human ever had in the history of the earth. He was ecstatic. The crowd went berserk. If he had had a cigar, he would have smoked it. But then almost immediately

---

[83] Procita holds the high-run record for most balls pocketed during a tournament, as opposed to most balls pocketed in any setting (which can also include exhibition play). Procita's historic tournament run was 182, came in 1951, and ironically enough occurred during a match against Mosconi.

word trickled from the crowd that Greenleaf's 277 was no longer the record but rather it was Crane's 309.

"It couldn't have been 308," Willie later said ruefully. "It couldn't have been 310. It had to be exactly 309."

•   •   •

Although always drawing purse-lipped scowls from the temperate ladies who passed by, Springfield's East High Billiards[84] in 1954 was seen by its male regulars as a fairly straight-up place. The wood floors were almost always polished, swept, and butt free. They said Clarence Newman, the rackman, always made sure the 4 by 8s and 5 by 10s (all Brunswicks, of course) had nice clean felt. There was a back room for gin and poker, but there was no beer and no whiskey. "The poolhall itself was frowned upon by the general population as a den of evil, although that was far from the truth—other than the smoking and the light gambling, it was a pretty decent place," said Dick Hatfield, a longtime regular. As is the case with many great poolrooms, it was upstairs. Right below it was Reco Sporting Goods and right beside that a greasy-spoon diner popular with the farmers and the high school kids.

When Willie scaled those stairs at East High Billiards on that chilly spring evening of March 19, 1954, he did so with shoes shined so bright they almost cast a reflection. His smart brown fedora he wore tilted only slightly. He was the undisputed best of the best—he understood this, and anyone who followed pool understood this, and yet it all was so exhausting. The intimidated regulars at East High looked upon Willie, who was there on exhibition, as they might look upon foreign royalty. Some held back, others crowded in. Willie pasted on a smile and greeted room owner Bob Haas with a warm handshake. He

---

[84] According to Springville resident and amateur historian Dick Hatfield, East High Billiards, as well as Reco Sporting Goods, encompassed both 111 and 113 East High Street. He said the poolhall probably got its start in 1948. The building was leveled in 1974.

gave a few pointers and signed autographs. He tried to make the crowd feel at ease. He understood the drill.

Willie would meet the hometown hero, a man named Earl Bruney, whom friends called Jake. The exhibition was set for 8:00 p.m. "Everybody was real excited, everybody was talking about it," said Bob Fry, Bruney's nephew, then sixteen years old and a senior at Springfield High. "Mosconi was going to be there, and so they wanted a hometown boy to play him, and they wanted the best player in Springfield. And old Jake, I tell you he was shooting pool all the time. He made money when he played pool. He was good."

Mosconi answered a few questions about his many world titles, then offered a tip or two, and eventually made his way to the Bally Six-Card Bingo machine, where, much to the amazement of the East High patrons, skillfully started ringing up points. He excelled at pinball, too, it seemed. "He was a big hit with everybody, very personable," said Hatfield.

Bruney, a water-department employee, actually reminded one of a farmer. He was then about forty-eight years old, was a bit overweight, and was fond of overalls. He had dark hair. Like Willie he didn't gamble much, although the locals considered him a top-notch player. The game, of course, was straight pool: Willie's game. The first to reach two hundred points wins. The referee was Art Mills, an appliance salesman.[85] As always, Clarence Newman racked the balls. That night he'd get a workout.

•   •   •

Bruney shot first and played a safety. Mosconi returned it, leaving Bruney nothing. They went back and forth like that a few times, ducking and stalling. Jake got the first open look and made three balls, but the fourth one he missed.

And then it was over.

"After that," said Hatfield, "Willie took command."

---

[85] Unlike Bruney, Mills was as close to a professional gambler as existed in the Springfield poolroom. "A real slickster," recalled Hatfield.

For an hour or more, no one at East High Billiards realized the significance of what they were witnessing. Of course, it was stellar pocket billiards, fantastic pocket billiards, with the balls gliding softly to the center of the pockets, the cue ball drifting away, but with precision, each shot announced with a soft tap, but with a different sound, subtly different from the sound made by amateurs. Clarence Newman kept the rack slung around his neck or sometimes draped on his arm. He would let it slide to his hand and rush to the table after every fifteenth ball. He wore a half apron smeared with chalk.

Fifteen-ball, side. *Tap.* Thirteen-ball, corner. *Tap.* Twelve, corner. *Tap.*

For an hour it went on. Then for two. And then for three. Willie played fast and with such total concentration that it was as if he played with no thought at all. It was if he had become mesmerized by the balls and so the crowd had melted away invisible, and the whole world was invisible, and all he could do was pocket balls, one after another, like Odysseus among the Lotus-eaters. It was almost as if he couldn't stop. It was almost as if it was easier for him to pocket balls than to miss them. *Rack, Newman! Rack, Newman! Rack, Newman! Rack! Rack! Rack!* No one at East High Billiards had ever witnessed anything like it. Nobody in the *world* had ever witnessed anything like it. Not then. Not since.

During the early morning hours of March 20, 1954, Mosconi completed a run of 526 balls. Again, that's 5–2–6.[86] It represented at least thirty-four racks of straight pool and maybe more, depending on how one does the counting. It is a record that has remained standing for more than five decades, and, in fact, may never ever be surpassed. It is pool's most cherished record and in all ways as startling as DiMaggio's fifty-six-game hitting streak, or the hundred-point game by Wilt Chamberlain.

"At 12:50 a.m., he missed the 527th shot—a six-ball in the corner.

---

[86] On November 13, 1953, Willie ran 365 straight, thereby surpassing Crane's old record. And Willie did so right off the break. Willie called the first shot—he said it was a one-ball in the corner pocket—and then he just kept going. His opponent, a man named Nixon Jones, looked on awestruck. Willie was in Wilmington, North Carolina, 530 miles from home. And so when Willie ran his historic 526, he already held the world's record. The new record surpassed Willie's old one by more than a hundred balls.

It tottered at the pocket but would not fall," said Hatfield. "At 1:10 a.m., the *Springfield News and Sun* was called to report the story." Fifty witnesses signed an affidavit attesting to the feat and that affidavit now resides at the Smithsonian Institute in Washington. Local A. Y. Lefty made a sketch of the missed shot, the fifth of the final rack. It jawed out of the corner. That's when Mosconi looked up, smiled apologetically, and said he was getting tired anyway. "I figured I'd go to 250 and quit," Mosconi said the next morning. "But then I reached that mark and went to 300. When I had 300 I thought about the record and went after it. . . . If anybody would have told me that more than 500 could be run, I would have told them they were nuts.

"I wasn't even thinking of a record," he continued. "I just wanted make a nice run for [room owner] Bob [Haas]. I know him very well, and I have played in his house many times."

· · ·

As much as anything, that 526 run made Willie Mosconi famous. Not many then understood the significance—least of all the residents of Springfield, but those 526 balls became one of the great feats of Willie's now legendary career, the sort that obituary writers would put right in the first paragraph next to the comma following Willie's name. It was a solitary feat, as was Willie's sport, his life, and his lonely character. "I'm lucky this time," he said after smashing the record in a town where no one much cared. "I got three days at home. I've only been home two days since January 25 of this year."

Less than a month later his third child, Gloria, was born. It was his second daughter and his only child with Flora. The blessed event came April 16, and within days Willie was on the road again, venturing out on America's wine-dark byways. "One day we counted up the days— sometimes he was gone 320 days a year," said Bill, his son. Flora maintained the home and tended to the newborn.

---

[87] The invitation-only tournament was in Philadelphia, at a venue called the Arena.

In the spring of 1955, Willie was called upon to defend his title,[87] and he came in second to Irving Crane in a two-man field. But he managed to exact his revenge later that year by demolishing the New Yorker during a five-day challenge match at Allinger's. Willie scored more than two points for every one of Crane's, the second-best pool player in the world. The final tally was 1,500–646.

The next year Willie won the world championship in Kinston, North Carolina, during a performance that bears note. Willie faced several old hands—Crane and Erwin Rudolf among them—but also some up-and-comers from the despised hustling world, including Wimpy Lassiter, sometimes mentioned as America's greatest-ever nine-ball player, and the terrifying John "Rags" Fitzpatrick, who was virtually unstoppable at one-pocket.

Here's a note from the first-day coverage in the *Kinston Daily Free Press:* "Willie Mosconi, the defending champion, had little trouble with Richard Riggie of Baltimore as he chalked up a 150–48 win." Here's the headline from the second day: "Mosconi adds second win in billiard action here." And from the third: "Mosconi blanks his foe." Here's a line from the fourth day: "It was the fourth straight win for the champ." And from the fifth: "Mosconi continues winning ways." The sixth day: "Mosconi boasts perfect record." The seventh: "Mosconi takes pool tourney win." And the ninth: "Mosconi . . . rolled over Richard Riggie of Baltimore."

The headlines kept on like a Mosconi high run, over and over, every day, for the entirety of the fourteen-day double round-robin. Mosconi swept America's greatest players—hustlers and tournament men alike. *He beat them all.* Willie held five of the fourteen daily high runs. Only the hustler Lassiter gave him a bit of a tussle, once scoring 145 points before Mosconi finally fell upon him like Ulysses on Antinous. On the last day Mosconi blanked the gambling Jimmy Moore, running 150 and out. He would not have these men in his house.

And even as he made ghosts of those hustling interlopers, the sport was collapsing beneath his feet. The prize money that year was a paltry $1,400, less than the purse of typical tournaments fifty years earlier. Nobody could touch Willie Mosconi. He had conquered all who had tried. And yet pool itself was failing him. By then he had won fifteen world titles. He held the world's record for the most balls run in a single inning, both in exhibitions and in tournament play. There are few athletes who have dominated *any* sport like Willie Mosconi.

"I have to ask—is this even *human?*" said historian Charles Ursitti. And then it was over.

Chapter 23

POLSKY'S LAMENT

> When the subculture died, the poolroom nearly died
> with it.
>
> — Sociologist Ned Polsky

When he married Flora, Willie Mosconi was still a youngish man whose skill was still arguably on the rise, but the sport was disappearing beneath him. He played plenty of exhibitions but to smaller crowds than before. He would play Billiard Congress of America[88] (BCA) tournaments, but they were becoming fewer and fewer. Quietly, quietly the world was changing. And for the nation's tournament perfectionists, for men like Mosconi—but also for poolroom scamps like Fats and Wimpy Lassiter—it was not a change for the better.

Consider this: 80 percent more pool tables existed in America during the quarter century before World War II than did in those years just after it.[89] And this: during the early part of the twentieth century, Ralph Greenleaf sometimes drew more spectators to his trick-shot shows than a professional football team brought to hometown stadiums.[90] The top

[88] The Billiard Congress of America was established in 1948 and supplanted the old Billiard Association of America.

[89] According to the *New York Post*, there were about five thousand licensed billiard parlors in the New York area during the 1920s. During the 1950s, there were about six hundred.

[90] According to the *New York Times*, "During the heyday of billiards, Mr. Bensinger drew crowds of more than 4,000, some of the spectators appearing in white ties and tails, to watch the world's billiard stars."

players of the nineteenth and early twentieth centuries were household names. No pool player, with the possible exception of Willie Mosconi himself, could make such a claim in the 1950s.

John Grissim, in his 1979 *Billiards,* devotes several pages to this confounding postwar transition. He wrote that the industry saw nothing but dollar signs during the war, that optimism and greed ruled the day. And then, for reasons that Brunswick, Mosconi, and the BCA did not grasp—it all went to shit.

"Hundreds of thousands of servicemen with middle-class backgrounds were exposed to the game for their first time during the war and many got hooked on it," explained Grissim. "Their enthusiasm was sustained by the exhibition performances by Willie Mosconi, Irving Crane and a dozen other billiard stars who toured military bases extensively at home and overseas. At the war's end industry prognosticators figured those legions of new converts would seek out their local poolrooms along with the prewar clientele and that business would once again be booming. They were dead wrong.

"Not only did the game's new converts avoid poolrooms, but the old crowd never fully materialized either. During the remainder of the '40s and into the '50s, splendid old rooms everywhere went belly-up, while attendance fell off dramatically at tournaments. For its part Brunswick decided to focus its energy on its bowling division, one which had been turning out a line of equipment since the 1920s."

The BCA failed to hold a tournament in 1954 and only intermittently held tournaments during the remainder of the decade. In 1956 it suspended them altogether. Rooms closed one after another. Those that remained were rough and filthy places, their once-proud burnished wood ruined with age and neglect. Table sales, the ultimate arbiter of poolroom success, had hit that glorious high in 1913 when Mosconi, Crane, and Minnesota Fats were born. But since then sales had trended down, down, down, until the 1950s, when they tumbled directly into the toilet. The *plop* was almost audible.

What was happening? The sport had persevered during difficult times and even flourished—but not now.[91] The poolroom industry and Mosconi, their Homeric champion, always blamed the riffraff. These men were usurpers, unprincipled and undisciplined, over-running Mosconi's great palace. When he called them thieves, he meant in a fashion beyond the merely literal. Hustlers would bring the sport low with their wanton cussing, with their spitting, with their shameless wagering. "The poolrooms can blame themselves," one pool expert told the *New York Daily News,* summing up the then-prevailing wisdom. "They catered to a bunch of bums in many places. They were blinds for horse rooms and other forms of gambling. They got a black eye, and they couldn't, or wouldn't, do a thing to achieve respectability."

●   ●   ●

Yes, true, all too true, that the hustlers threatened the dignity of pocket billiards. It was also true that the hustlers threatened the dignity of Willie Mosconi himself, and that they were a sleazy bunch of bastards. *But it was also true that they had always been so.* Minnesota Fats and the hustlers were as much a part of pool as Willie Mosconi himself. That whole sorry element had always been a part of pool. They were so associated with the game that they had come to define it.

Just as no other human sport requires such perfect mastery over the precise movement of a sphere, no other human sport has become so associated with the random and chaotic elements of wagering. These are *facts.* Pool is about perfection, as Mosconi understood perfection. Pool is also about gambling, as Fats would have it. Pool is about *both* things at once, and it's always been about both things—even as far back as American Colonial days, and even before then, when it was played by the sharpers and the blacklegs and by all the princes of the land.

---

[91] During the Depression men could ill afford to buy new tables but nonetheless would spend their meager earnings in public rooms. And during World War II, when many men were getting shipped overseas, the military bought tables and installed them on bases. The navy town of Norfolk, Virginia, became the nation's greatest mecca for poolroom vice, indisputably because of the war. But now all that was over, and some suffocating thing had descended upon pool like a heavy blanket.

So if not the riffraff bringing the game down, then who? Sociologist Ned Polsky gives us the startling answer. It was not a who, he says, but a what. It was *marriage* or, more specifically, the decline of bachelor culture. This is what doomed pocket billiards.

In his *Hustlers, Beats and Others,* first published in 1967, Polsky lays out the argument. Briefly, it's as follows: During the late 1800s, when pool rivaled baseball for the nation's attention, the proportion within the general population of single males, aged fifteen and above, stood at 42 percent. In the 1950s it had plummeted to 25 percent. Men were also getting married earlier, so there were fewer "bachelor years" among those who eventually settled down. Citing a 1959 study on marriage and divorce, Polsky notes that the average annual marriage rate among single men rose from sixty-four per thousand in the 1900s to sixty-nine per thousand in the 1920s, dropped again during the Depression, and then soared upward in the 1940s, to ninety-two per thousand.

Now, the settled-down suburban life stands at odds with the poolroom life. During the 1950s America was becoming a nation of settled-down suburban dads. It wasn't the persistence of the so-called sporting element that killed pool but rather the *decline* of it. Loafers and hustlers may not add much to the overall economy, but they certainly add to the poolroom one. They spend their days in poolrooms and their nights there, too. They shoot one-pocket, and they throw down fives and tens, and they pour their lifeblood into the game. Like the barbershop and the neighborhood tavern, the poolroom became a gathering place for working-class bachelors. But Polsky stresses that the poolroom wasn't just *one* of these places but rather "*the* one, the keystone." So when the bachelor culture fell into decline, so too did the American poolroom.

"The once-great attraction of pool and billiards, both for spectators and players, was in large part factitious," wrote Polksy. "It had not so much to do with the games themselves, as with the poolroom's latent function as the greatest and most determinedly all-male institution in American social life. The poolroom got so thoroughly bound up with this function that it could not readily adapt itself to changed conditions; when the subculture died, the poolroom nearly died with it."

It's not as if these men stopped being sports fans. It's just that with the growing popularity of television, they didn't need to wander off to the neighborhood poolhall to fulfill their cravings. Men could pop open their beers and settle down on the couch and watch the New York Jets on TV. Men are typically a shiftless and lazy lot. Now they could be thus at home. So it wasn't the hustlers but marriage, TV, and suburbia that threatened pool. And in the 1950s, as world-class tournaments became increasingly few and far between, America was becoming irreversibly a suburban, TV nation. Willie Mosconi was at the top of his game but had fewer places to play it.

Chapter 24

THE BITE ARTIST

"One mark of trickster's mind, then, is that it exploits
. . . opportunity."

— Lewis Hyde, *Trickster Makes This World*

"Hey, Johnny, lemme sell you this watch. . . ."

Lanky John Ogolini, who had been on his way to the post office to mail a letter, eyed Minnesota Fats's timepiece with mild irritation. Ogolini had learned from long experience that any potential financial transaction involving his fat friend should be approached with a great deal of skepticism. On that day Fats had accosted him halfway up the steps to the Du Quoin post office. "This is a *good* watch," Fats hissed. "See? Got it right here. . . ." It looked to be gold plated and with diamonds—but who knew? If Ogolini were to guess, he would say Fats had won it in a card game.

"C'mon. I need the money. *Gotta go to Florida.* . . ."

"Well, I dunno, Fatty. . . ."

What was Fats doing during these lean middle years? As Willie conquered the world, what was Fats conquering? Those who knew him, those like Ogolini, said first and foremost Fats was being a terrific mooch. He could be generous when he had money, but when he was broke—which was somewhere between often and always—he was quick to put the bite on his friends. He was maniacal about it. The word for it in later years was hyperactivity. He kept on, and he kept on, and he kept on. Ogolini said Fats would come up to him; he'd start pestering Ogolini something awful. Fats was like an annoying little kid.

"He says, 'I got to go to Florida, I got some action,' and you know how he gets: He won't let up. He says, 'I gotta go. I gotta go. I gotta go and have some action now. I gotta go. I gotta go to Florida and win some money.' He'd keep that up, you know. . . ."

"And I said, 'I don't want that damn watch. I told him I already had a railroad special.' At that time you had pockets, you know, and you'd pull that railroad special out." As he tells the story, Ogolini mimes how a man might look at a railroad watch. "And I told him, 'Look at this here—your watch had a different kind of band on it. I can't wear that. That band was irritating. I don't want it.'"

But this is how Fats was. He stayed home making himself fat. He leeched off Evelyn, and he leeched off Orbie, Evelyn's mother. He lived for free in their Dowell home and even pestered Orbie to sign over the title. Orbie hated Fats with an enthusiasm bordering on religious zealotry. He didn't work. He didn't help around the house. He spent Evelyn's money when she had it. "Orbie couldn't *stand* him," said one longtime resident. "She hated, hated, hated him." And then he would pester Evelyn for the title to the house, just pester her over and over again, just like he was pestering Ogolini to buy that damn watch.

Although she stuck with him, Evelyn was none too patient with Fats. When he drove to nearby Johnston City, Evelyn and Orbie would commiserate about what a no-good, lazy son-of-a-bitch he was. When Fats would come back from a long afternoon of shooting pool with his friend George Jansco out in Johnston City or from playing cards with Blackie in Heron, the two would fight and scream. It wasn't like Fats helped around the house, helped with the bills, helped with anything . . . except himself to what was in the refrigerator. "And so Evelyn didn't treat him well," said one longtime friend. Those who knew Fats said he was lazy. And this, even by the very high standards of very lazy hustlers. Luther "Wimpy" Lassiter partnered plenty with Fats during his Norfolk days, and sometimes, he said, Fats was too lazy *even to shoot pool.*

Mostly, Fats wanted just three things from life: to play cards, to shoot dice, and to eat. And so that's largely what Fats did during those middle years when Willie traveled the nation breaking records. Fats ate fried chicken, and he spent Orbie's money, and he sat on his fat ass. As Willie Mosconi fought for a sport then in decline, Minnesota Fats was putting the bite on his luckless friend John Ogolini.

"So Fats goes home, and the next day he comes back, and he caught me again at the post office." Ogolini is laughing now. "This is typical, typical Fats. He says to me, 'I gotta go to Florida. *I gotta go . . . ,'* and then he changes his tack, and he says, 'Johnny, why don't you go with me?'

"Now at that time Fats had a beat-up old Chevy, and he wanted me to go with him. I said 'No. No way.' So then he wants to borrow $5,000, and I said 'Fats, there ain't no way.' I was just starting out, you know, and I didn't have no money then. He wanted to borrow $5,000, and I just didn't have it.

"But he kept it up. He kept talking and talking, and the next day he said, 'Johnny, just take this watch. Gimme $500 for this watch, and go to Florida with me.' And I said, 'In that old junky car?' You know, he had a beat-up old car. I said, 'I wouldn't go to Clarksville and back with you in that car.' But, shit, you know what: I bought that damn watch off him. He pestered me every time he saw me. That's just the way he was, and that's what he done. I gave him $500 for that damn watch, and he went with my money and that beat-up old Chevy, and then he came back with a brand-new car. He won that car with my damn money! He was driving a beat-up Chevy that looked about ready for the junkyard, and he took it with him—and then he comes back with a brand-new car."

Chapter 25

THE STROKE

He was perfect in everything that he tried.
— Bill Mosconi, recalling his father

It was a cozy little three-bedroom house in the middle of a tree-lined drive right on the west side in Haddon Heights, which in the spring-time could seem like the most pleasant small town in all of New Jersey. There was a grassy terrace out front and a sycamore tree and blooming azaleas. Young Candace Mosconi walked to public school every morning and eventually graduated from Haddon Heights High. Older brother Bill attended the all-boy St. Joseph Preparatory, at Seventeenth and Girard Avenue in North Philadelphia, and he did okay there, too . . . though he didn't much care for it. ("I'm going to leave it! I'm going to leave it!" he'd always threaten.) But Bill stuck with it, and the priests didn't throw him out even though they wanted to, and Candace stuck with her school, too, and little Gloria ended up going to St. Mary of the Angels, and mostly the Mosconis had a pretty good life . . . even though Willie himself was only infrequently a part of it.

Their father only had himself for company when he was on the road, and he typically seemed eager to keep that company when he returned home. He was like a seafarer too long exiled. He lived in hotels, and he ate in cafes, and he smoked cigarettes one after the other. As Bill grew up playing Little League, Willie played faraway exhibitions, sometimes three hundred per year. He was away from home, vanished, and absent . . . *almost always*. "He was just gone," said son Bill. "For six years he wasn't home at all." And even when his father was home, even during those infrequent stolen days here and there—even *then* he could be absent. Twenty thousand miles is simply too much driving for any man. And Willie Mosconi drove those miles most years. Sometimes more. If Willie came home tired and irritable, who could blame him? If he came home incommunicative, who could blame him? "He didn't seem to know me, and I didn't seem to know him," reported daughter Candace. "He'd talk, but you really wouldn't have a conversation with him," said Bill.

Willie Mosconi confronted only one burning question when he was on the road, and he seemed still lost in it even after he pulled into the driveway on Prospect Ridge right next to the sycamore and the azaleas.

How do I stay perfect?

Powerful men on long solitary voyages must by necessity make their own rules. This was especially true for Willie Mosconi. Through the tournament victories and the endless road show, Willie came to the understanding that he was in some ways greater than other men. Like long-suffering Ulysses, Willie didn't wander through this lonely life by settling for the lowly standards of others. Rather, Willie Mosconi succeeded in life because he commanded a focus so total and complete that the heat of it made others falter. He won because he insisted that other men lose.

But to make it happen, to win night after night, he had to maintain that focus, *always*. To be world champion, Willie had to be right, *all the time*. If ever he showed anything less than magic during an exhibition, then the crowd became surly and grumbled. If he had an off night and let a local hotshot come close, then the railbirds whispered and clucked. "He's losing his edge," they'd say knowingly. "He's past his prime. He doesn't play like he played before." Willie Mosconi had to show everyone that he was absolutely and utterly the best. This was the sort of life he endured on the road: perfection on command. It was his fate as the child prodigy of pool, or as the hometown hero at Frankie Mason's, or when setting records in Springfield, Ohio. Beating all comers was simply the price of greatness.

But for a man entering middle age, it could be unbearable. Willie Mosconi could win at will—but he also discovered that to keep winning he must will it always. So is it any surprise that when Willie came home he became withdrawn and distant? Is it any surprise that his daughter would complain that she didn't know him and that his son said conversations were a rarity. He said there were days that Willie wouldn't answer the phone or come to the door.

But then sometimes Willie would toggle on and become engaged in the world but not without aggravating those around him. Willie insisted on perfection, always. But if he had no pocket billiards match on which to focus that insistence, then he would turn it on family. It wasn't that he was abusive or tyrannical. He didn't hit the children. Bill said it was more that his father was *uncompromising.* It was as if his father had become trapped by perfection. The trait would manifest itself in unexpected and sometimes comical ways, said Bill.

A few examples:

In the spring of 1956, just a few months after his spectacular showing in Kinston, Willie purchased a seventeen-table poolhall at the intersection of Broad and Rockland in Philadelphia. The poolhall was aptly called Superior Billiards, and Willie did his best to keep out the riffraff. One afternoon a pair of corrupt Philadelphia cops came with an envelope in hand. But Willie wasn't there. It was just Bill, working the cash register. The cops insisted that Willie's son open the box and hand over some money. It was that vulgar and that simple, a classic shakedown, and Bill wasn't sure what to do.

So he called his father at home.

"Pa, the cops are here!" he said. Bill then was in his late teens or early twenties.

Willie's response was uncompromising, unthinking, and stubborn. "Tell 'em to go to hell," he said. Willie always saw the world in black and white.

"And so the next thing you know, Dad was bailing me out," said Bill.

Bill also tells the story of the baby shoes.

"Gloria was a baby, and me and my Dad had to polish up the baby shoes, make them white, and I had to lace them up. I finished lacing up one shoe, and my father was still there with his laces. And he said to me, 'look at your laces. They're not even straight.' On his shoe, both ends came out exactly as they should be. He said: 'when you do it, you have to do it right!"

And then there was the round of golf.

"I went to play golf with him one time. I was in college, and we went to play golf, and I mean I had played golf maybe ten times in my life. So I hit the ball off the tee, and I shanked it to the left, and I was nervous because my father was there. And he said, 'You don't even know how to swing the club right!' We went about two holes, and then I said, 'Dad, I quit. This is not any fun playing with you because I'm not perfect. I've got to change everything and do everything, and we're just out here to have some fun.'

"And he said, 'No, this is not for fun. You have to play it right.'"

And then, of course, there was pool. Willie never encouraged his children, even though Bill and Gloria expressed an early interest.

"There was a point when I thought I was pretty good at pool; you know, I could run twenty or thirty balls. And so he came home one day, and I said Dad, 'Let me show you.' And I went to put the ball on the table and went to shoot the cue ball to break them, and he picked the cue ball right off the table, he picked it up before it made contact and he said, 'You stink.' He said it just like that. And I said, 'But Dad, I can run a couple of racks. I wanna show you.'

"And he said, 'You stink. You don't even know how to hit the cue ball right,' and he asked if I really wanted to learn to play. He told me to learn how to hit the cue ball, and he showed me how to stroke, and he said, 'Now, you practice this, and don't even put any balls on the table.' And so I did that for a couple of weeks.

"Afterwards he said, 'Now you know how to hit the cue ball.' He said, 'Now you're ready to learn how to play.'

"But I said, "Geez, Dad, now I don't want to.'"

•　　•　　•

His father, quite simply, brooked no compromise. He spent his entire life setting his own rules, both on the road, where he vanquished every adversary that came against him, and even before then, when he saved a family from starvation. The world had become black and white for Willie Mosconi. People were either on for him, or they were off. Dirty cops could go to hell, even if that meant sending his son to jail, and baby shoes had to be laced up perfectly. "When you do it, you have to do it right!" And for crissakes don't swing a golf club unless you know what the hell you're doing.

For Mosconi, there was no in-between. This trait permeated all aspects of his character and even his conception of games and leisure. Bowling, golf, and most especially pool: none of it was about having fun. "That's how he was about everything," said Bill. If he faced Irving Crane and he was up eighty balls in a match to 150, then Willie wanted to win by ninety balls or by a hundred. "When you are playing somebody, you do your best every second, and it doesn't matter what it is," he told Bill. "There is no reason, there is no rationale reason, not to play your very best."

Shortly after he purchased Superior Billiards, Willie told a reporter he might leave off playing tournaments altogether. Over the years winning had become a burden. It's just the same as an addiction: there's euphoria afterwards, but for a man like Willie—a man who wraps his entire identity into it—the panic of going without, of not winning, blots out the final satisfaction. "Maybe I'll just quit tournaments altogether," he told the reporter. "What do you think about that?" How can a man pour one's soul into anything, to strive constantly, and not also become depleted? Willie may have looked relaxed during tournaments, but he was a bundle of nerves. Willie lived his life with a focus so total that it became something like blindness. Victory was maddening; failure was worse.

●　　●　　●

There's nothing more tragic and magical than a drunken woman. And there she was, Evelyn Grass Wanderone, the most beautiful woman in all of Little Egypt, the coveted Gingham Girl wife of Minnesota Fats: drunker and weepier and more frail than lanky John Ogolini had ever seen her. She may have been on her fifth or sixth highball when Ogolini walked through the front door of the Du Quoin's Depot. She was sitting alone, a tragedy in and of itself.

"Evelyn, Evelyn, Evelyn—what the hell are you doing?" John stood there at her table. She didn't quite seem to recognize him at first.

"Fats is back there playing cards with that damn Greek," she managed finally. "He's over at the St. Nicholas, and he's playing cards, and he don't know how to play that game, and he don't know nothing about how the Greek plays it, and the Greek is just beating the hell out of him."

"That's it? He's losing?" Ogolini had heard that one before.

"Well, I'm also mad," she said. "And I'm drunk."

While Willie Mosconi traveled the nation, shooting exhibitions and winning world tournaments, Fats mooched and gambled and made Evelyn insane. He fought with his mother-in-law. The weak and the sloppy were not welcome in Willie's black-and-white perfect world. Fats, by contrast, lived by a code that was really no code at all. He was untrustworthy, he was a braggart, he was undisciplined. He took instant cash over long-term gain. He never held a job, not a real one at least, and on many nights the pool hustler couldn't even muster the energy to play a decent game of pool.

Where Willie was perfection, Fats was frivolity. As Willie conquered pool during those dreadful fifties, Fats accomplished nothing of consequence. He collected ducks, dogs, cats, and a squirrel. He loved Evelyn but often became madly jealous. "She was," as one longtime high school friend would recall, "the most beautiful girl that ever walked the earth." Sometimes Fats would drive out to the country to buy watermelons. Sometimes he spent the night trading aces and jacks at the St. Nicolas Hotel. For Willie there was not a thing in this world worth doing unless he could do it right. Fats did nothing unless easily done.

Willie Mosconi saw the sport as permanent and perfect, but in reality it had begun to evaporate away. It was as if Willie Mosconi was protecting the dead, and it's in the contrast to this attitude that one finds the greater nuanced significance of Minnesota Fats, the trickster. Fats was a man for whom truth always held ambiguous sway. He was a seducer, unmoved by the world, and yet ubiquitous in his appeal.

Sociologist Charles Lemert tells us that for a trickster, "a time can only be right when times are expected to change." Pool was disappearing, disappearing from underneath Willie Mosconi's feet. So perhaps it would soon be time for America to change its view of it, to accept the sport as something other than the perfect, wholesome, *uncompromising* sport that Willie, through his celebrity, had come to embody.

"No trickster . . . can deceive for the good if his trick does not call out a truth shared by the many who listen to his story and live to tell it," writes Lemert, writing in his *Muhammad Ali: Trickster Celebrity in the Culture of Irony.* "Times such as these reveal what most human beings spend a lifetime denying—that everything is impermanent. . . . Celebrities can be, and usually are, worshipped. Trickster-celebrities though they may be, do their magic only when they expose the terrible news that all of us shit and piss and fart and want to fuck—the most earthy of human things, the very things by which we spill the remains of our bodies back to the dust from which we came.

"When it happens that a celebrity manages, for whatever reason or cause, to keep the trickster alive, it happens (and probably only happens) when, as the saying goes, the time is right, when, that is, the social order of things demands it. And when this occurs, things are never what they appear or ought to be."

●　　●　　●

It felt like a great sea wave had struck him square on, like a violent whirling typhoon—except it was washing around inside his brain—and then it knocked the great Willie Mosconi flat on his back. The forty-three-year-old world champion had been quietly polishing a pool ball, rubbing it to a keen shine as he sat at the front counter of his North Philly poolroom. Then his focus washed away, and his world went all helter-skelter, and suddenly men were huddled about him, and they were speaking to him. But Willie could not talk, and he could not move. This came in 1956.

"It was out of the clear blue sky, a vascular accident, a sudden surge in blood," said Willie, speaking to the *Philadelphia Inquirer*'s Maralyn Lois Polak for a February 26, 1984, profile on him. "I keeled over. It was like a roaring noise in my ears. I didn't know what it was. I stiffened up and fell off the stool. But I never lost consciousness; I knew something was happening to me. I couldn't speak, couldn't do anything, couldn't move. Fortunately somebody saw it and came on over and tried to help. And they called the police, and the police got their ambulance, and they rushed me to the hospital."

Flora said, "I was home when they called me from the hospital. They said he didn't lose consciousness, but he had fallen down. We rushed right over there, and he could hardly talk. His tongue was swollen. I thought, 'Oh God! Oh God!' He was very out of it. They told me it was an aneurism and that it was in his head but that he was very, very lucky."

Although first diagnosed as a stroke (and that's how Willie would always describe the incident), what happened that day, as Willie's daughter[92] said, should probably be more accurately described as a "temporary ischemic attack." She said more came during her father's twilight years, and she suspected that the culprit was an old head injury, most likely the one he suffered in a car accident while on the road with Ralph Greenleaf. She said her father's symptoms were never precisely strokelike but rather involved moments of paralysis and befuddlement.

And like a sea surge, the episode also shifted Willie's center of gravity. He had to learn to walk again, even to stand. Doctors ordered more tests, kept him under observation, although Willie said he refused physical therapy. "What's this for?" he told the doctors. "This is ridiculous." Flora Mosconi said her husband was out of bed in three or four days, although he remained at Philadelphia's Mt. Sinai Hospital for two or three weeks longer.

She also said that for a brief period her already taciturn husband stopped speaking altogether and instead sat eerily staring out the window. This despite his speech having returned within just a few days of the incident. Eventually, Willie took to long walks around the neighborhood, and he began squeezing a rubber ball to regain strength. "Finally got it so that I regained the use of my arm, and also my leg, just by walking," he said.

Two of his fingers remained numb for years afterwards, but much more horrifying to Willie was the loss of self-confidence. He had spent his life not just conquering opponents but utterly humiliating them. He would walk into strange rooms each and every night, he would turn on that *focus*, men would stand in awe as he ran hundreds of balls. Willie Mosconi was America's greatest living player, perhaps its greatest player ever, and now suddenly he found himself unable to fully control his own body.

Bill Mosconi said his father feared one thing more than all others: death. Any contemplation of it, especially after the 1956 collapse, could throw him into a panic. Willie had broken records, he had transcended his sport, he had gained a measure of immortality. Why else strive for greatness if not to create something that lives on? Why is there anything worth doing? For Willie, failure and death were one and the same. And this may have been why, ultimately, he did not surrender in 1956.[93]

"I remember he finally said, 'I got to keep playing,'" Flora said. "He had this engagement in Michigan, and he said, 'I'm keeping it.' He did not want to cancel, but he was nervous about it. He had made the

---

[92] As her father got older, the episodes came with greater frequency and intensity, she said. "He [eventually] lost his ability to understand certain things. He had great posture, and he would walk around real peppy, but he lost his capacity for certain things. He never lost his speech, but he would get disoriented."

[93] During his recovery, Willie read biographies of other sports figures confronting death. "I like to read autobiographies of other people, like Babe Ruth and maybe Lou Gehrig," he told the *Philadelphia Inquirer*. "They had a lot of courage. They knew they had it and they knew they were going to die, and they faced it strongly."

commitment." She said she feared another episode, and he should skip the appearance, but he insisted on it. So Flora drove Willie out to the airport loaded up with medication and the phone number of a Detroit neurologist just in case. "It was amazing," she said.

As it turned out, however, Willie never needed to contact the doctor. He said he was off his game and dizzy, but neither did he embarrass himself. He recalled that he appeared on television in Detroit and then returned to New Jersey and began practicing daily. This is something he would have never done ordinarily unless there was a tournament at stake. Willie rebuilt his stroke. He started putting together long runs. His confidence remained shaky, and that can be a fatal weakness for a pool player, but he attempted to play through it.

"I always blamed it on the business that I had, the pressure I had owning the business," he told the *Philadelphia Inquirer*. "Worrying about it, worrying about the people getting back, and doing things myself to protect it. That could have brought it on. But I wouldn't stay in bed. I wouldn't feel sorry for myself. I made up my mind I was going to get the hell out of there and try to do something. And it was tough! When I got sick, I was down the deepest I could probably get. I couldn't be any worse. So I said, I'm going to do *anything* just to get the hell out of this bed and stop feeling sorry for myself. And that was that."

•　　•　　•

In 1958 the Billiard Congress of America sponsored a straight-pool championship in Philly, called it the First National Invitational Pocket Billiards Tournament, but only invited four pool players: Willie, Wimpy Lassiter, Jimmy Moore, and Irving Crane. The association still considered Willie the reigning champ and considered the last real title event the one held in Kinston, North Carolina—the one Willie won so spectacularly before collapsing on the floor of his poolroom.[94] But these were strange times for pocket billiards. The public was losing interest in the sport. Room owners were going bankrupt. And straight pool, Willie's game, that wonderful subtle sport requiring such overwhelming precision and steadiness of nerve: that game in particular had slowly lost its hold on the public imagination. The pool world as Willie understood it, the world that he in fact had come to embody, had begun to evaporate away like a ghost. And so the 1958 affair was remembered as somewhat depressing, with crowds about half the size of those of previous events.

On April 11 Willie Mosconi confronted Cowboy Jimmy Moore, a hustler. As always, Willie played fast and seemingly without thought, but the knots were formed hard in his shoulders, and his arms and legs felt like lead. His eyes stung him. And despite Willie's better than 20–20 vision, he couldn't see the shape, not like before. He couldn't seem to map out the table eight shots and nine shots in the advance. *Where's the goddamned key ball?* Nothing made sense.

And so Jimmy Moore, *the hustler* Jimmy Moore, that usurper who supposedly had won some tin-cup match against Luther Lassiter in Chicago,[95] unceremoniously crushed Willie Mosconi with an unfinished run of 110. The final score was Moore 150, Mosconi 11. On April 15 Moore beat Willie again, this time in just thirteen innings. *How you like that, Mosconi?* The final humiliating score was 150–113. It was torture. It was making Willie almost physically ill.

Self-doubt blurred Willie's focus, and focus is what gave him that intuitive sense for which shots go and which shots do not. For years his ego and his towering skill had granted him the illusion of invulnerability. But after death had left its calling card, and after he caught that glimpse of oblivion while powerless on the floor of Superior Billiards, something had changed. "Something like that bothers you mentally— you lose so much self-confidence, and you need all of that you can get to shoot pool," he told one reporter. Shots that looked 100 percent

---

[94] Now it's also true that Lassiter and Moore, the two hustlers in the field, had traded what they considered the title at two later competitions. But neither the BCA nor Mosconi recognized their victories.

[95] According to Charles Ursitti, this challenge match was held March 27–April 5, and the final score was Moore 3,000, Lassiter 2,634.

right before his collapse now looked slightly off. And Jimmy Moore, *the goddamned hustler Jimmy Moore,* had made a fool of him.

There was nothing fun about any of this: not playing pool, not competing. But like a drowning man, Willie had to succeed. He had no choice. He drove each day from his Haddon Heights home, where he did not speak and he did not smile. The kids, Bill and Candace and young Gloria, all kept their distance. Flora kept her distance.

On April 13 Willie Mosconi beat Wimpy Lassiter in six innings. Lassiter had given Willie a tussle before. He had an eagle eye, same as Willie. He was as straight a shooter as any man in America. But Willie beat him 150–19. On April 19 Willie beat Wimpy again, this time by a score of 140–13. And then came Irving Crane, who knew nothing but joyless dispiriting mind-numbing defense. On April 10 Willie knocked Irving's lights out. It took ten innings, with Willie scoring nearly three balls to every one of Irving's. The final score was 150–52. On April 14 Willie beat Crane again, this time in sixteen innings but by an even greater margin. The final score: 150–25.

Willie somehow had reached down and rediscovered that same awful power he always had, that truly terrifying power born of hate and grim determination. His brain wasn't working like it was before. His shot making was off. A hustler had beaten him. And yet on April 16, 1958, William Joseph Mosconi won his fifteenth world title. It was his last great victory, and it came during the last great championship of America's waning age of straight pool.

Shortly afterward, the Billiard Congress of America suspended tournaments altogether. America, it seemed, had given up Willie's game.

Chapter 26

THE HUSTLER

Jackie is a top-notch pool player.

— Willie Mosconi on Jackie Gleason

Paul Newman staggers forward, arms outstretched. "Fats," he pleads. "Fats . . . you can't quit me!" The stink of failure clings to Newman like day-old sweat. He's exhausted, and he's pathetic, and he begs, he begs. . . . "You can't run out on me, Fats. C'mon. I got $200 here. C'mon." And that's when it happens: Newman topples forward; he hits the floor—but hard. There's that loud thump. *Blam*! The balding Myron McCormick rushes over. Jackie Gleason is there, too, but he exhibits not the slightest trace of compassion. The fat actor straightens his overcoat after a moment and then walks away.

Other than the hollow tap-tap of Fats's well-shined shoes, no sound disturbs the scene. It's a brutalizing horrible silence, and it suffocates everyone and everything in the dingy poolroom.

A second passes during which the actor does not stir. It seems as if he might have actually injured himself.

Another second. Newman remains prone.

Another second.

And then, finally . . . "Let's do it again, Robert." The actor jumps to his feet but does not dust off his pants. There's that million-dollar smile. "One more time, Robert. I don't think that was it." Paul Newman is ready to go.

The year was 1961, a year that was shaping up to be one of the bleakest ever for American pocket billiards. The fat Rudolf Wanderone was marking time in Dowell and Du Quoin, mostly stuffing himself with fried chicken and making his mother-in-law crazy. But really, why do otherwise? The sport had fallen into an abyss. Rooms were going bankrupt, equipment sales were nearly nonexistent, and Willie Mosconi, the great maestro himself, hadn't played a national tournament in three years. That's because there were no national tournaments.

"It was a lean year for the sport," said Cy Kalmet, co-owner of Paddy's poolhall, shortly before the film's release. "During the Depression a billiard room was a poor man's club. He met his friends here and passed away the day. Now the old neighborhoods and the corner halls are gone. The family plans its entertainment in advance, and they all go out together, and the only thing you can be sure of is that they're not coming in [to the poolrooms] any more."[96]

And now Director Robert Rossen and Actor Paul Newman were working on a film that could make matters even *worse*. They were haggling over the perfect take, and Newman must have hit that hardwood floor six times, maybe ten, and industry leaders were suffering a collective thrombosis because this would be a dark, dark film about all the worst elements of their sport.

One-flight-up on West Forty-fourth Street in Manhattan (and smack-dab center in the middle of this industry-wide plague), the fifty-three-year-old director had created the sort of poor man's club that Cy Kalmet had warned about. The poolroom was Ames, but Rossen had changed it to look more like Chicago's Bensinger's. The director spent $20,000 jointing up the New York room, giving it an exhausted feel. He even went to Chicago specifically to see Bensinger's, which was one of the last of the nation's old-time poolrooms, and he copied some of the tournament posters hanging there. He also ordered a fresh coat of cracked paint for Ames. The crew installed one sign that said "Please do not spit on the floor" and another instructing patrons that both gambling and minors would not be tolerated.

Rossen replaced good chairs with rows of decrepit ones and somewhere found a knee-high spittoon.

Gleason, no stranger to poolhalls, said it was important to create an atmosphere that comported with Americans' expectations of the game. "Poolrooms usually assume a dirty antiseptic look," he said between takes. "[There are] spots on the floor, toilets stuffed up, but the tables are brushed immaculately—like green jewels lying in the mud." It was also precisely the sort of image that the industry was attempting to run away from, the sort of image that Mosconi spent his life denying.

The Hustler[97] was based rather faithfully on a 1959 novel by Walter Tevis, which he wrote as part of his University of Iowa master's thesis, and which he based on his observations of poolhalls in his native San Francisco and Lexington, Kentucky. Although the public was indifferent and the book at first sold fewer than six thousand copies for HarperCollins, Hollywood saw promise. Within a week of publication, Tevis had offers from five separate studios.

"When I was eleven, my closest friend had a pool table in his basement, and I became a pretty good player," Tevis explained. "Also, when I was a student at the University of Kentucky in Lexington, the best job I could get to help support me through college was at a poolhall at night. I worked there for about a year and a half. I met a number of pool hustlers, and in a writer's cynical way I cultivated their acquaintance, thinking I might use them for material sometime."

Twentieth-Century Fox hired Newman for the Fast Eddie character and Gleason for Fats. Director Rossen did almost all of the camera work on location in New York City—either at newly dirtied-up Ames or over at McGirr's, which had recently switched from a location on Broadway to newer digs at Forty-fifth Street. There was also a midtown

---

[96] In a Feb 14, 1959 *New York Times* article, old-timer Joe Procita said: "Television and bowling have taken over. You can't make money in the sport any more. I used to get $700 a month to travel around the country and give exhibitions. Now I just manage to eat on what I make from a few lessons and a tournament here and there. . . . I just play to keep my hand in."

[97] The producers at one point wanted to call the film *Sin of Angels*, which they had culled from William Henry Davies' poem "Ambition."

Greyhound bus station and an Eighth Avenue bar and grill. Besides powerhouse actors Gleason, Newman, and George C. Scott, the film featured the delightfully frail Piper Laurie and a cameo appearance by the retired boxer Jake LaMotta, who played a gruff bartender.

The director also contacted Willie Mosconi during an exhibition at Jullian's and explained that he needed help in setting up shots and training actors. Willie has said variously that he was offered a flat $10,000 fee for the film or $833 a week for four weeks. He did not say yes to Rossen immediately, but he did say yes eventually—despite the fact that the movie represented all the corruption and vice that Mosconi hated. Willie fought his entire life against the stink of pool, against that vague crookedness associated with it from the sport's very beginning, the sort embodied by Newman's dramatic collapse onto the poolroom floor.

And now Director Rossen would project that disaster nationwide.

"The people at Brunswick were really upset when they found out I was technical advisor for that film," Mosconi would say later. "And when the movie finally came out, some of my friends in the industry looked at me like I was a traitor." There would be poolhalls in *The Hustler* but only of the worst sort. There would be pool players, but the kind Willie denigrated at every turn. *The Hustler* would become the single most important symbol of poolroom vice ever created, a love letter to all those whom Mosconi despised. It was a dark film, and Willie Mosconi had become its secret heart. The *New York Times* would even refer to Willie as the most important member of the film's production staff, the man who made it all seem so very, very real.

• • •

Before shooting on the $1.5 million production could begin that March,[98] Newman would have to double-quick learn the secret of pool. He practiced kick shots and open-handed bridges and had to learn which end of the cue to grab and how to stand up and a new way to walk. This is where Mosconi's assistance proved essential. "Keep that elbow up,

Paul," Mosconi would snap. "Look down your cue! Keep that leg straight!" For two frantic weeks Mosconi showed Newman how to pocket balls, how to push them around the table. Other than the pool table Newman had recently installed in his home (much to the chagrin of his wife, actress Joanne Woodward), which he switched out for the dining-room table, the actor's only exposure to the game had been years earlier as a billiard-room manager at his alma mater, Kenyon College. He claimed to have "racked balls and cleaned tables" but not much else.

The first order of business was finding a spot away from Newman's gawking fans. After a false start at the Lambs Club in New York, Willie settled on the basement recreation room of Dr. Roland DeMarco, an old friend who also happened to be president of Finch Junior College, a girls' finishing school on East Fifty-seventh Street. Newman would appear there each day in dark sunglasses and wearing a leather jacket. He rode up on a motorcycle, dashing as all hell, and then slipped into De-Marco's campus residence through a back entrance. "He'd come in every day on a motorcycle, and he and my father would go to this little room, and the girls there never knew that Paul Newman had been there for hours," recalled Bill Mosconi, who was then about twenty. "If the students would have known he was there, it would have been a mass panic."

•   •   •

Gleason, by contrast, never needed Willie's help. The fat actor could already run forty balls when he fell into stroke, and his prowess with a cue is clear to anyone who watches him do so in *The Hustler*. Mosconi did, however, recommend Gleason for the role of Minnesota Fats.[99] He had known the actor for years, knew firsthand his love for

---

[98] Rossen apparently opened the set up to reporters on March 18, as articles appeared the following day in both the *New York Times* and the *New York Herald Tribune*.

[99] Willie also recommended Frank Sinatra, another celebrity friend, for the role of Fast Eddie. Sinatra would sometimes call the house in Haddon Heights and once almost gave Willie's poor mother-in-law a heart attack. "Hello, this is Frank Sinatra; is Willie there?" he said when she answered the phone. Willie's mother-in-law repeated the Frank-Sinatra-is-on-the-phone story for ten years. Willie also had a friend make a custom cue for Ol' Blue Eyes.

the sport, and figured he'd be perfect for the role. "He's a top-notch player," said Willie.

The story of Willie's first meeting with Gleason is a famous one. As it turns out, Gleason and Mosconi had a mutual acquaintance in native Philadelphian Toots Shor, a man who made a name for himself by moving to New York and opening a twenty-four-hour restaurant famous for its celebrity customers.[100] Now Shor fancied himself a pool player, and Gleason, who was a regular at Shor's restaurant, used to hustle him a little bit before he made it big in Hollywood.

The rest of the story gets repeated over and over. Here's one version from Peter Finney that appeared in the *New Orleans States-Item*:

"At the invitation of Toots Shor, Willie was once part of a pool hustle that involved Jackie Gleason. At the time, Gleason was earning his eating money betting Shor at pool. Toots introduced Mosconi as 'Mr. Shuman,' a wealthy clothes salesman from Philadelphia.

"After cat-and-mouse talk, Jackie bet 'Mr. Shuman' $100. Playing his role to the hilt, Willie messed up a few shots but managed to squeak by. Gleason was hooked. He bet another $100, whereupon Willie proceeded to run one hundred balls, the last thirty left-handed.

"Shor was in stitches. Suddenly, it dawned on Jackie he had been taken. Turning to Toots and pointing to Willie, Gleason said: 'I don't know him, but he's doing all right under the name you gave him.'"

•   •   •

The character played by Paul Newman, Fast Eddie Felson, spends his days suckering the unwary. He considers it a mark of high character that he drinks JTS Brown directly from a bag. His aimless girlfriend Sarah, a cripple, drinks more fiercely than even he does. Eddie wolfishly picks her up at the bus station and then without much more than a fifth of bourbon seduces her. There's also Bert Gordon, played with aplomb by George C. Scott, and Minnesota Fats himself, whom Gleason imbues with that soul-deadening combination of cruelty and amicable civility.

Between them the characters stage a circus of deceit and betrayal. Eddie comes to New York with a mission: He proposes a high-stakes challenge to Minnesota Fats. He figures to win $10,000, maybe more, because he knows Fats gambles high. Eddie is California's greatest pool hustler, a self-assured shark, and he knows Fats has a reputation for being America's greatest pool hustler. "Who can beat me?" he says. "Huh, Charlie—who can beat me?" But Eddie's first match with Fats goes south. After beating the overweight hustler for hours, after winning $10,000 and more, the glory, the booze, and the exhaustion take their toll. Eddie's lack of character beats him, not Minnesota Fats, and he loses everything.

The remainder of the movie chronicles Eddie's single-minded quest to get a rematch, to wreak vengeance on Fats, to force him to cry uncle. It becomes an obsession for Eddie, like Ahab and the White Whale. But with no money and no prospects of getting any anytime soon, Eddie enters into a Faustian bargain with the black-hearted Bert Gordon, who agrees to back the hustler in exchange for nearly all the winnings. Gordon controls everyone around him: Fats, Eddie, even Eddie's girlfriend Sarah. They become pawns on a great chessboard. Eddie eventually gets his rematch, but as with Captain Ahab, his obsession betrays him.

This is a bleak, bleak movie. Thumbs get broken. There's betrayal at every turn. And yet it's also a glorious film and one that the critics immediately fell in love with. Ann Masters of Chicago's *American* said it never occurred to her that the game of pocket billiards could be so fascinating. "The scenes in which Paul Newman and Jackie Gleason pit their skills against one another in the dim, silent poolroom are intensely dramatic," she gushed. *Newsweek* called the film "honest,

---

[100] Toots Shor was owner of a famous Manhattan restaurant near Broadway popular during the 1950s with celebrity ballplayers, athletes, and aspiring actors. Gleason was a longtime regular there and would often hustle Shor at straight pool. The restaurant was at 51 West Fifty-first Street and was literally a steak-and-potato place—but with cocktails. The drinking at Toots Shor's Restaurant was a thing of beauty. In one famous incident Toots was said to have literally left Gleason on the floor after a drinking contest. Shor's was mostly a bachelor hangout when the culture of the permanent bachelor was still alive.

sensitive, and beautifully executed." *Chicago Sun-Times* critic Roger Ebert exulted that *The Hustler* is "one of those films that seem to have such psychic weight that they grow in our memories."

Pool is a glorious and poetic sport, but that alone did not make *The Hustler* great. The film succeeds not because it's about pool but rather because of how it uses the game to explore larger themes. For at its heart *The Hustler* is about excellence and respect—Mosconi would always deny they existed in the sort of poolhall portrayed by *The Hustler*, and yet, here they are. In the Ames of *The Hustler* (as in the real-life Ames and the real-life Bensingers), these rich virtues are commonly celebrated but always before a select few. This is always the way of the poolhall.

Great hustlers are like other greatly skilled men: they have ambition, they strive for excellence, they voraciously crave the esteem and acclamation of their peers. But unlike others, hustlers live in shadows. Their subculture is partitioned away from decent Americans, so their virtues are only their own. Fast Eddie may earn the respect of his peers, but that respect does not extend beyond the front door of Ames. Minnesota Fats is great but not in the way that most people would know or respect or understand. The irony of *The Hustler*, as in the irony of pool in general, is that hustlers can live utterly depraved lives and yet also become greater than life.

• • •

The jointing-up of Ames won *The Hustler* a "Best Set Decoration" Oscar. The film also won for cinematography. Its principals—Newman, Gleason, Scott, Laurie, and Director Rossen—received Oscar and Golden Globe nominations.[101] Rossen and Newman also won British Academy awards. But beyond the awards and the critical acclaim, the film was also a commercial success: it helped catapult Newman to

---

[101] Unfortunately for Rosen, Newman, Gleason, Scott, and Laurie, 1961 was also the year of *West Side Story*, which pretty much swept the Academy Awards that year.

A-list status, made millions for the studio, and actually prompted a new craze in America.

And yet Rossen found himself defending the film. In an interview with the *Bowlers Journal,* the director said that far from representing an insult to pool, it shows the sport in all its glory. "This movie won't give billiards a black eye," he told the magazine shortly after the film's release. "As a matter of fact, I think the skill of playing will come across so well that people will be amazed. I think the movie will attract people rather than repel them. I also think the background will be fascinating to so many people.

"[And here's] another plus factor: never before has there been a movie with a pool background or pool players as the main characters. In the movie, I try to give people an insight into the skill of pool. The film doesn't say that poolhalls are cathedrals. It would be unrealistic to say so."

Industry leaders had convinced themselves that the film would doom their already doomed sport. Brass at Brunswick even threatened to fire Willie over it. "The movie will set the billiard industry back 150 years!" quaked one. "It's awful, awful, awful," said another. The jittery bigwigs at Brunswick saw the film and immediately reached for their antacid tablets. Willie said he had gotten Brunswick's permission beforehand, but it didn't matter.

"You have no idea how many calls I got from people all over the country accusing me of ruining the game," he said.

What the brass didn't understand was that the game was already on its last leg. Just before 20th Century Fox released *The Hustler,* there were just eight thousand pool centers in operation nationwide. Compare that to the forty-two thousand before 1930. In New York, the pool-playing capital of the world, there were just 247 rooms when Fast Eddie and Minnesota Fats went head to head at the jointed-up Ames. Four decades earlier there had been four thousand! So it's clear that what the industry was selling prior to *The Hustler* people were no longer buying.[102] It's also clear that the film had the exact opposite effect of that feared by the equipment manufacturers.

Far from killing sales by associating the sport with conmen, the movie drove up sales by letting Americans witness firsthand how those virtuosos plied their trade.

"So rapid has been the resurgence of the billiard boon that deliveries of tables and equipment are slow and skilled workers difficult to find," the *New York Herald Tribune* reported on July 14, 1963. And this wasn't a gradual change, the newspaper reported. This wasn't an adjustment measured in single percentage points. One manufacturer reported a jump in sales of more than 1,000 percent, from $329,000 before *The Hustler* to $4 million shortly afterward. About two thousand new pool centers popped up nationwide within the course of six months.

The renaissance had begun.

---

[102] Here's a side note about those awful years. In an effort to rejuvenate sales, Brunswick began marketing a new family-fun line of bowling equipment. Suddenly billiards—that sport that Brunswick had always dominated—became an adjunct to ten-pins. Brunswick may have characterized the strategy as an aggressive attack on flagging sales, but it had all the hallmarks of a retreat. Speaking to a *Bowlers Journal* reporter in September of 1961, Mosconi perversely noted that pool was a flourishing pastime for those waiting to bowl. He said he hardly even gave exhibitions in poolrooms anymore. And he didn't seem to miss it in the least. "Some of these [bowling alleys] are so gorgeous they have carpets on the floor and partitions around tables for semi-privacy," he told the reporter.

Chapter 27

HUSTLERS AND SCUFFLERS

> There's two different types: there's a scuffler, and there's
> a hustler. A hustler is one who's always in action. . . ..
> And then there's a scuffler. He never gets it, ya under-
> stand? All he ever does is waste his time. He gets in
> everybody's way. He goes through life, and he's a failure.
>
> — Minnesota Fats

Fats did nothing of consequence, and yet he captured the heart of the most beautiful woman in Little Egypt. He *achieved* nothing, and yet the good people of Dowell exulted in his conquests. "He was a natural entertainer, and by the time you got through interviewing him he had got you sucked in," said Mayor Luciano Lencini. "He could get people believing him. It was like he could do anything." For Fats, it was all about perspective, about how people saw him. It was a *trick*—even though many who knew him insisted one could find the remnants of truth in everything Fats said and everything Fats did.

His friend John Ogolini remembers the time Fats dared him to take a peek inside the grocery sack. It was the morning after Fats had placed fourth in a tournament, one of the few Fats ever entered. "He had stayed after the tournament gambling all night. He just stayed, and he played, and he gambled. Fats was there till about five in the morning. And then the next day he came up to me, and he said 'Lookee here,

John.'" Fats looked like a proud cat who had just killed a pigeon. He was smiling so broadly it looked as if he might start laughing.

Inside the grocery sack were five-dollar bills, and tens—but there were also hundreds. *It was a damn grocery sack.* Ogolini figured there was $10,000 in there at least. And Fats had won it all, or so he claimed, gambling after coming in fourth during some bullshit tournament. "He would never tell you if he lost—he'd only tell you if he won," said Ogolini. "I told him when I looked in that bag, I said, 'Man, Fats, you sure like to brag.' It seemed like he was always winning."

What Fats did as well as anybody living was hustle, particularly when it came to others' perception of him. His wild boasts took on lives of their own. Fats won bags of cash and shot dice on sinking ships, and he beat Happy the Chinaman. He was like a shaman mesmerizing the world with his claims. And not long after Willie completed work on *The Hustler*, and 20th Century Fox released the film, Fats made the most startling claim of all. It would become his most famous trick.

Minnesota Fats, that is, the Minnesota Fats made famous by Jackie Gleason, was the *perfect* player. No one in the country shot straight pool like him. Nobody gambled more fearlessly. He went through life with the sort of refined dignity one might associate with an orchestra conductor or an undertaker. "Jackie Gleason is excellent—more so than you first realize—as a cool, self-collected pool expert who has gone into bondage to the gambling man," wrote the *New York Times*. He is also the figure from the film that most captured the American imagination, really even more than Newman's Fast Eddie character.

But shortly after the film appeared, Rudolf Wanderone—the man who had so far done nothing consequential with his life—told a reporter that he *was* Minnesota Fats. Wanderone claimed he was the real-life model for Gleason's character, that he was the cool, self-collected expert described by the *New York Times*. His friends may have known him as New York Fats, or Chicago Fats, or even Johnston City Fats, but he said in reality he was *Minnesota Fats*.

He made this startling claim despite never having set foot in Minnesota. Neither was Wanderone a particularly good dresser, and he certainly had none of Gleason's haughty grace. But these were the deterrents of lesser men. At the urging of his friend George Jansco, Wanderone quickly set up a picket in front of the Egyptian Drive-In where they were showing *The Hustler*. "You want Minnesota Fats? You're looking at him!" he'd shout to cinema patrons as they pulled in along the gravel entrance. He also made the claim to *Sports Illustrated* writer Tom Fox. And then suddenly, everybody was reporting it: *Esquire* magazine, the TV men, newspapers. An appearance on *The Tonight Show* soon followed.

That the man who wrote *The Hustler* insisted that he had invented the character from whole cloth made no difference. Walter Tevis said Fats was a work of fiction—that he was as real as Donald Duck—and that if the character resembled anybody, it would be dignified Willie Mosconi. But the pool craze was on, and no one cared what Tevis had to say. Reporters were desperate for a story and down in Johnston City, the fat Rudolf Wanderone gave them one. "I was automatic champion one-pocket player of the world," he told one. "They never had any tournaments. I always had to give great odds, most of the time two balls. The great champions would never play me. They dodge me at all times."

The terrible irony, of course, was that Willie Mosconi himself was an unwitting party to what may have been a monstrous deception. In an interview with the *Long Beach Independent-Press-Telegram*, Mosconi said the Fats character "was patterned after a real live pool hustler known as New York Fats." He would regret those words for the rest of his life. In later years he even carried around a note from Tevis that supposedly disproved the Wanderone-Fats connection. Mosconi kept the note in his wallet like a talisman to ward off unpleasantness.

But too late, too late. In the language of the folklorist, it was as if Fats had used the trick of perception to slip the trap of literalness. He had taken *The Hustler* and Mosconi's own words as a springboard. He used them to launch himself onto the grandest of stages. And all of it—his fame, his image, the name that is now part of the national vernacular—is the product of his hustle. Minnesota Fats made his appearance magically to America like money at the bottom of a grocery sack.

• • •

A pool craze sparked by *The Hustler* swept across the nation. Suddenly, suddenly: People wanted to go to tournaments. ABC aired pocket billiards. Jim McKay went out to Johnston City, close to Fats's hometown, where a pair of promoters had begun staging circuslike hustler tournaments. He wore his yellow *Wide World of Sports* jacket, the one with the black emblem over the heart, as he interviewed unapologetic gamblers like Boston Shorty and the newly christened real-life Minnesota Fats. By virtue of making his startling claim, Wanderone had positioned himself at the center of this revival. In a flash he had become its leading figure, the very embodiment of it.

Mosconi had won world championships, had crisscrossed the nation every year for the last half of his life. He had neglected his family, punished his body, got up every morning, put on that coat and tie—*Hey, how ya' doing; I'm Willie Mosconi*—but now that people were actually paying attention, now that the public actually wanted to know about pool, all they ever asked him about was Minnesota Fats. "Ever play Fats?" they'd say. "What do you think of Fats? He says he can beat you." "What kind of player was Fats?"

Willie started out feeling annoyed, but his regard for the fat hustler quickly plummeted to disdain and then finally hard-landed somewhere between abhorrence and repugnance. Mosconi had broken every record there was to break. He had run more balls in a single inning than any man alive. He was the fifteen-time champion of the fucking world. And now when he arrived for exhibitions cue in hand and ready to entertain the crowd, he found himself confronting some variation of the same maddening question.

"Ever play Minnesota Fats? I hear he hustled you once."

A sizable percentage of the profiles written specifically about Mosconi after 1961 also mention Rudolf Wanderone. In the earlier pieces Mosconi would typically respond to Wanderone questions with some level of diplomacy. In later ones his antipathy became more well defined. "I call him Wander-phoney," he'd say. Or: "He has contributed nothing to the sport." The newspaper accounts show it over and over again. "He didn't respect him because Fats was all hype," said Charles Ursitti, the promoter. "Fats could play decently, but he was no Willie Mosconi. Then again nobody was a Willie Mosconi. But Fats was smart enough to exploit the game."

• • •

When *The Hustler* appeared in the nation's theaters and the pocket-billiard renaissance swept the nation and kids started rushing back into the poolrooms, the great Willie Mosconi was already retired from tournament play. He had had that last victory in 1958 and then no more. And in a true sign that he had become bigger than the sport, the BCA had not scheduled another bona fide tournament without him. That meant Mosconi was displaying his expertise only during his never-ending exhibition tours. But after *The Hustler* the tournaments began again. There were the famous Johnston City events, known as The Hustler Jamborees.[103] Besides straight pool and nine-ball, the jamborees also featured prominently one-pocket, which Mosconi considered a hustler's gimmick. Of course he'd have no part of it.

In early 1966 Willie got a phone call from a West Coast promoter who was on a mission to lure him out of retirement. Arnie Satin said he was planning an invitational event and that Irving Crane would be there along with the relatively clean-cut Harold Worst, who was then the world champion at three-cushion billiards. Satin also invited schoolteacher Steve Mizerak Jr. and Joe "Meatman" Balsis, who had earned his nickname working as a butcher in his hometown of Minersville, Pennsylvania. But there'd also be gambling Eddy "Knoxville Bear" Taylor, perhaps the finest-ever banks[104] player; the

---

[103] See *Hustler Days*.

[104] A variation of pool whereby all balls must be pocketed through a bank or kick shot. Taylor would frequently run eight and out playing banks.

hard-partying Richie Florence, a young player from Torrance, California; and Bill "Weenie Beenie" Staton,[105] the hustling hot-dog salesman from Alexandria, Virginia.

Mosconi at first said no way. He said he absolutely would not return to organized competition. Mosconi was doing fine playing exhibitions, making plenty of money, and he figured he didn't need the grief. He was a gum-chewing bundle of nerves whenever he played, and those nerves became more and more frayed as he grew older. Satin said he'd pay Willie's expenses and guarantee him several thousand dollars—win, lose, or draw. Mosconi said no. Satin upped the guarantee. Willie said no. Finally, Satin made Willie a $10,000[106] offer, and that did the trick.

"You say $10,000 isn't a lot of money, but in 1966, you could buy a brand-new Cadillac for $3,000," said Charles Ursitti, the promoter. "If you made $10,000 for a whole year, that was good income. But it took a lot of money to get him out of retirement. He once told me, 'Charlie, whatever I needed to accomplish, I have accomplished. If I win, I'm expected to win—but if I lose, I'm an old man expected to retire, and I'm a bum.' I guess that's true of any sport."

The newspapers grandly described the venue as "Burbank's House of Champions," but it was actually an abandoned out-of-business supermarket. Satin installed bleachers and swept up the place, but Mosconi clearly considered the venue beneath his dignity. He sniffed that the carpeting was drab, that tacky green plastic swayed overhead only to disguise the harsh fluorescent lighting, and that it "was as far removed from Allinger's or McGirr's as California is from the East Coast." He said the venue was "hardly what might be considered a classy room."

Mosconi also found Arnie Satin irritating to the extreme. The promoter was about Willie's size, perhaps even a bit smaller, was a nervous man and something of a know-it-all. He wore a ridiculous cheap toupee. Mosconi was a proud man, did not much care for Satin's familiar ways, and Satin was probably irritated that the champion had made such stringent money demands. "Mosconi was a prima donna,"

---

[105] See Appendix II.

said Ed Kelly, one of the competitors that year. "And he got way the best of it. There were afternoon and evening sessions, and Mosconi said he wasn't playing in the afternoon. He would only play prime time. After he hit some balls on the table, he made them change the cloth."

Jay Helfert, another longtime Los Angeles player, said in those later years Mosconi's real-life persona bore very little resemblance to his common portrayal by the news media. "He was easy to irritate," said Helfert. "When he was playing, Willie expected the rapt attention of everybody present. And if he had any problem at the table, it was never his fault. It was always the balls, the lighting, anything but him. Mosconi really had an attitude. And when Willie arrived in Burbank, the first thing he asked for was the check. He said it before he said hello, and he wouldn't say it nice. He said 'Gimme the money.'"

Mosconi began the tournament as he always began tournaments: by winning. "Mosconi Ends Retirement in 150–68 Billiard Victory" read the Associated Press dispatch of April 9. The news service said in Mosconi's opening inning he ran ninety-two balls. The next day he won again, this time 150–56 against Onofrio Lauri. Then he beat a Los Angeles player by the name of Bob Woods and then ran over Weenie Beenie 150–80. He had an opening run of forty-five in that game. On April 13 he beat Richie Florence by the embarrassing margin of 150 to minus 3.

On April 17 something strange happened. Mosconi lost. Cicero Murphy, America's first African-American pool champion, pinned a 150–89 defeat on Willie. A United Press International news account suggests that Murphy got stuck several times—either frozen on the rail or facing too much green—and then escaped with spectacular long-range sniper shots. Murphy ended the match with a twenty-four-ball run. Mosconi then won two more, first against Jack "Jersey Red" Breit,[107] one of the nation's great pool hustlers, and then the next day beat Steve Mizerak. On April 23 Mosconi dropped another one, this

---

[106] Some put the guarantee at $6,000.

[107] See *Hustler Days*.

time to Irving Crane. This defeat put him in a three-way tie with Jimmy Moore and Joe Balsis for the tournament lead, and there were only two days left. On the next day Mosconi beat Moore. But Balsis also won his match (he destroyed Crane 150 to minus 4), and that meant Mosconi would have to meet the Meatman from Minersville on the last day to determine the tournament champion.

Mosconi undoubtedly already had a pretty good piss-off going when he made his appearance that day. He didn't much like the venue, didn't much like the promoter, he felt the equipment was subpar. And to add insult to injury, Balsis had managed to surpass one of Mosconi's world records. "Mosconi was probably doubly pissed because Balsis averaged 22 balls per inning, which broke Mosconi's record of 18.34 that dated back to 1950," said billiards historian Mike Shamos. "Balsis also had the tournament high-run of 137 and a two-inning game."

Mosconi in his memoirs said there was no Hollywood ending for him. He said he took an 87–73 lead, but then Joe Balsis, a hall-of-fame pool player, ran sixty-three balls and then fourteen. And that was it. Mosconi had come out of retirement, and for his effort he'd placed second. Mosconi said he felt as if something was missing from his game, that he didn't want to win like he did before. "It's harder to maintain your intensity," he wrote in his memoirs. But the truth of the matter is probably quite the opposite. Willie remained the same as ever. He had that unquenchable thirst to win. The problem was that he had a more difficult time maintaining his nerves. He simply could not abide losing. It made him crazy. It made him hate the game. It made him hate everyone around him. Losing was still not an option—even when he lost.

There are several versions of what happened at the end of that 1966 tournament, of how Willie proved to himself that he was no longer fit for tournament play. But all the versions point to a near total loss of composure by the tightly wound king of pocket billiards.

"I talked to Arnie Satin about it," recalled Helfert. "The tournament was over, and they were handing out awards, and Arnie didn't like

Mosconi, and so he made some kind of sarcastic remark when he gave Mosconi the runner-up prize. I don't know what he said, but it was a little bit of a slur. And so Mosconi took that smaller trophy and swung it at Arnie. I mean, he just swung it at him. And then when he didn't strike Arnie, he tried to hit him with his hand.

"Mosconi struck him, but Arnie said he deflected the blow. It kind of went off his shoulder. I don't think Arnie was hurt. But there was a big audience there. There was a room full of people. Some people said later that Mosconi hit him right in the head, but Arnie said it was a glancing blow and that he deflected it a little bit."

Ed Kelly recalls the same story, although he cautions that he was not an eyewitness. He said that Arnie, who died in the 1990s, spoke of it often. Kelly also said he heard the same story from others who were present. "Arnie gave him the second-place trophy, and he said, 'C'mon Willie, take your second place,'" said Kelly. "And Mosconi said something along the lines of 'Stick that trophy up your ass.' He said it in front of all those people. And then Mosconi tried to fight him, and he threw a halfhearted punch. Willie was a hothead, and he was mad that he came in second. Mosconi had beaten everybody on earth. He was the greatest straight-pool player who ever lived, that's for sure. And he wasn't used to coming in second."

Bill Mosconi wasn't there, but he doesn't doubt the story. He recalls once hearing of his father going berserk because an audience member started heckling him while he was trying to shoot. "He went over there with his cue stick like a spear, and they had to grab him," said Willie's son. "He was just holding it like a spear and he was ready to toss it at the guy, and they grabbed him, and they had to grab the cue stick out of his hands. He would have killed him, that's how intense he was."

Mosconi's son said that one thing he learned over the years was never to cross his father after he lost. Never. This would have been useful information for poor ol' Arnie Satin.

"When he lost, you had to stay out of his way—it wasn't like he could laugh it off," said Bill Mosconi. "He wasn't a good loser. He went off to a corner, and he would be by himself. He didn't want to talk about it, but he analyzed what he did, and he tried to figure it out. You didn't even say, 'Good game, Willie'; you just got out of his way. We did, and we were his own family. If he lost, you didn't talk. He went into his room, and you went into another, and that would last for two weeks. That's no exaggeration. My father was consumed by it. It was inconceivable that he would lose at anything. He never changed, and it didn't make any difference what he was playing. He was a killer."

Chapter 28

WILLIE'S TRAP

Ain't Nixon hustling, ain't he out shaking hands twenty-
four hours a day, trying to get to be the president? Huh?

—Rudolf "Minnesota Fats" Wanderone, speaking with
a TV newsman in Johnston City, Illinois

At about the same time that Mosconi was losing his mind in Burbank, Minnesota Fats was writing his autobiography. This was quite a neat trick given that Fats was very nearly illiterate. "Fats couldn't read a menu, and he couldn't read road signs," said promoter Jay Helfert, an old friend of the hustler. Fats never made it past grade school, never opened a book, or read a newspaper. He used a rubber stamp to sign autographs. And yet here he was authoring an autobiography. Willie Mosconi had so far never managed such a feat.

But increasingly Fats was replacing Mosconi as the public face of pocket billiards. While Willie made two-hundred-ball runs in bowl-ing alleys, Wanderone could garner a hundred times the publicity plying his bullshit to *Esquire*. While Willie appeared as a special guest on TV sports programs, Wanderone became the star of his *own* shows. Typically, they featured Fats playing celebrities. Both Fats and Willie appeared on Johnny Carson, and they both were the subject of flattering magazine profiles. But increasingly it was Fats whom the media loved.

"He was a big celebrity—everybody knew who he was," said Jay Helfert. "I remember sometimes we'd be at a restaurant, and within a couple of minutes, somebody would say, 'You're Minnesota Fats, aren't you?' I swear to you, within minutes people would get up from their booths. There would be a huge crowd. It looked like people crowded around a fight. It would be like a big circle. And I remember seeing it once at a gas station. He just started talking, and within fifteen minutes, you couldn't get a car in that gas station."

As a consequence Fats was gaining an ability to define the sport. Not Willie's vision of what pocket billiards should be, not a dignified game for gentlemen, but what Fats said pool actually *was*. This is what it meant to be replaced. A lifetime of hard work, fifteen world championships, countless miles on the road . . . and now Willie Mosconi was playing a *hustler's* game. What's worse is that Fats was gaining a truly sickening ability to define Mosconi himself.

The fans would ask Fats, ask him all the time: *Why don't you play Mosconi? Have you ever whupped him? Can you whup him still?*

"You find him, and I'll play him," he crowed in Chicago. "He couldn't beat a drum," he told a *Los Angeles Times* reporter. Helfert also said Fats was fond of telling a story about "Willie the Wop," the greatest pool champion in the world who also happened to be the world's biggest choker. "His stories were so demeaning to Willie the Wop. It was only later that I realized that he was talking about Willie Mosconi," said Helfert.

So now Fats was writing an autobiography, collaborating on the project with *Sports Illustrated* writer Tom Fox. Wanderone told the stories; Fox did the writing. When Wanderone became surly, his wife Evelyn filled in the blanks. World Publishing released *The Bank Shot and Other Great Robberies* in 1966, and it contained more of those wild claims of Fats's supposed conquests. It made Willie livid.

"Me and Willie are about the same age and back in our younger days we played every game on the table together, only every match was for the cash which meant I was the automatic winner," Fats boasted on page 74. "Willie Mosconi is a tremendous pool player . . . but when it came to playing for the cash I was in a class by myself. So every time I played Willie for the gold in Philadelphia I whacked him out clean."

Fats claimed that he "beat Willie so much that his old man figured losing like that might not be good for Willie's ego." He said "the old man even had a little talk with me and asked me not to play Willie for the cash" and that "the old man figured Willie sure didn't need the experience he was getting losing the cash matches to me and he told Willie he should let me alone."

On page 75 Fats said "back then he couldn't come close to whipping me in one-pocket, only Willie wouldn't quit." He wrote that he would "whack him out again and again." He said that Willie kept telling him, "I know I can beat you at this game, I know it."

"But Willie never did," he said.

To an outsider such outlandish claims about thirty-year-old pool matches might seem a trivial thing. To Willie Mosconi they were deadly serious. Fats, he believed, was ruining everything. His dreadful book and his awful TV appearances and all the lies represented a direct challenge to his legacy. They represented a challenge to the very dignity of the sport. Desperate to make Fats pay, Willie sued for $450,000.

But the suit came to nothing.

And then Willie offered to play Fats for $20,000, winner take all. He would humiliate the fat hustler before the entire world—or at least to those who would show for the event, which he proposed for the ballroom of Philadelphia's Sheraton Hotel. The champ sent a registered letter to the hustler proposing a two-thousand-point match of straight pool. A friend of Willie's had put up the stake money, and Willie said he'd even spot Fats 250 points. When he received no response from Fats, Willie increased the offer to five hundred points.

But if Willie had hoped to set a trap, it did not work. Fats never responded to the letter, and he never showed up. Willie was left to make trick shots by himself for a handful of perplexed bystanders. Willie drove home by himself, his anger building.

Chapter 29

THREE WEEKS IN JOHNSTON CITY

Fats played with him like a child—that's what happened.

— Ed Kelly, recalling a high-stakes
match featuring Minnesota Fats

The usual crowds weren't there when Ed Kelly showed up. There was no tournament, no drinking, no newspaper men. It was just Johnston City's semiabandoned Show Bar, the two 4½-by-9-foot Gandy tables set low in the pit, and Minnesota Fats.

Some put the year at about 1970.

"We were in Alabama, in Mobile, Richie Florence and I, and they call me up from Johnston City, and they say Fats has been coming around, and he's got some money," said Ed Kelly. "So Richie stays in Alabama, but I went over there, and I gave Fats 9 to 7. That's two balls, you understand."

And so that's how it began: Champagne Ed coming up from Mobile, Alabama, coming the 650 miles straight north direct to Johnston City, Illinois—and giving Minnesota Fats two balls. Kelly then was one of the finest players in the nation and at thirty-one years of age was just coming into his prime. But he would not be alone there challenging Fats. Following Ed Kelly in short order to Johnston City were Ronnie Allen and Richie Florence, two other men of daunting skill. And each came toting a suitcase and a fat bankroll.

Fats may have never showed up to play Willie Mosconi, may have never accepted his $20,000 challenge—but this was not because he wasn't then gambling against top-rated players. Was he really the world's greatest hustler or simply a blowhard? Could he really beat every man living, or was Fats unwilling and incapable of playing anybody good? Back in 1970 at just about the same time that Fat Minnie was dodging Willie Mosconi, he was confronted by three other would-be assassins. During three weeks in Johnston City, they would explore that space between what others said about Minnesota Fats and what Fats said about himself.

●　　●　　●

Ed Kelly said Johnston City was pretty much empty when he arrived. Paulie Jansco was around—hell, Paulie was *always* around—but other than that it was a ghost town. Not that Johnston City was a sprawling metropolis even during the busiest of times. The rural southern Illinois town had no more than five thousand residents, a population that grew slightly each November when George and Paulie Jansco held their famous Hustler Jamborees down at their Show Bar. But when Ed Kelly showed up to play Fats, the tournament had either just concluded or had not yet begun, and so the Show Bar was pretty much abandoned.

Jansco's famous roadhouse was a large boxlike building improbably located along the rural Herrin–Johnston City road, just west of town. Fittingly, it had a red farmhouse roof. Surrounding it were a few houses, all in vague states of disrepair. It had an unpaved parking lot, all grimy gravel and dirt. During the eleven months of the year when there was no hustlers' tournament, it remained mostly empty.

And so Fats would have looked every one of his nearly sixty years when he wrangled himself huffing and puffing from the driver's side of his Cadillac and made his way to the front door. His home was over in Dowell, just thirty minutes away, and that's where he would have been leaving Evelyn every night. Much to Paulie Jansco's surprise, Fats in recent days had started coming around the Show Bar to knock balls around. He suddenly seemed willing to step up against anybody who had the nuts to play him. Paulie couldn't believe it, and this is why: In recent years Fats had fallen into the extremely annoying habit of appearing at the Show Bar only when there was no one important to see him. That is, Fats had refused since at least 1964 or 1965 to attend the Janscos' annual tournaments. His presence then would have attracted media attention, but Fats always claimed some other bullshit commitment. Paulie and his brother Georgie had always seen it as a snub.

So maybe that's the reason Paulie made the call to Alabama looking for someone to rob the man he ostensibly counted as a friend.[108] Paulie was pissed off. He knew he couldn't beat Fats straight up, no way, but he knew Ed Kelly sure as shit could. After all, Champagne Ed had won the world nine-ball championship in 1965, had won the Johnston City one-pocket and nine-ball divisions in 1966 and won the Los Angeles World Pocket Billiard Championship in 1969. It was like finding a hired gun. Champagne Ed was not a man to be trifled with.

• • •

Kelly said that Fats demanded two balls. He said that he wouldn't play him for anything less than 9–7. The game was one-pocket, which was just about the only game that Fats ever wanted to play.

"And well, he beat me," Kelly confessed. "I wound up getting broke."

• • •

Impossibly, there was another shark from California said to play even more terrifying one-pocket than Ed Kelly. This other player was the winner of the 1970 one-pocket division in Johnston City and the

---

[108] By then, Georgie was already dead. He was the victim of a stroke in 1969.

winner of the 1966 Stardust Open in Las Vegas,[109] then the richest tournament in pool. This other player was known for his high-stakes backroom wagering and typically could not even get players like Ed Kelly or the phenomenal Jersey Red to the table without first offering *them* a spot. His name was Ronnie Allen, and some believed him to be the finest one-pocket player ever.

Fats was impressed enough to make the same deal: 9–7 or nothing. After all, Ronnie Allen was the man who *invented* power one-pocket. He could move several balls at once to his pocket. He could see runouts in the subtle and beautiful one-pocket patterns that no one else could see. Two balls or nothing, Fats said.

"And so that was the end of that," said Kelly. "Fats beat Ronnie 9–7. He busted him. He just beat Ronnie's brains out."

• • •

Twenty-five-year-old Richie Florence came to Johnston City just behind his elders, and he was brimming full with his own supposed greatness. He was a quiet kid, mostly, but probably also giddy, having just completed a polishing-off of gambler Cleo Vaughn down in Alabama. He had beaten other players, too, including the grand old Wimpy Lassiter himself, and once ran a hundred balls straight during four different games in the U.S. Open. He told Fats he was willing to play for as long as Fats was willing to gamble.

Richie also had loads of cash, maybe some of it Cleo Vaughn's, but much of it the result of his long lucky streak in Vegas. In the book *Billiards* John Grissim wrote that Florence had won maybe $4,000 shooting dice at one casino, maybe $6,000 shooting dice at another. The Young Turk reportedly had $20,000 cash, much of it loose in his pocket, and he told Fats he was willing to play him for it for as long as Fats was willing to gamble.

---

[109] The Stardust Open was held at the Stardust Hotel and Casino on the North Strip. It was torn down by way of implosion on March 13, 2007.

Richie started playing Fats cheap $100-a-rack games. He gave Fats one ball, not two. Fats won the opening lag and broke, and he sent whitey gliding to that sweet spot just between the top two racked balls. He used just enough force to push all the racked balls drifting over to his side of the table but without so much force that the cue ball went spinning wildly around the table. Instead, it hit one rail and then two and then came resting along the long rail closest to Richie's side. It was a textbook defensive break: nothing dropped, but nothing was really expected to. The point was to move all the balls closer to Fatty's pocket while denying Richie an offensive shot.

Richie turned the break back on Fats. He knocked a ball to his side, while leaving the cue ball stuck down near Fatty's pocket. And that's how it went, back and forth, with both Richie and Fats trying to get the upper hand, both trying to find that opening where the game goes badly for the opponent but very quickly. Balls went toward Fatty's side, and then they went toward Richie's. Sometimes a ball drifted up-table, and sometimes one dropped uselessly into some other pocket besides the corner. Eventually, of course, someone made a mistake, someone left that open shot, and then Fats made a ball or two, or Richie did, and the first game was over double-quick, and then the second came and went as well.

Fats would win two, three, four games—not win by much, but he'd win nonetheless. Then Richie would knuckle down and win a few. Sometimes Richie would demolish Fats with quick run-outs, or sometimes he'd just barely eek out victory by a single ball.

Finally Richie fell confidently into stroke and looked to double the wager. Fats played him a few games that way, for $200, but then complained that he was getting tired. *I'm an old man, sonny. I'll play you tomorrow.* When Fats left that night, tired but not beat, he was up just a little. Maybe $1,000. Maybe less.

The next day Fats did not come back. He called in with some bullshit excuse about a business appointment. Richie didn't know whether it was true or whether Fats was dodging him, but by then he probably didn't much care. By all accounts Richie was happy to play anybody who would play him. He was drinking and partying and having just one hell of a time goofing with Ronnie Allen and Champagne Ed and Paulie Jansco. Richie spent the day drinking and the night too, and then got back to his hotel room for two or three hours' sleep.

The next day began much like the previous one, with no Minnesota Fats, but plenty of other friends with whom to share a cocktail. Richie played and goofed and partied in a way that only twenty-five-year-olds seem capable of. And then as Richie Florence was ready to turn in, just as he announced that he had to get some sleep—that's when Fats came strolling in just like royalty. *Let's play some, Junior.* Richie went fishing for his stake money, and he started out winning. They were playing $200 a game this time, and Richie was stroking the balls in, playing fast and fluid. Sometimes he'd run four, sometimes five. Then Fats starts complaining that his stomach was grumbling. *Hey, kid, I gotta get a sandwich,* he said. *I can't take this. I gotta eat.* They stopped for a while, and Fats got a Coke and a white-bread sandwich, and when they finally got to playing again, Richie wasn't shooting so well anymore. Fats would miss a ball here and there, but Richie, who had been up partying for days and days, missed a fair bit more. Fats would pick up maybe four games to Richie's three, or sometimes three games to Richie's two. Slowly, slowly, the money started flowing back the other way, like a river dammed upstream.

Fats went home that night $1,000 richer.

No one then watching, not the railbirds, not the road players, and not at first Ronnie Allen and Ed Kelly, realized what was happening. Richie was the superior player, everyone figured. He was young, tough, and fearless. *He had heart!* But for two or three weeks the pattern continued: Richie stayed out partying, Fats went home and slept. Richie would get two or three hours sleep, Fatty came in rested and fresh and ready to go. Richie won a few, and Fatty won a few more. Richie got hot—the kid played some pool, he couldn't help but get hot—but always, always: only when Fatty's stomach was grumbling.

And so almost every night Richie Florence went home $800 or $1,000 lighter. Nobody then saw what was happening, and Richie least of all. But quietly, gradually, almost imperceptibly, he was going broke.

Fatty took maybe another $10,000 from Ed Kelly and Ronnie Allen, and then he took another $20,000 from Richie Florence. But he did so *quietly*. The trickster Minnesota Fats robbed Richie with subtleness, which was all the more surprising given that Fats was anything but subtle.

"Fats played with him like a child—that's what happened," said Ed Kelly. "If he saw the game was going a certain way, he'd pull out and then come back the next day, bright and shiny. You know, Fats never partied. He maybe had one drink in his entire life. But Richie might have been out partying the night before. Fats would dictate when they would start playing, he was always in the driver's seat, and so he just managed Richie.

"When Richie got hot, Fats would say, 'I got to get another sandwich. I got to take a break to eat.' If Richie got on a roll, if Richie started shooting, Fats would quit him. He'd say, 'I'll play you again tomorrow.'

"He got Richie doing what *he* wanted Richie to do, see? Fats was a champion at it."

Chapter 30

THE DEATH OF WILLIE'S GAME

> You are what you are because it was in the cards. Every livin' creature has a destiny. Understand? But some never know what it is. That's the sad part.
>
> — Minnesota Fats

Straight pool is that multirack game in which every ball counts for a point. The player targets any ball just as long as he or she calls it first. When only one ball remains, the player reracks the remaining fourteen and then continues the run. It became the official tournament game in 1912, just one year before Willie's birth, and it grew in popularity just as Willie came to dominate it. Likewise, straight pool faded from view when Willie retired—in large part because he was no longer around to draw crowds. So this means that the fortunes of straight pool largely followed the trajectory of Willie Mosconi's career. It also appears that the game's period of decline generally corresponds with the release of *The Hustler* and the growing fame of Minnesota Fats.

Mosconi said no other game requires such intense concentration and position play. He said the game does not reward luck. Arguably, not any skill associated with any other sport—not shooting free throws, not putting, not pitching—demands such subtle control over the movements of a ball. Willie was a gentleman and a perfectionist, and he found everything about straight pool inherently dignified.

Fats said the game was the most boring known to man. He sneered that he had known old brokes who wouldn't even bet a ten-cent pack of cigarettes on the outcome of a hundred points of straight pool.

•　　•　　•

Georgie and Paulie Jansco were the first important promoters to heretically condemn straight pool, so perhaps it's not surprising that they conducted the first of their famous tournaments not in the elegantly dignified Allinger's or Ames, but rather in a flat little building that Fats described as a beer shed. As the tournament grew in popularity, the Jansco brothers happily moved to bigger digs and installed bleachers and a bar. But there was never any burnished wood and no chandeliers in their southern Illinois tournaments. And while the brothers included straight pool during those events, they did so only reluctantly.[110] Instead, they favored the hustler's games of one-pocket and nine-ball.

Despite never having received sanctioning from the Billiard Congress of America, despite holding the month-long events in a tiny backwater, the Jansco brothers' jamborees attracted network television, writers from major newspapers, and coverage in *Sports Illustrated* and *Playboy*. Thanks to the growing interest in hustling, *The Hustler*, and Minnesota Fats, the jamborees became three-ring media circuses—albeit ones where the carnies had taken control of the Big Top. The attention Willie was drawing during those years exhibiting his straight-pool prowess came nowhere close to it.

The shit-talking Red Raider came up from Houston for the jamboree, as did Boston Shorty, the Tuscaloosa Squirrel, and Ronnie Allen, who had decided to go around calling himself Fast Eddie. Minnesota Fats came too, of course. After all, it was Fats who helped convince George Jansco to hold the damn thing. And the cameras!

---

[110] And Paulie Jansco dropped straight pool altogether in his even bigger Stardust tournaments, which the brothers began holding in Las Vegas in the mid-'60s.

ABC's *Wide World of Sports* filmed the first events, and they strung lights everywhere. Jim McKay showed up in his yellow blazer. CBS took over in later years.

"Once a year, all the big-time pool hustlers in the country and those trying to earn a name in the game gather at Jansco's Show Bar in Johnston City for the hustlers' world championship nine-ball and one-pocket pool tournament," reported Dick Kay of Chicago's News 5 TV. "Only a few care about the tournament itself—that's just an event to get them all together. The hustlers are interested in the fast action that begins when the official games end. Many come to town broke or traveling light, as they say, and they try to hustle the entry fee. Some bring a moneyman to handle the side bets or stake them in the action."

Kay reported "a Texas carnival owner will give you a $200 bet faster than Fast Eddie can chalk his cue, and the hustler will shoot as long as the action will last." Kay noted that "more money changes hands in the stands in one hour than the cashier at the Bank of Johnston City sees in a week." He called Minnesota Fats the king of the hustlers. "But he never plays the tournament. He waits for someone to win the $20,000 prize money, and then he hustles him for the cash. That's his hustle, but then everybody has one."

There were plenty of fine pool players there—some of the best players then living came to the tiny town of thirty-eight hundred, including the dignified Irving Crane—but never Mosconi. This was the arena of his fat rival and all his sorry compatriots, so Mosconi would have nothing to do with it. But the Johnston City tournaments continued to grow, and eventually it expanded beyond the confines of Little Egypt to the almighty and glorious Las Vegas itself. As the Jansco tournaments gained in popularity, and as the TV cameras broadcast the inner hustling sanctum to the outside world, Willie's beloved straight pool continued to waste away.

• • •

Now part of the Janscos' complaint was that straight pool is just flat-out boring to watch. A top pro might confront a long table-length shot or a difficult cut, but that should happen only rarely. Instead Mosconi or Irv Crane or Joe Balsis would simply tap in multiple shorties . . . *three-ball, side; two-ball, corner* . . . and to the untutored eye it all seemed just so very ridiculously simple. Of course, anybody who has ever actually *played* the game, anybody who knows anything at all about it, knows that straight pool is far from simple. Seventy balls in a row? Forget about it. It would be more useful to pray for a hole in one.

But difficulty does not equal excitement, and tough or not, straight pool has an undeniable sleep-inducing quality. It also didn't help that the casual players whom the Janscos might hope would buy tickets or watch on TV couldn't really be expected to understand the game. So when the promoters de-emphasized straight pool in their Johnston City event and when Paulie dropped it altogether from his more glamorous Stardust tournament, they were just giving the people what they wanted. "The Janscos didn't do anything unless it was based on money . . . and so they favored whatever was going to be popular," said one Johnston City veteran. Eight-ball also was just then gaining ground, driven in large part by the growing popularity of coin-operated tables. The smaller size of those tables and the need to continually feed them quarters made them particularly unsuited for straight pool. [111]

Thanks in part to the continued promotion of the Jansco brothers and Minnesota Fats—and Willie Mosconi too—the *Hustler*-inspired craze continued for about a decade. But by the early 1970s it had nearly run its course. The Janscos held their last Johnston City event in 1971, and Paulie[112] suspended the Stardust events shortly after that. After a while Fats's TV appearances also began to drop off. Likewise

---

[111] Dave Courington, promotions director for table-maker Valley-Dynamo, says coin-operated tables didn't really didn't take hold until the late 1950s. That would have been exactly during the break in pool history when the public was mostly indifferent to all varieties of pocket billiards. When the sport came roaring back during the 1960s, many of the new players gained their first exposure to pool playing on the bar boxes and so were unfamiliar with big-table games like straight pool. This also put a knife in the back of the gentlemen's game.

[112] George died unexpectedly in 1969.

that organization for which Fats and the Janscos had very little use, the stuffy Billiard Congress of America, fell on hard times.

The successor to the old Billiard Association of America, the BCA had begun sanctioning tournaments again during the resurgent 1960s, ironically enough, because of the public's newfound fascination with hustling. But the trade group continued insisting on straight pool rather than those varieties favored by the undignified money players, and it was that insistence—coupled with a particularly dreadful U.S. Open in 1973—that nearly killed pool for television. And not just straight pool, but *any* pool.

The 1973 event, the U.S. Open broadcast from the Grand Ballroom of the Sheraton-Chicago Hotel, featured Luther Lassiter and New Jersey schoolteacher Steve Mizerak. Promoter-historian Charles Ursitti recalled that the players traded a mind-numbing succession of safety shots. They also played horribly. As Matt Racki III in an August 1973 edition of *National Bowlers Journal* noted, "play was pretty sloppy at times, especially during matches you would least expect—and when ABC-TV cameras were switched off, there weren't any surprises as winners stepped forward to receive their checks."

Ursitti said it made for dreadful, soul-crushing television.

"It just took too long to film," he said. "They used to televise the U.S. Open on ABC for years . . . and for years, it was straight pool and only straight pool. And for the die-hard fan, that's what you want to see. But it can get boring, and in 1973 they got into about eighteen minutes of safety play. And of course, eighteen minutes of playing safe is extremely hard to edit. What people want to see is offense. They want to see a lot of downtown shots. And so [the networks] abandoned it. CBS and ABC said, 'That's it. We're done.'"

•   •   •

During pool's dark years of the late 1950s, back before *The Hustler*, the wife of billiards legend Joe Procita had proclaimed that only a miracle or a patron saint could bring the sport back from the dead. In the

Hollywood movie she got that miracle. In Rudolf Wanderone, as Minnesota Fats, she got her patron saint. But the resurrection was not to everyone's liking. It came without Willie's glorious gentlemen's game, it came without the tuxedoes, and it came without the respect for the men who wore them. The dignified world that Willie would speak of with such fondness was part of a dead past. Who could blame Willie for his anger? What he was selling, what he had spent a lifetime selling in city after miserable fucking city—people simply were no longer buying. Why drive twenty thousand miles a year? Why spend three hundred days away from home?

When the hustlers resurrected pool, they did so by overturning the beautiful house over which Willie Mosconi ruled. Fats had made a mint by playing on the trick of perception. He redefined himself even as he redefined the game. Fats claimed he was the greatest hustler, and so he became it. By contrast the great champion spent the 1970s doing trick shots with Roone Arledge, and nobody much cared. Mizerak and Lassiter sloppily beat each other's brains out playing Willie's beautiful game, and the world turned away. Who could blame him for wanting his vengeance?

And Fats: his fame grew and grew and grew. The Miller Light people even contacted Fats about a commercial, and Fats *turned them down.* He was then hurting with prostate problems and so referred the call to Steve Mizerak. The famous "Just Showing Off" spot was one of Fats's cast-off opportunities . . . and it changed Mizerak's life. It may have been the first time in history that Fats turned down good-paying publicity, but then again he could afford to do so. "He loved the fact that people didn't know who Mosconi was, but they sure knew who he was," said one longtime friend.

And Willie's anger, which had continued to rise through the humiliating 1960s, would inch up that much further with each ignored challenge, with each new upbraiding, with each new insulting question from a reporter about whether he had played Minnesota Fats and whether he thought he could beat him. "He's a phony," Willie would insist. "He's a big bag of no show." He hated Fats, and he always would.

And now, the crowning humiliation, the worst of it: Hal Cayton, Jim Jacobs, and Charles Ursitti had hired him in 1977 to do color commentary for Fats and another hustler. And Willie Mosconi would do it because he needed the money.

Was it any wonder that Mosconi became unhinged? When that wire came loose, or the camera broke, and Charles Ursitti had asked Fats to entertain the crowd, he might as well have lit a stick of dynamite. A lifetime's worth of insults and jibes roiled up within Willie Mosconi, and when Fats said he had played them all and beat them all, it would be Burbank all over again. Mosconi would be Secretariat from the starting gate. He would physically attack Minnesota Fats.

"We were in a portable sound booth, and they had brought in four chairs—one for each player, and there were two extras for interviews. . . . And we were just talking, just talking normal, and I was sitting next to [Mosconi], and we were talking to kill time," said Ursitti. "I was asking about nostalgic stuff and learning about Greenleaf and Ponzi and the players who had passed on. It was chitchat, you know, and then [Fats said what he said], and I swear to Christ, for a guy sixty-something years old, Mosconi would have beat Carl Lewis the first forty feet."

It was then that the notion came to Charles Ursitti: Let Willie play Fats. On Valentine's Day, 1978, the world's greatest pool hustler would confront the world's greatest tournament player. All paneled wood and chandeliers at the Waldorf-Astoria with $500 seats and humming cameras and *Howard Cosell*, two gray-haired warriors go head to head. *"Ain't gonna play in no* SUIT,*"* Fats would yelp. *"Shut him* UP,*"* said Willie. The Great Shoot-Out promised spectacle, decency versus its opposite, the sort of occasion over which schoolchildren would argue and old men set their wagers.

The trap was sprung.

Chapter 31

1978

I'm telling you that there never was a Minnesota Fats.
Nobody ever heard of this guy before the film. He just
took over the identity himself. He's a windbag. Real
name is Rudolf Wanderone. I call him Wanderphoney.

— Willie Mosconi, interviewed in the *Toronto Star*, 1982

So everything was set. Everything. And as the day drew near, the Holford family—Bill, Meda, and Brad—began making their preparations. It was as if the whole little town of Du Quoin and the even smaller town of Dowell had begun to vibrate. *What about Willie Mosconi?* they'd ask. *Who's that?* they'd say. Boys took side bets in the high school cafeteria. Fats was topic No. 1 in the barber's chair. *Fats will win two out of the three! Naw, Fats will take all of 'em!* The buzz was everywhere, all throughout southern Illinois and across the Ohio River and down in Houston and on the West Coast and in Atlanta, Miami, and Charlotte. The bestirring in small-town Du Quoin became the bestirring of America. Ursitti, the promoter, and Arledge, the producer, had unwittingly struck a rich cultural vein. It was like *The Hustler* all over again.

"This was what *Wide World of Sports* was created to do—it was huge," said Dennis Lewin, the program's coordinating producer. "*Wide World* was the biggest thing in sports television, period, and Mosconi was going to play Fats. We got buzz, and we had a great promotions hook with Fats playing Mosconi. . . . You can't get that sort of ratings today for anything. There's nothing like it."

This is how Mosconi figured to exact his revenge. Fats and the hustlers had taken possession of his sport. They were residing at the center of his beautiful kingdom built with his fifteen world championships. For thirty relentless years Willie Mosconi wandered a sea of poolhalls, shooting trick shots and performing exhibitions and becoming arguably the most wondrous pool player ever to wield a cue. And now he was like Ulysses dressed in rags. No one recognized any of it. No one recognized *him*. And everywhere, everywhere, he was confronted with the same ridiculous, maddening questions: *Ever play Fats? Can you beat Fats? What about Fats?*

Would a lifetime of struggle prepare him for nothing else than to become a foil for an imbecile? Willie could hardly even say the name without spitting. "Fatso you mean! That phony! He's just a con man!" He would meet Fats on TV, and with millions upon millions of Americans watching, he would disprove the lies once and for all. He had waited for years for the opportunity and finally now, before the biggest audience Willie would ever know in his life, it had come. With the eyes of the nation upon him, lost Ulysses would finally reveal himself.

Willie Mosconi's world championships and his exhibitions in luxurious billiards academies and his public appearances as the industry's clean-living front man—none of it generated the broad public excitement that erupted spontaneously in those days leading up to The Great Pool Shoot-Out. It helped that Cosell was on board. He was the most famous sportscaster then working. It also helped that *Wide World of Sports* was hyping the shit out of the event[113] and that the Big Fights team of Jim Jacobs and Hal Cayton had reserved the luxurious Starlight Roof of the elegant Waldorf-Astoria to add an ironic dash of dignity to the proceedings.

But while Willie hoped to take the opportunity to finally define Minnesota Fats, in some ways The Great Pool Shoot-Out would really

---

[113] "Willie Mosconi vs. Minnesota Fats—two of the legendary pool-playing greats go at it for the first time in 30 years," read one of ABC's breathless newspaper ads.

define a great deal more. A capacity crowd, schoolyard children, Joe DiMaggio, and twenty-one million families, all asked the same question: *Who would win?* Charles Ursitti and Roone Arledge had pitted the forces of respectability and *stability* and decency against the wily trickster, the man-child who had lied and had cheated and who represented everything gone wrong about the American Dream.

Willie Mosconi vs. Minnesota Fats. Who would win?

•   •   •

The Holford family would be accompanying Fats to New York, all courtesy of Big Fights, of course. That meant that fifteen-year-old Brad had to tell his coach he'd be missing football practice and he had to make arrangements to cover his school work and he could boast endlessly to envious friends. Father Bill and mother Meda made sure the Kentucky Fried Chicken would run on its own for a few days. The small-town family would stay at the Waldorf, and they'd get to see the blinking lights of Times Square and tour the financial district. Fats, good ol' Fats, had gotten it written right into his contract: Brad and his parents would get free airline tickets, free hotel accommodations, free meals. It was like being friends with Willie Wonka, for crissake. "He was always helping our family," said Brad. "That's just the way he was."

Fats was generous, sincerely so, but his was a generosity that also bolstered the illusion. It was like he carried around a magic bag of money. And it was bottomless. Fats's sometimes flashy generosity was a symbol of his purported ability to overcome any opponent, any circumstance, any odds. "He would carry $50,000 and $60,000 around in his pocket—I mean wads of $500 and $1,000 bills," said Brad Holford. "I remember he had his lawyers who were trying to give him $1,200 for a [rare] $1,000 bill. I don't even know if they make those bills anymore." Brad said he never figured Fats for a millionaire, but he sure lived like one. He lived rent free in his mother-in-law's house, paid for its remodeling, and then began tirelessly buying Cadillacs. When he got bored with Cadillacs, he switched to limousines. Brad said the long cars would collect like leaves in his driveway because Fats either was too lazy to sell them or because he liked the way they looked. And then his perverse opulence would mix with his eccentric generosity, and on cold days Fats rolled down the windows of his abandoned limos and all the smelly neighborhood dogs would jump in.

Pool promoter Jay Helfert has another story about the Cadillacs and the dogs. Helfert said he was driving cross-country to Oklahoma, and unexpectedly found himself in the vicinity of Dowell, so he figured he'd stop and pay Fats a visit. He called for directions. "So Fats says, 'When you see a stop light, stop there and turn right and just go down that road and out into the country.' He said, 'You'll come to a driveway, and you'll see all these Cadillacs. You'll see a blue Cadillac. You'll see a gold Cadillac, and you'll see a yellow one. That's my house.'"

Fats showed Helfert his pool table. There were newspapers and memorabilia stacked up high on the felt. Helfert said it didn't look as if he had done any actual playing on it in a long time. Evelyn was there, too, but she didn't say a word. "So I spent the day with him . . . and then at about five in the afternoon, he said, 'Would you give me a hand with something?'" Fats led him to the garage, where he kept two huge, heavy plastic buckets. They smelled awful, and Helfert said he was almost afraid to look inside. "They were full of hamburger meat. And each bucket has a trowel inside. And Fats says, 'Grab one of those buckets, and do what I do. Just do the same as me.'"

And then, get this: Fats starts spreading meat on the driveway. He spreads it all along a line, right next to the Cadillacs. "I had no idea what I was doing out there. He says spread it out to here, just like this, and so we both make these lines of meat about thirty feet long. *Lines of meat!* And then he puts two fingers in his mouth. He makes a whistle, that real loud whistle that people do, and pretty soon dogs appeared from everywhere. I mean, dogs just came running from across the fields. Dogs come running down the road. Dogs from everywhere. Maybe there were two dozen—and they all come running to his driveway. And they all start eating that meat. He was feeding them all."

Fats may have been *nouveau riche*, but it would have been a step up in class for him to be considered so. The abandoned cars did little to add to the allure of the Wanderone homestead. If anything, they made it look like an auction site for the newly bankrupt. The barking dogs proved his eccentricity. He spent money like crazy, bought stuff for anybody who would ask, mooched when he was broke, gave candy to little children.

And he fed dogs with food fit for men.

"It was like he ran the damn pound," said Helfert.

•   •   •

It was snowing the day Fats and Brad Holford and Brad's mom Meda and Brad's dad Bill packed into one of Fats's fat limousines. With Bill driving they made their way north and west on Interstate 64 to Lambert Airport in St. Louis, and their plan was to fly up from there to New York. But first things first. At Lambert Fats immediately cashed in Evelyn's airline ticket. He didn't even inquire about the flights, the weather, or the onboard meal. Evelyn had not accompanied them and so he wanted that money.

And then the second interesting thing that Fats did was to order up a room and room service for himself and the Holfords at a pricey Hilton hotel near the airport. Brad said they had gotten snowed in, so they were stuck in St. Louis for the night. "But everything was paid off," said Brad. The weather cleared the next day, and they boarded the flight—it was American Airlines—and suddenly Brad, Bill, and Meda found themselves settling into the sumptuous accommodations of the fabulous Waldorf-Astoria. They flew first class, and they lived first class.

And then the *third* interesting thing Fats did was to reach into his pocket, fish out that giant wad of $500 bills, and peel them off one after another for the red-haired woman who then appeared mysteriously at the Park Avenue hotel. Brad said that she came by with her husband the first day they were in New York and that she visited with Fats in his hotel room well into the evening. The woman treated Fats with great affection. This woman claimed to be Fats's daughter.

"She said he paid for her to go overseas for her schooling," said Brad Holford, although he acknowledged that seemed awful hard to believe given that Fats really didn't have a pot to piss in before *The Hustler* came along. "I don't know if that was in her childhood or teenaged years or for how long. She basically acted like she was crazy about him, but she said that she never really had any time with him."

Brad said the woman came back to the hotel the next day, but this time without her husband. He said she squired them around the city. It was like having a tour guide. "I remember we were just stunned. We never knew about her. He never said anything about her. . . . You know, Fats was pretty well self-centered about everything. I mean he was good to me, and he was good to my family, but everything was based around Fats. I can't imagine him being any kind of devoted father."

It was a wonderful day for Brad and his family. His country family wasn't so sure about the subway, and then, right on cue, Fats's hidden daughter arrives like a genie in a big new Fleetwood and chauffers them around. The Holfords didn't know where to eat, and she takes them out to Chinatown. The Holfords didn't know what to see, and with Fats's daughter it was like they saw the whole city. "She took us everywhere," said Brad, still beaming as he recalled the day.

And then the mysterious woman showed up once more. The next day she was wearing her fur stole and was looking majestic, and Brad remembers eagerly pushing the lit-up button on the hotel elevator. Together they went up, up to the eighteenth floor, and there Fats's supposed daughter and Brad, Bill, and Meda settled into their front-row seats and watched wide-eyed as the ABC technicians whispered into headphones and made last-minute adjustments to the blazing hot lights.

The big show was about to begin.

Chapter 32

THE GREAT SHOOT-OUT

The scene set is the Starlight Roof of the Waldorf-Astoria,
one of the most famous rooms in the world for great
social occasions. We're on Park Avenue, in the heart of
New York City. Hello again, everyone, I'm Howard Cosell.

— The famous *Wide World of Sports* commentator
speaking before The Great Pool Shoot-Out

There would be no loose wires this time, no broken cameras, no technical snafus. Of this Director Chet Forte and Coordinating Producer Dennis Lewin and the other professionals at *Wide World of Sports* had made sure. Lewin's crew had the TV lights blazing bright and hot. The tuxedoed Charles Ursitti rushed around barking last-minute orders. He was squat, and he was bespectacled, and he was bearded like a beatnik, and it was as if those lights had warmed his blood. Jim Jacobs was there too, as was Hal Cayton, and right at center stage like a crouching beast (although more imposing and magnificent than most) was a $20,000 pool table courtesy of Brunswick Billiards. It was a 4 by 8 with a ball return. "Everything was jelling just right," said Charles Ursitti, who could sit still during the big event only with the greatest of difficulty. "If you had to pick the magic formula, then we had the ingredients for it: the timing was right, the players were right, and God was on my side. We just got lucky."

Get your popcorn. Settle in. The Great Shoot-Out was coming at you direct from the luxurious Starlight Roof way up high in the beautiful Waldorf-Astoria. This was Park Avenue, New York City, the very center of the known universe. This was *it*. Charlie Ursitti could not have known the sheer volume of men and boys who would tune in for his big show. He figured that sure, it would sell. "For a couple of weeks before the show they were pumping it constantly," he said. *Everything on* Wide World of Sports *sold*. But even so Ursitti and Roone Arledge and Jim Jacobs had no inkling of the millions upon millions upon millions of television sets that would warm to life.

And for . . . of all things . . . *pocket billiards*.

Cosell got there early, of course. He had his assistants apply makeup with thick brushes. They draped a paper napkin around his neck like a bib. Sandy-haired Brad Holford took an early peek at the Starlight Roof, where they had hard-backed chairs lined up five rows deep. The fifteen-year-old marveled at the chandeliers sparkling like diamonds. There must have been a dozen in there, at least, all fashioned from Austrian crystal. "It was like a banquet room, and there was probably room in there, for, I dunno, hundreds of people," Holford said. "They had separate chairs, individual cushioned chairs, you know—restaurant chairs, and they were placed on separate levels. It was like bleachers."

Cosell dramatically declared it "one of the most famous rooms in the world for great social occasions," and after taking the elevator eighteen floors up, after emerging into that beautiful marble rotunda—who could really doubt it? When configured as a theater, the six-thousand-square-foot rectangular Starlight Roof held about 550 people. The décor was definitely art deco, but with stunning woodwork. It was a shrine to a more elegant age—never mind that *Rolling Stone* journalist Robert Sabbag in a piece about The Great Shoot-Out uncharitably compared the heavy drapes to the sort one typically finds in "the finest whorehouses." That wasn't the real Starlight Roof Sabbag was describing. That wasn't the real Waldorf-Astoria. Rather, what Sabbag sensed was the ancient stigma of pool. Before even a shot was fired, it had permeated the room like the smell of a raw onion. It was unmistakable.

ABC and Howard Cosell had hyped it as the match of the century, had in fact produced a spoof newspaper with the front-page headline to that effect. (*"Willie Mosconi versus Minnesota Fats: Why Not?"*) ABC and Cosell knew very little about pool and cared even less. They could not identify any of the great figures of the sport. They knew nothing of its history. And yet they confidently made this crazy claim—*the match of the century*—because one thing ABC and Cosell did understand was show business. And so the famous sportscaster, towering like a tree during interviews, set forth first to establish the rivalry and the stakes. "Willie, it's been said that each of you have everything to lose and nothing to gain by this match," he said. "In other words, you are the greatest straight-pool artist of the world. Everybody knows your record. Fats is one of the most renowned and colorful figures in the history of the game. . . ."

"Well, yes, that's right to a certain extent. But I look at it from a different angle," says Willie. "This is something that I haven't done in a long while. Howard, I look at this as a *fun* thing. This is something a little bit different. He may think he has everything to lose. I certainly don't."

Willie was five foot eight and had put on a few pounds over the years. Fats claimed to be taller than Willie—*I'm five feet eight and a* HALF, *ya understand*—and had lost weight. So now, besides being almost precisely the same age, Willie and Fats had begun to look like one another. They both shot blazing fast, too, although Willie angrily stalked his shots, pure focus, looking to all the world as if he might at any moment pound his fist into the table. Fats by contrast shot pool as if the pool match had slipped his mind—there was no focus there *at all*, and he waddled around the table like a perverse penguin with his whole upper body rocking, at first left and then right. He was like a damned human metronome. He walked like a man with bunions on both feet.

"Is it going to be possible under our rules of procedure for you to remain quiet while Willie shoots?" asks Cosell.

"Let me tell ya a secret," says Fats. "I can play as if I was deaf and dumb. I can play as if there was a gang war in the jernt. Dat don't mean nuttin' to me. Whaddever you wanna do, I can do it, see? I do it nice. And when I leave, I leave with da cash. *Ya unnerstand?* I don't care what goes on. I don't care if dey was shootin' bows and arrows and dey was having Western movies. Dat don't bother me." Fats drawls out the vowels at the end of each sentence. It's as if he wants to savor his words before they vanish away into the ether.

"Ya unnerstand—ninety-nine out of a hundred pool players ain't even allowed to *breeeaathe,*" he says.

• • •

First off, The Great Pool Shoot-Out wouldn't be just Willie's game, straight pool, nor would it be just one-pocket, Fats's game. Instead, the Odd Couple of Pool would start out playing a set of nine-ball, then they'd switch over to eight-ball, and then rotation. Only if there were still no victor would Willie and Fats turn to straight pool and then finally one-pocket. The player who wins three sets wins the event. Each set was best of nine. So, for instance, if a player wins five games at nine-ball, he wins that set. But he then would have to go on and win five games of eight-ball, rotation, straight pool or one-pocket to win the entire event.

Mosconi also insisted that all shots must be called, even nine-ball shots, and that balls made on the break get spotted back up. This is not how most Americans (or most humans for that matter) play *fun* pool, especially not nine-ball. But Willie wanted to limit the cruel power of luck. He figured to turn The Great Pool Shoot-Out into a contest of pure skill, a contest that he figured he stood little chance of losing. The Great Shoot-Out was not a *fun thing,* despite Willie's claims to the contrary. He had traveled too far, sacrificed too much, paid too high a price. Losing was not an option. He had become a stranger in his own land, but he aimed to set things right.

And that's why he practiced hard for weeks before the Shoot-Out, practiced to meet a man whom he always insisted was nothing more than a third-rate hustler. "He's a bum. He can't play. He's a phony."

But Fats, by all accounts, did not practice. Neither did he argue when Willie insisted on turning nine-ball and eight-ball and every other sort of fucking game played that day into a variation of call-shot straight pool. Fats was just as impatient as Willie but more cocksure and full of bluster. He said he didn't care what the rules were. "He didn't even want to hear the explanation in advance," said Cosell. Fats said he'd play by any rules Willie set. Fats said he'd beat him anyway.

•   •   •

But that's not to say that Fats would allow Willie to define the Great Pool Shoot-Out. Willie wanted a test of skill. Fats wanted a circus. Willie demanded decorum. Fats demanded attention. So even before the first break shot of the starting game the Fat One had started up. *"Hey, Howard,"* he screeches. *"Hey, HOWARD!"* Fats is wearing an expensive polyester leisure suit that doesn't come close to fitting. He looks like a dark blue waddling egg, except one with skinny spindly arms.

"The noise in the background, ladies and gentlemen, is Minnesota Fats," says Cosell.

"I ain't gonna play in no coat, Willie. When I played in your joint at Seventh and Morris, I didn't have no coat on. *A coat.* Why, a coat on a pool player is like ice cream on a hot dog."

Fats won't sit still, Fats *can't* sit still, and Willie, who has played his entire career in a coat, looks as if he might burst another vessel. The Shoot-Out hadn't even begun, the balls hadn't even started falling . . . and already Willie was ready to strangle him.

"Tell him to put his jacket back on," he says.

"When I played polo, I didn't play in no evening attire—that's for *monkeys!*" says Fats.

Jim Jacobs gets between the two to mediate. Fats is running around the table, ranting. "His jacket goes on," says Willie.

And then Fats *really* starts up.

"I mean, ain't that *ridiculous?* Ain't that the most ridiculous thing ya ever heard? A jacket on a pool player?" Jim Jacobs has begun pleading:

first with Fats, then with Willie. The Starlight Roof audience looks on, aghast but fascinated, sort of like bystanders around a car accident. "Imagine playing Ping-Pong with a tuxedo on!" yelps Fatty. Willie says he won't play unless Fats puts on his jacket. Fats says he won't budge. "Understand I let everybody make the rules, 'cuz I'm going to win anyway," says Fats.

There's a confused murmur in the room, like a low rumbling, and then that murmur turns to nervous tittering. With desperation, Jacobs turns to Mosconi. Jacobs knows there's nothing in the ground rules about the wearing of jackets, so Fats has a point. "C'mon, Willie," he pleads. "It's okay, Willie."

Mosconi has sometimes appeared in a suit jacket, sometimes a tuxedo jacket—but never, *ever* in his shirtsleeves. Not during any exhibition, not during any tournament, not during any public appearance during a lifetime of public appearances. As the face of pocket billiards, it was his duty to represent it in the most dignified fashion possible. And so when Fats appeared in that polyester suit that looked like shit, when he removed his jacket—an action that drew all eyes to his protruding belly—it was not as if he was showing just Willie Mosconi great disrespect but rather disrespect for the entire sport. That's why Willie continued to insist on the point for five long awful minutes. It was as if Fats had come into his home and then pissed on the carpet. And it was only Howard Cosell who would break the impasse.

"Okay, Willie agrees, there will be no wearing of coats," the famous sportscaster said finally, as Willie removed his jacket to a smattering of applause. Fats would not wear a jacket, but neither would Willie. That was the deal. But it's interesting to note here that nothing prevented Willie from wearing his jacket, while Fats played in his shirtsleeves. The problem with that, of course, was it would have given a slight advantage to the hustler. Fats was right: it's easier to play pool without a jacket. And giving any sort of advantage to Minnesota Fats was clearly out of the question. So The Great Shoot-Out of 1978 marked the first time in history that the great Willie Mosconi would play in shirtsleeves. That's how important it was for him to win.

• • •

"Fatty, wanna get in your seat now?" says Ursitti.

And then Fats starts up again.

"Now I got to sit down now, too? The places I played you had to go play with a *gas mask*. We didn't have no evening attire. Sit down? When I play Istanbul for the sultan, this is how I sit."

"All right now, a little quiet," says Willie, and he breaks open the nine-ball rack and the colored balls go exploding in nine separate directions. It's a crisp break, but not thunderous (nine-ball, after all, is not Willie's best game), and nothing drops for him. Fats waddles up. He takes a moment to size up the lay, but just a moment, and then banks the one-ball cross-table into the side. He makes the shot effortlessly, almost as if he's distracted. It's as if he's playing the crowd more than the game. It's as if he's thinking about what he's eating for dinner that night or figuring how to make his daughter laugh. She just happens to be sitting right there in the front row with a fur stole draped over her shoulders. As always, Fats stands almost straight up as he shoots—an odd, unorthodox stance for a pro. He extends his stroking arm out like the handle of a teacup. He wears a shiny diamond on the pinky of his left hand. *"Two-ball, corner,"* he says.

And now Fats begins griping, presumably to himself, but it comes out in a great stage whisper so that all five hundred people craning from their seats at the Starlight Roof can hear exactly what he's saying, and everyone who will watch on TV hears, too. It has finally occurred to Minnesota Fats that he finds Mosconi's rules ridiculous beyond compare. This revelation comes to him as the two-ball drops on a fluke. "You try to hit it, and you just hit it," he mutters to himself, but *loud*. "You can't call it, that's it. But we're going to have to be here all night, anyhow. I ain't going no place. I *cancelled* my reservations." He takes his seat, and now it's Mosconi's turn, and he starts shooting fast. The muscles in his jaws tense like the cables on a suspension bridge. His lips turn white as he stretches them tight over his teeth. Willie does not talk. He does not mug for the camera. He addresses the crowd but only to get them to quiet down. It's 1978, and with nothing at stake but honor, Willie entertains the crowd. It comes in the way of a beautiful explosion.

"Two-ball," he says.

"Three-ball, corner pocket," he says.

"Four-ball," he says.

"Fats is looking on intently as Willie is doing away with the balls one by one," says Howard Cosell.

"Five-ball," says Mosconi.

"Six-ball."

"If this is a fun thing, Willie doesn't show it. His attitude could not be more serious," says Howard Cosell.

And now comes a spectacular table-length bank—*bang!*—followed by the tiniest hint of a knowing smile. The crowd is clapping now, enthusiastically so and with great gusto. But even still Willie doesn't slow down. It's as if the crowd has vanished away, invisible.

"Game to Mosconi!" shouts Ursitti.

And then again: seven, eight, nine.

"Game to Mosconi!" shouts Ursitti.

And Cosell whispers in his deliberate halting cadence, stressing every other syllable, enunciating perfectly. "You can't give Mosconi an opening—not with his ability at straight pool," he says. "That's *his game*. In effect, this has become straight pool for Willie. Fats is beginning to look a little dubious but dubious in the sense of whether he can compete."

Chapter 33

BEHIND THE EIGHT-BALL

Fats loved the fact that people who didn't know who
Mosconi was knew who he was.

— Brad Holford

Finally, a ball gets away from Mosconi. He had plowed through the
third rack without a miss, got down on the case ball, and then the yellow nine drifted away to the right, four inches from the pocket. It was
an inexcusable miss. "If Nicklaus can miss a four-footer, then the great
Willie Mosconi can flub an easy shot," says Cosell. And so Fats wins
his first game, and the set goes 2–1, still in Mosconi's favor. The tournament champion wins the fourth game, too, but then grabs the rake
in the fifth and miscues. Fats runs the five, the six, the seven, and the
eight. He jabbers all the while.

"Game to *Fats*," says Charlie Ursitti.

Fats wins the next game after that, too, but this time he does so by
running the table. He does so without shutting up. It seems he's inca-
pable of shutting up. "Everybody beats me," he yelps. "That's why I got
so much *money*. I got six brand-new Cadillacs. Every time a bird flies
over, I get another one. I let dogs and cats sleep in presidents' limousines." The set goes 4–3, still Willie's favor, but now the Fat One is
making great shots, impressive shots: a tough table-length bank splits
the pocket, a skittering delicate inside cut, a combination bank goes
cross-corner as if by magic. The crowd gasps, but Fats hardly seems to

notice. He lines them up like a drunk, fires without thinking; he yammers with every stroke.

A man in the third row or the second sounds like he might have a
heart attack, he's laughing so hard. Fats has got them, got them all:
there in the Starlight Roof and at home watching on TV, too. "What
about Detroit Slim?" someone shouts. They wouldn't dare move a muscle when Willie was at the table, but with Fats there, they're *shouting*.
"Broke him a thousand nights in a row—Detroit Slim went into share-
cropping," says Fatty. And then, finally, he misses one. Willie Mosconi
steps up, chalks his cue, and wordlessly runs the table.

"Set to *Mosconi*," says Charlie Ursitti.

•   •   •

Was this the trick? Simply getting under Willie's skin? Brad Holford
remembers Mosconi tried to counter, tried to use some psychological
warfare of his own—but it was pointless. "Mosconi would take Fats's
chalk and throw it under the table," said Holford. "But it didn't bother
Fats. He didn't care. He never cared." It was as if the game itself was beside the point, said Holford. "He didn't care who won or lost. He was
like, 'Hell, I'm MINNESOTA FATS' . . . but I remember, Fats would always call Mosconi 'MOUTH-sconi,' and *that* sure was irritating."

And so Fats keeps pushing Willie's buttons, over and over again.
The whole event is a sham, he tells Willie. *It's a carousel*, he says.
Straight pool? Straight pool? Why, that's a cancer, he says. "He was like
saltwater up my father's nose," said Bill Mosconi. Fats was, without a
doubt, the pool player in this world whom Willie Mosconi detested
most. This was not ABC bullshit. This was not show-business hype.
That was reality, pure and simple, and Fats understood this reality, even
as he remained disconnected from it. Fats had been pushing Willie's
buttons not just that evening but for the last fifteen years—ever since
The Hustler came out, and *The Tonight Show* began clamoring for him.

Fats loved it that he was becoming more famous than Willie
Mosconi, and the corollary was also indisputably true: Willie's hatred

was born from Fats's ridiculous fame, built on nothing. Fats had pulled the wool over America's eyes, another trick, and with every newspaper interview, with every TV appearance, with every magazine article, he besmirched the great reputation of the champion's sport. He had given it over to the hustler, the game that Willie had spent a lifetime building. And so, yes, *oh hell, yes,* Fats pushed Willie's buttons. Over and over again he pushed them. Fats used his big mouth to charm the railbirds but without actually playing. That was a trick, and it unbalanced Willie.

•   •   •

About midway into the second set, it gets ugly.

Mosconi is already up two games to none in the eight-ball part of the competition, and he and Fats can't stop bickering. He tells Fats to sit down. He tells Fats to shut up. "I'm sorry I *disturbed* you," says Fats. Willie asks Charlie Ursitti if he's going to let this go on, if he's going to let Fats make a mockery of the proceedings. "Okay, Willie, that's it," says Fats. "Let's go for *crissakes.*" Fats fishes a wad of $500 and $1,000 bills from his pants, the big denominations he always carries, and there's $35,000 in there at least. It's wrapped together with a rubber band. "I want to play you some one-snatch for $1,000 a game. Right now." Fats spreads the cash out on the green felt. "C'mon, Mr. Exhibition!" Fats sneers.

Willie is stammering angry. It looks like he might have another stroke.

"We'll finish it right here," says Willie, referring to the ongoing eight-ball game.

"Ha! *This?!*" says Fats.

And then Fats gets on Willie again. "I'll play you some banks or some bank-every-other ball. That's half straight pool and half banks. Let's go, Willie. What's the matter? What are you waiting for?"

Willie says he'll play some high-dollar straight pool.

"*Straight* pool? I wouldn't play you straight pool if you gave me ninety-nine to a hundred."

"I better go interject," says Cosell.

"Take your seat, Fats," says Charlie Ursitti.

And then somewhere in there Fats calls Willie's beloved straight pool a throwback to a long-dead era. "Ain't no living human playing it," he says. And somewhere in there he says he beat every living human, Willie included. And he says he's played the sultan and the Terrible Turk. "I was playing $500 a game," he says. "I was playing $1,000 a game."

Howard Cosell tries to quiet him down. Jim Jacobs tries to quiet him down. Willie's tense, tense like he might throw a punch. The veins in his neck have begun to throb. Cosell notes that Willie's lips and much of his face have gone ghost white. "Are you going to let this go on?" Willie repeats, his eyes blazing. Willie's ready to storm off.

Fats retrieves the cash from the table, turns to the crowd, dares the tournament champion to play him for the big money. Willie says he's not in the habit of carrying around his entire life's savings in his pocket.

"And don't no monkey get no *ideas,*" says Fats, waving his bankroll to the crowd. He's drawing laughs again. "I'm the toughest son of a bitch on *earth.* You don't even know the rest of the story . . . *on earth.* . . . I whipped every son-bitch in New York a hundred times, and *he* knows it."

Fats points a handful of green at Willie.

"I whipped every son of a bitch in New York and Philadelphia and anywhere else, so don't get no funny ideas. Tell you, you ain't *never* seen one like that. Fought in two revolutions and went down on two ships in the middle of the ocean. Ain't *never* seen one like me. . . ."

It's pure torture.

• • •

Cosell rubs Fats's belly, as if for good luck. The hustler smiles with the biggest shit-eating grin the world has ever seen. Finally, he's back in his seat. He's retrieved his money. "Mosconi likes total quiet; Fats likes to destroy the opponent with talk," whispers Cosell. But when the very obviously flustered Willie Mosconi fires away and misses, Fats sees his chance. He's back to the table but quick, and he's firing away, bam, bam, *bam, bam.*

"Game to *Fats!*" says Ursitti. And then again—one, two, *three*—Game to *Fats!* The hustler plays expertly, more expertly than Willie and the Fats detractors would ever suppose. But he also has luck on his side: some from the gods, some of the self-made sort that is the province of the Trickster. And he yammers as he works.

"Antarctica, I been there," says Fats, pocketing a ball. "One hundred and twenty-five *below.* Played cards aboard ship, never got out of the dining room." He pockets a few more. "I hustle cards and everything. I'm an expert, world-champion card player, beat anybody living playing *cards.* Never lost one for money in my life."

●　　●　　●

ABC reported afterward that 11.2 million households tuned into The Great Pool Shoot-out. Nielsen Media Research said it received a 36 share, meaning that more than one-third of the TV sets in America were tuned into the Waldorf-Astoria. More people watched the Willie & Fats Show than watched most games of the 2005 World Series. The viewership of The Great Shoot-Out rivaled that of national college football championships. In 1978 only the title fight between Leon Spinks and Muhammad Ali, that other great trickster-athlete, had better ratings on *Wide World of Sports.* And remember, *Wide World* was the hottest show on sports. "Today, you would die for ratings like that," said Lewin.

The ABC marketing men had made a startling claim, one made in ignorance and in the service of show business. They had promoted The Great Pool Shoot-Out as *the* match of the century. But look at the numbers. Look at the viewers. Charlie Ursitti and Roone Arledge had improbably tapped into something. The marketing men were impossibly, ridiculously . . . *correct.* The great Willie Mosconi had challenged the incomparable Greenleaf—but never like this. Minnesota Fats had challenged Ronnie Allen, Ed Kelly, and Richie Florence—three hustlers at once—but not before an entire nation of railbirds. Nowhere in books, nowhere in newspapers or in the minds of historians, *nowhere,* will one find evidence of such broad public interest attached to a single match of pocket billiards. And so those two worlds—that of tournament pool and that of hustling—really had combined on the grandest of stages. It was true. And in that crazy arena where sports and showmanship come together, one can find no greater figures than Willie Mosconi and Minnesota Fats.

●   ●   ●

Willie remained pretty much speechless for the remainder of the eight-ball segment, which he won, and the rotation block, which he also won. The final score was 5–3, 5–2, 5–2, all Willie's favor. It was a clean sweep. There would be no straight pool. There would be no one-pocket. Willie had made his case to the world, finally, and in grand form.

"That's it," said Howard Cosell. "Willie Mosconi won the Great Shoot-Out. In point of fact, this has been one of the most fascinating events we've had on *Wide World of Sports*. . . . And Fats, at the start you expressed every confidence in victory. And then during the course of the competition you sort of backed off. . . ."

Minnesota Fats, the man who would never stop telling lies, finally would have to speak the Truth.

"I never back off at all—that's just like it is," said Fats. "This man is a tremendous player. Everybody who's got any sense knows this man might beat anybody alive. I might beat anybody living. I ain't never lost in my life, and so he beat me. What you want me to do?"

Willie had set forth to reconquer his sport, to wrest it back from the greatest symbol for all that had gone wrong with pocket billiards, and in this he had finally succeeded. Willie had been a mariner lost at sea. Now he was returned, and he had put his house in order.

"Everybody living on earth knows this man has been champion," said Fats. "He's sixteen times champion now. I been champeen of the earth ever since the turn of the century. Now he's champeen of the earth."

Chapter 34

WILLIE AND THE TRICKSTER

> You tell Mosconi, if it ain't for me, he'd be looking for work. I'm the greatest money player on earth. I'm the one that put Mosconi on television. Without me, none of them would be on television. He was the best tournament player and exhibition player. I'm the greatest money player on earth.
>
> — Minnesota Fats

The ratings in 1978 were fabulous, stunning, and wholly unexpected. They were ratings for which the ABC brass could only have dreamed. Obviously, there would be a sequel: Willie versus Fats Round 2, the big show—*but this time in Vegas!* They came together again in 1979 at the Flamingo Hotel. Willie got an eight-foot practice table set up at the hotel. "Willie asked me if I'd rack a few balls for him—he wanted to get in stroke for the show," said promoter Charlie Ursitti. "And then he set up a break ball and proceeded to run fourteen straight racks."

That's fourteen racks. That's two hundred balls, give or take. "Before he opened the rack for the fifteenth, we stopped to order coffee and a Danish from room service," said Ursitti. "And he kept shooting, and I kept racking. When I'd rack, he'd stop for a sip of coffee and a bite of Danish.

"After eleven more racks, still without missing a ball, we decided to call room service again and get some sandwiches. He kept shooting them in, only stopping to take a bite of food while I racked, until he'd run seventeen more racks. Then he said, 'That's enough; I'm getting tired,' and fired the break ball in the pocket. That's forty-two perfect racks—589 balls, unfinished. Petey Margo was on the show, and he came in and watched for a while. So did John Oganowski,[114] and Steve Mizerak stopped by a couple times. Willie did it all so effortlessly; he was so fluid."

It wasn't an official record, not like Willie's 526 in Ohio, with the affidavit attesting to the feat, and the witnesses listed at the Smithsonian. It was just Willie Mosconi, age sixty-six, knocking balls around a practice table and eating a room-service Danish. It was as if Willie could not help but plow through racks. In 1979 Willie again won each of the divisions, but this time it was one-pocket, straight pool, and nine-ball. The final score was 2–1 at one pocket, 125–60 in a single game of straight pool, and 5–2 in nine-ball.[115] Willie practiced beforehand, not for the sheer joy of it, not because he wanted to improve his game or to impress Charlie Ursitti, Pete Margo, and Steve Mizerak. Willie practiced for the same reason that he had quit playing in tournaments—because he could not abide losing.

In the following year, in June, Willie, his impossibly perfect wife, and the promoter Charlie Ursitti crowded together into a booth at the cafeteria at the Sands Casino Hotel in Atlantic City. Charlie was sitting on one side, Flora and Willie on the other. A television crew that week had begun taping another sequel to the Fats & Willie Show but this time with more pros for added flavor.

Ursitti said it was Flora who saw Minnesota Fats first.

"It's breakfast, and there in this long line was Fatty waiting to be seated. Flora looks up and says, 'There's Fatty!' and she starts waving.

---

[114] The father of professional Loree Jon Jones, formerly Oganowski.

[115] According to the March–April 1979 edition of *Billiards Digest*, the event was held on February 10 and 11 and aired again on *ABC's Wide World of Sports*.

She says, 'Fatty, Fatty!' and Willie says, 'Jesus Christ, Flora, what are you calling *him* for?'"

Imagine the scene. Willie is trapped in the booth, held captive by his eggs and bacon, and *here comes Fats*. Ursitti recalls that Willie gets so perturbed that he starts mumbling to himself. As far as Willie was concerned, Atlantic City wasn't big enough for the two of them. All of *New Jersey* wasn't big enough. Willie would just as soon not even breathe the same air. Fatty sits down across from Willie, and of course he starts up right away.

"There he is—there's *Mosssscoooni!*'" he says, drawling out the vowels. Willie does his best to ignore him. He won't even make eye contact and so wordlessly glowers into his menu. It looks as if Willie is contemplating mass murder "Look at *Mosssscoooni*," says Fats. "Mooosconi is making faces at his menu. Mosconi even gets mad at the menu. . . ."

• • •

Over the years Fats and Willie would appear together at banquets, roasts, and hall-of-fame dinners . . . and Willie always insisted he be seated as far away as possible. "That man really rubbed him the wrong way," said Flora. She said her husband didn't even want to be housed in the same hotel as Fats. As the years progressed, there would be other challenge matches: in Vegas, in Atlantic City. Sometimes the competitions featured only Mosconi and Fats; sometimes they featured Wimpy Lassiter and U. J. Puckett and eventually even Jean Balukas and Loree Jon Jones, two of the greatest-ever women players. ABC aired the first four as part of its *Wide World of Sports* programming. Later Ursitti took the programming to the nascent ESPN, the inheritor of *Wide World*'s legacy.

Instead of straight pool these later competitions featured new games like seven-ball and six-ball, games that played out quick for the TV cameras and that rewarded luck as well as skill. During one Fats came within a single ball of beating Mosconi. It was an unexpected turn that likely took a year off Willie's life. And then in 1984 Fats won his series against Mosconi outright. "You've just witnessed a miracle, like Moses parting the Red Sea," said one stunned onlooker.

That was probably another year right there.

•   •   •

"So I go in there one morning, you know, I went into town and I was talking to him a little bit." Lanky Johnny Ogolini said Fats had returned to Little Egypt, returned after having gotten his ass beat during one of the Shoot-Outs. And yet Fats seemed not the least bit cowed. He said the match settled nothing. It was as if Fats lived in a different world. "You know I was kidding him a little bit, and I said to Fats, I said, 'You went out there, playing Mosconi, and I told you before you left you were going to get beat,' and he said, 'Johnny, I was just playing for fun. I don't care about it. For money, marbles, or chalk, I'll defeat him any time I want to.'

"And I said, 'But you *ain't* got no money. You're broke.'"

Johnny said Fats lets out a snort. A real-live snort. "*Broke?*" he says. "*BROKE? Minnesota fucking Fats ain't never fucking broke.*"

"He was going through the mail when we were talking, you know, just opening letters, and he pulled open one, and there was a damn check for $35,000. It was just right there in the mail, in front of me."

"I'm broke?" he said. "*Lookit this.*"

With Fats the trick never ended. He could lose, and yet he remained unbowed. He could lose, and yet he insisted, he *insisted,* it did not matter. *Let's go, Willie, you and me,* he had said as he laid out his bankroll. When the green was on the table in stacks, when he was playing *his* game, Big Minnie said he was unstoppable. *And don't you monkeys get no ideas.* And so it absolutely did not matter if Fats's claims were true or even verifiable. It absolutely did not matter if Fats really had beat every man living, if he really had gone down with the ship, or if he ever played the Terrible Turk or Happy the Chinaman. With Fats it was the *truth* that was ridiculous.

Fats the Trickster confronts authority. Fats the Trickster reinvents the world and his place in it. Fats the Trickster tears away at contradictions and hypocrisy. Tricksters are found in every nation and throughout history . . . but Fats the Trickster is uniquely American. His stories are those of consumerism gone berserk, of larceny, and of deceit. He tells of chicanery, of the tension between sex and Puritanism, and, most of all, of an American sort of freedom. And Fats the Trickster stood for everything that Willie Mosconi did not, and so his beef with Mosconi was not only about who was the better pool player—not even mostly that—but rather about *ideas.*

Fats understood this: that the desire to gamble is like a hunger. It's universal. But among society's civilizing forces so too is that instinct to supress gambling, hence the laws in every state and nearly every nation regulating or outright banning the activity. And nowhere is this tension between gambling and society more apparent than in the world of professional sports, where elites like Willie Mosconi understand both gambling's inherent attractiveness and its inherent corruptive and addictive qualities. The elite not only frown upon wagering on their own sports but consider it taboo. Wagering on one's own sport is what gets professional players banned for life. It's the sort of activity that can only end in disgrace.

And so here then appears the crux of the matter.

Freud says that taboos are those prohibitions that come about before the existence of civilizations, before the gods appear to ban objectionable behavior.

And the function of all tricksters is to break them.

No wonder such a stigma has been historically attached to pocket billiards, that sport which more than any other has embraced gambling. Not just Fats but *all* of pool's leading figures have been secretly or proudly gamblers: Mosconi, Ralph Greenleaf, Ponzi, Irving Crane. The greatest-ever nine-ball player, Wimpy Lassiter, was a pool hustler. Its greatest one-pocket players—Ronnie Allen, Rags Fitzpatrick, Jersey Red, and Marshall Carpenter—all were hustlers. Brunswick Billiards tried to hide the fact, went so far as to change the sport's very name, but all of them, everywhere, even Brunswick's own stable of stars, *they all gambled.* Pool is nothing without gambling. That is its truest nature—even in the face of its history of long denial.

Freud defines taboos as cultural prohibitions from antiquity, prohibitions which were at some time externally imposed upon a generation of primitive men by the previous generation. Freud writes that taboos always "concerned activities towards which there was a strong inclination" and that "anyone who has violated a taboo becomes taboo himself because he possesses the dangerous quality of tempting others to follow his example." So of course Minnesota Fats was despised by Mosconi. As a hustler, Fats had *proudly* broken the taboos. He had the temerity to crow about it, to expose to ABC's *Wide World of Sports* and Howard Cosell and Johnny Carson and the whole damn world that *other* side of pool and that other side of all human competition. Fats understood what sells, what speaks to the human soul, what differentiates between the Kentucky Derby and the simple running of swift horses.

•　　•　　•

But of course: sports is also nothing without true skill and artistry. The truth of Fats is not the *only* truth. Willie Mosconi—that wanderer who hoped to use his skill to run the rabble from his home—he came to symbolize the purity of sports excellence. *You had to play*, he believed. *You had to be a champion*. In every aspect of his life, in tournaments, at exhibitions, on the road, and at home, that's all Willie Mosconi believed. That's all he *understood*. "There is no excuse for not playing your best," the father told his son. Otherwise, competition becomes as hollow as fake wrestling.

The hustler could not have accomplished what he accomplished, none of it, without Willie Mosconi. Fats needed the legitimacy of *The Hustler*, that film that Willie Mosconi helped create. Fats needed Willie Mosconi to tell a California reporter back in 1962 that the Jackie Gleason character really and truly existed outside the illusion that was popular cinema. No player other than Mosconi possessed the stature to make such a claim. And then Fats's fame grew in lockstep with his years-long rivalry with Mosconi, the sport's greatest champion.

With cue in hand Willie Mosconi truly was an illusionist, not a pretend one like Fats. Willie was a man who could step up to the table and between bites of a Danish run nearly six hundred balls straight. *He would kill you with hundreds.* But Wille's mistake was thinking that he could beat Fats through that monumental skill alone. That's far too literal.

Some time after that first Great Pool Shoot-Out, a reporter walked into a bar in Philadelphia. The reporter had arranged an interview with Willie, but the great champion hadn't yet arrived. So the reporter strikes up a conversation with the bartender, and the bartender mentions that he's heard Mosconi's name somewhere.

Remember: this was Philadelphia, Willie's hometown.

"He was formerly the greatest pool player in the world," says the reporter.

"That must have been before Minnesota Fats, right?' says the bartender.

Mosconi had traveled the nation, shooting trick shots, performing exhibitions, trying to save pocket billiards from the awful rabble. He won the straight-pool world championship fifteen times—more than any man living. When he finally beat Fats on nationwide TV, he was like Odysseus cleaning out the suitors from Ithaca. He *thought* he had restored his home, he *thought* he had proven to the world the truth as he understood it.

But ask anyone in America to name one pool player—*just one*—and that pool player will not be Willie Mosconi. Fats would bug Willie about this. He loved it that people didn't know Willie's name but knew his. "You gotta have fans, Willie," he'd say. And so when Willie helped create the fame of Fats by giving him a soapbox from which to operate, and when Willie met Fats in the most watched pool event in the history of the nation, Willie Mosconi helped seal his own defeat.

And that was the trick.

EPILOGUE

> Hermes is the god of signposts: i.e., he is, specially for
> a traveller like Ulysses, the point at which roads parallel
> merge and roads contrary also. He is an accident of
> providence.
>
> — James Joyce

In 1986 the sport got another shot in the arm—and again it came from the movies. Touchstone Pictures released *The Color of Money,* a sequel to *The Hustler.* It starred Paul Newman and Tom Cruise and had Martin Scorsese directing. Newman, passed up for an Oscar in 1961 for the first pool movie, won the best-actor award for the second. The new film got generally great reviews and was a commercial success, although Fats and Mosconi both despised it. Willie thought it included too much gambling. "I walked out," he said. Fats thought it included too little Fats. By then the pair were no longer making money off challenge matches, were no longer appearing much on TV, were no longer much in the public eye. A new pool revival had come but this time without them.

Fats was already split from his wife, Evelyn. He could be self-absorbed under the best of circumstances, but after he became famous, he was positively insufferable. "They didn't scream and yell, but it was more like a business relationship," said Brad Holford, recalling the end of the line for Minnesota Fats and his sweet Eva-Line. Suddenly Fats was a big TV star and seemed anxious to show off for the fans. When the admirers came calling, Evelyn disappeared into a back room; when

Fats caught a flight for an out-of-town exhibition, he left Evelyn behind. Sometimes they argued over the house: It was in her name, but he had invested thousands of dollars into it. He suggested that it get transferred to his name. She said no fucking way.

"They would fight off and on. It wasn't a close relationship," said Holford. "Part of it was Evelyn's house. He paid for everything and redid everything and modernized it, all with his money. But the actual property was in Evelyn's name. And then maybe a year or two before she booted him out, he got in trouble with the IRS. He almost went to jail.

"I was there when the IRS agent was there. Evelyn called me into the house. She put me in a bad spot. She said, 'Brad, come in here. I want you to see how Fats is acting.' And he was going berserk. I guess the IRS agents were used to stuff like that, but he was ranting and raving. He was going, 'Look at this cocksucker, mother-fucker. . . .' You know, *boom-boom-boom*. He was going off. He was really mad.

"In the last couple of years, they got along really bad. I don't know what was the last straw, but it was an overnight deal. I mean it was, today he was here, and tomorrow he was gone. I remember that Fats said one day that he was going to Nashville and he said, 'I'm never coming back to this place.' It broke my heart."

Fats ended up in that city's famous Hermitage Hotel, where he spent some of those final years feeding pigeons and stamping his autograph onto the scraps of paper and dollar bills pushed into his hands by curious guests. He lived in a $100-a-night room for $400 a month *. . . nothing but first fucking class for Minnesota Fats, you unnerstand . . .* and he spent his nights at the nearby Bull Penn Lounge where manager Mickey Goodall kept his table set aside special. On March 26, 1993, he ended up marrying the much-younger Theresa Bell. Everybody just called her called T-Bell, and she owned her own home.

He died there three years later.

•   •   •

Willie spent his retirement in Haddon Heights, being cared for by Flora, his savior and the savior of the entire Mosconi clan. She made him dinner, tended the house, cared for the new batch of grandkids. Son Bill said Willie spent much of those years shooting golf at a private club in Philly then popular with retired athletes. Willie held forth there for his cronies, drinking beer sometimes, telling stories. On June 2, 1985, the nearly scratch golfer hit a hole in one. "What's not to love about that life?" said Bill.

But Willie was slowing down, perhaps affected by that old road injury that he sustained when he and partner Ralph Greenleaf hit a pig and rolled their car. Daughter Candace blamed the trauma for the transient ischemic attacks that now unbalanced Willie with alarming frequency. And so the family eventually checked Willie into a retirement center out in Cherry Hill, which was maybe six or seven miles from his Haddon Heights home.

"He was in St. Mary's probably part of the last year of his life—it was a retirement center, you know, assisted living," said Bill. There was a pool table set up there for the residents, he said.

"The people in the nursing home wanted him to play on that table, and he would say, 'I don't want to play.' He'd say, 'You've got to pay me if you want to see me play.' But the little girls, the grandchildren, who were five or six years old—they pretty much got whatever they wanted. They'd say, 'Please, Grandpa, play, play, play!'"

And so finally Willie relented. He was seventy-three years old, hobbled by age, tired and cantankerous. Somebody racked the balls, and then it began. Boom. Boom. Boom. BOOM. "He ran them off in like fifteen seconds," said Bill.

It was an amazing feat in a lifetime of amazing feats, one of the most amazing things Bill Mosconi said he'd ever seen. He said his father died not long afterward. "I thought it was unbelievable. It was unbelievable that he could do that. His vision was incredible still. He just got up, and he tore them off. He could still get the cue ball to go wherever he wanted it to go. It was second nature.

"And then I remember he put the cue stick down, and he said, 'That's it.' And it was.

259

APPENDIX I

The following biographical pieces come from the author's "Untold Stories" columns, published in Billiards Digest *in 2006 and 2007. All articles appear with permission of the magazine.*

The Forgotten Lowell Kid: Andrew St. Jean

This is the story of Ralph Greenleaf's drinking partner, a man who was a gambler and a contender for the national championship. He was a hell-raiser of the old school—of the *very* old school—a product of Prohibition and of the Roaring Twenties. Sometimes he wore a tuxedo, sometimes a mask. He almost always carried a flask.

Welcome back to "Untold Stories." This month I'm profiling Andrew St. Jean, one of the most colorful almost-champions of our most colorful sport. In 1928 St. Jean was runner-up for the title, being bested only by the great Ralph Greenleaf himself. St. Jean also was among that stable of players contracted by the Coca-Cola Company to don masks and appear in poolrooms. They played anonymously as "Masked Marvels" as a promotional gimmick.

For this month's column I have interviewed New Englander Ray Desell, one of the nation's few experts on the life of St. Jean. I also have consulted Willie Mosconi's memoirs and those of Minnesota Fats. I gathered a few more details on Steve Booth's Web site, onepocket.org, and from the *New York Times*.

These things we know for sure: St. Jean was of French-Canadian extraction and of working-class parentage. His was a family of immigrants. His parents spoke French, and the language was also probably St. Jean's first. He was born in 1902, died in 1954, had a lifelong love of booze and gambling, was treacherous as a player but also extremely skilled. He was said to have the ability to run seventy balls one handed and during his later years made his living playing three-cushion billiards with only one hand.

And it was cirrhosis that killed him. He was buried in his home of Lowell, Massachusetts (also the home of Jack Kerouac), in his family's plot at St. Joseph's Cemetery. "He only lived a few miles from where I live now," says Desell, a resident of Lawrence, Massachusetts. "His father owned a poolroom in Lowell and . . . he liked to drink and he partied with Greenleaf many times. They both liked to go out and drink—even before they did exhibitions they would go out and get tanked."

Desell said St. Jean was the oldest of four known siblings: he had a brother and two sisters, and the sisters later became nuns. The sisters, now dead, told Desell that they lost track of St. Jean over the years, although one recalled seeing him play against Willie Hoppe during the 1920s. St. Jean also was said to frequent a social club in Lowell popular with French-Canadians. It's called the Pastetempe Club, and it's still there in downtown, looking pretty much the same as always. "He was dyed-in-the-wool Canadian, just as his whole family was," said Desell. "The French-Canadians worked in factories there, textile factories in Lawrence, Massachusetts, and Lowell. They were all textile cities, and there were many ethnic groups there, mostly working class."

One of the few known photos of St. Jean (provided to us courtesy of Mike Shamos and the Billiards Archives) reveals a man with a long nose, a rising hairline, and sleepy, languid eyes. His dark hair is rigid and slicked back. There's a straight ruler racing-stripe part on the left. Unlike many modern players, St. Jean appeared to shoot crablike, with both knees bent. In the photo he seems quite focused and plenty dignified, although I imagine he might have had a little bottle tucked away somewhere beneath the folds of his elegant coat.

Like Greenleaf, St. Jean was very much a product of the Jazz Age. Both men enjoyed celebrity (although St. Jean's was nowhere near that of Greenleaf's), and both were showboaters. St. Jean, for instance, was known to attempt spectacular and ridiculous shots that any cautious player would pass up. But then again St. Jean loved applause almost as much as he loved whisky, and he was clearly addicted to both. There were few in the pool world who could keep pace with Greenleaf when it came to drinking, but St. Jean certainly was one of them.

"I got this from people who knew him and played him, from Portland, Maine, and everywhere else. I talked to them, and they all said the same thing: St. Jean was an alcoholic . . . and he squandered his talent," said Desell. "Mosconi said the same thing. St. Jean was the greatest player in the world from the neck down. He had the physical ability."

Several old-timers, the late Eddie Taylor among them, also tell us St. Jean was a world-class one-handed player, perhaps one of the best ever. Norm "Farmer" Webber, a fixture at Cochran's in San Francisco from 1955 to 1963, said he played St. Jean just as World War II was coming to a close. "We played a match together in Portland, Maine, at Dube's Billiard Parlor in 1944 or '45," said Webber, who was interviewed by Steve Booth of onepocket.org back in 2004. "He came to play an exhibition, and I played him straight pool and beat him. . . . He was sober at the time I played him. I only beat him by one ball, 100 to 99."

Taylor, the so-called Knoxville Bear, provided Steve Booth more evidence of St. Jean's prowess. "I didn't know him, but you know who told me that he was a tremendous one-handed player? Fats told me, and another guy named Dayton Omstead, and Dayton was a pretty damn good three-cushion billiards player. He [Omstead] told me that he played St. Jean even up, and he was running three and four and going five rails and whatever, playing one handed."

Desell himself said he was told by the late Bob Ingersoll of Boston that St. Jean once ran seventy balls against him *one handed*. To my knowledge not Willie Mosconi, not Ralph Greenleaf, nor anyone else, anywhere, had ever managed such a *Ripley's Believe-It-or-Not* freak run. Fats could play one handed . . . but not like *that*. "During the 1940s

St. Jean would play three-cushion billiards one handed for $4 a game because nobody was going to play him any pool; that was just impossible," said Desell. "But you'd be asking for trouble, because he could run fifty balls with one hand. He'd just take a cue off the rack, and if you promised to buy him a beer he would do it."

In 1927, probably one of his best years as a professional, St. Jean proved that physical ability. It was in that year that he bested Greenleaf not once but twice in handicapped matches. On one occasion St. Jean didn't even need the spot, as he beat Greenleaf 1,250 points to 1,232. The following year, on April 3, St. Jean won the Eastern States Championship, which probably then was considered the most prestigious regional event in the nation.

Here's a sample of the coverage, this from the *New York Times* on April 4:

> "In one of the most sensational pocket billiard matches of the present season Andrew St. Jean defeated Arthur Woods to win the pocket billiard championship at Kreuter's Billiard Academy last night. St. Jean scored his victory 125 to 71 in only two innings, and took the championship with a record of nine victories and one defeat.

> "St. Jean was forced to watch Woods attain a run of 65 points in the first inning of their match. St. Jean, however, replied with 118 points on his first trip to the table. Woods got only six in his half of the second, and then St. Jean ran out with seven."

The article noted that St. Jean's 118 was the high run of the tournament and that he went through his ten games making 90 percent of his shots.

The *New York Times,* in an article published a few weeks later, reported that Greenleaf was keen to meet St. Jean for the national championship. Greenleaf was still smarting from those two previous exhibition losses, and it's likely that the two had posted a sizable side wager on their outcome. That means the losses probably cost Greenleaf more than just his pride. An April 23, 1928, the *New York Times* noted that Greenleaf, then the national champion, was expected to sign papers finalizing the title-match event featuring St. Jean as challenger.

"It is known that he is especially keen to meet Andrew St. Jean, twice his conqueror during the past season in handicap matches," the *Times* reported. "Charles S. Kline of the Strand Academy said yesterday that he was willing to stage another meeting between St. Jean and Greenleaf and that he intended to wire an offer to the champion. Promoter Kline said he felt certain that St. Jean would play."

St. Jean got off to a spectacular start against Greenleaf, putting the great champion on notice that he was not a man to be trifled with. Again, this from the *Times:*

> "Andrew St. Jean, who has twice defeated Ralph Greenleaf, six times champion of the world in handicap pocket billiard matches, started his scratch encounter with Greenleaf at the Strand Academy and got off to a 75-point lead, even though he divided blocks with Greenleaf.
>
> "The total score is 252–177. This is part of St. Jean's attempt to place himself in the forefront of leading challengers for the world's title. . . . St. Jean played an unbeatable game to win the opening block, 131 to 30. So efficiently did St. Jean perform that he ran out the block in nine innings."

St. Jean ended up losing the match 1,058 to 1,500. It would mark the closest he'd ever get to the summit of American pocket billiards.

Desell said that St. Jean had more success as a gambler, but even then he would sometimes beat himself. He simply lacked the discipline to stay away from tough shots. "You know, sometimes he'd be running forty balls ahead of the guy and he'd play some crazy shot and the guy would beat him," said Desell. And sometimes he'd play *too* well, as he'd scare away the cash.

Take, for instance, the story of St. Jean and the two bookies. Desell said all three had driven into a small town and checked into a hotel, and then the bookies went off to set up the game. Apparently they had gotten a line on a pigeon.

"They said, 'Andrew, stay in the hotel, order something to eat, and take it easy. We'll be back.'

"But St. Jean gets a little restless, and he went downtown, and he had a few drinks in a bar. And then he went into the street and hit another bar. And so he [gets drunk] and he's shooting pool, and he's showboating. The guy he was supposed to play there sees all this, and so the match was cancelled."

And finally there's St. Jean, the Masked Marvel. The Coca-Cola Company for several years would hire topflight players to appear unannounced in poolrooms. There these players would anonymously challenge the best local player. The Masked Marvels also performed trick shots. Afterwards the Coca-Cola promotional people would hand out free soft drinks, and the Masked Marvels would mysteriously slip away.

"The Coca-Cola Company had a few Masked Marvels—I don't know how many—but they would pay them a stipend and St. Jean was one of them," said Desell. "He also did a lot of exhibitions in New York City during the 1920s and the 1930s. He would do three-cushion exhibitions in the afternoon and he'd play at night. He really was nothing short of spectacular."

The Late Great Weenie Beenie

He wasn't the most graceful of players. He wasn't a child prodigy, didn't suffer a hard-luck life, and didn't drop out of high school or brawl. He never hustled for his next meal.

But still Weenie Beenie was a pool player of the old school, a successful business owner and one-time college boy who could get just as comfortable mingling with the country-club set as in those backwater rooms where men carry cash loose in their pockets.

This month's "Untold Stories" I devote to the paradox that was Bill "Weenie Beenie" Staton, a man simultaneously charming, dapper, and educated—but also wildly competitive, fearless, and, ultimately, a predator. He was that rare poolroom animal who could seamlessly and gracefully straddle both the straight life and the sporting one. His very name spoke to it.

One by one they're leaving us, those old-time '60s roadmen. Jack "Jersey Red" Breit died from cancer a while back; complications following a blood clot took Eddy "Knoxville Bear" Taylor last year; Billy "Cornbread Red" Burge is gone, and so too is Larry "Boston Shorty" Johnson. And now it's Weenie Beenie's turn, God bless him; Beenie passed away February 18, 2006, at Grand Strand Regional Hospital near his home in Myrtle Beach, South Carolina. He was seventy-seven.

During his life Beenie wore many hats: he was a college student, a business owner, a TV trick-shot artist, an avid golfer, a devoted husband, a father—the list goes on and on. In the pool world, his highest *official* accomplishment was his victory at the 1972 Stardust Open one-pocket tournament in Las Vegas. But Weenie Beenie also won the Virginia State Pool Championships five times, placed in the money at various national-class events, and frequently left with the cash during after-hours match play. Last year Beenie became one of the first inductees into the national One-Pocket Hall of Fame.

Steve Booth, the man behind onepocket.org and its much-appreciated hall of fame, said that in contrast to his playful-sounding name, Weenie Beenie was one of the game's most dignified and well-respected personalities. And by his willingness to wager giant pots against monster competition, said Booth, he earned for himself a reputation for fearlessness.

"He was a fantastic example of someone who can be successful as a pool player, as a gambler—but also as a parent and businessman," said Booth. "He was a real gentleman . . . a real ambassador for the game. He would fit in with any sort of crowd; he probably made more TV appearances than anybody outside Fats and Willie Mosconi. But he was also a threat to beat anyone, at any time."

For many of the truly greats—players like Steve Mizerak or Jean Balukas, for instance—pocket billiards takes hold very early on. This was not the case for Weenie Beenie, whose hometown of Concord,

North Carolina, allowed neither whisky nor wine nor poolrooms. Rather than the late-night forays so common to his contemporaries, Staton instead got a high school diploma, did his stint in the air force, and studied business at the University of North Carolina. In 1950 he migrated to Arlington, Virginia, where he teamed up with his brother Carl to open a twelve-by-twenty-foot hot-dog stand.

At the time, the area's main poolroom was Michaelson's, on Ninth Street NW. There was also Brunswick's on Irving Street, or the second-floor joint over at H Street and Thirteenth NE. Weenie Beenie eventually matched up with men like Earl Schriver at those rooms or one-pocket legend John "Rags" Fitzpatrick. He played Wimpy Lassiter and Marshall "Tuscaloosa Squirrel" Carpenter and Big Nose Roberts.

But that would come later, much later, because first Staton would have to play another role . . . and one that few national-class road players would ever admit to.

First, Weenie Beenie Bill Staton had to play the role of *sucker.*

This is what happened: Staton, then twenty-three years old, got an 11:00 p.m. call at his home. It seemed that Buddy the cook had failed to show up for his regular shift. Keeping the hot-dog stand running was Staton's responsibility. He was, after all, a *businessman.* And so he went out to Buddy's favorite haunt, a nearby poolroom named Lyle's. There he found the fry-cook deep into a fifty-point game of straights.

Now Staton knew nothing about pool, straight or otherwise, and so was unprepared when a man named "Woodbridge" approached him. Buddy said he needed another fifteen or twenty minutes to finish up, and Woodbridge quite kindly offered to help him pass the time. Maybe $2 a game?

It all seemed so innocent.

"I lost the $55 I had with me," Staton told me back in 1998, during an interview for *Hustler Days.* "I knew how to chalk up. That was about it, and he just whipped me. So I went out and bought myself a pool table, a Brunswick Anniversary table, and I practiced up. And then he whipped me again. I practiced some more, and he whipped me some more."

Staton spent better than $1,000—and that's *1950s dollars,* mind you—to recoup a $55 loss. He practiced on that top-of-the-line Brunswick, and kept practicing, and Woodbridge kept beating him. So too did just about anybody else. But Staton kept at it, he took his lumps, he took lessons, he gambled, he got better. He may have played like a chump at age twenty-three. Not so by age thirty.

"I became seriously interested in pool when I first lost money at it," he explained. "I started playing anybody. That was 1952, 1953. And it didn't make any difference who it was. I'd play people I didn't know. I would walk into poolrooms, and they would service my account. They were hustlers, and they would come from all over the country. I got to know most of the big players; players who had no way of making a living back in the 1950s. . . .

"But I was very fortunate I did not have to depend on pool to make a living. I was able to be a businessman-player. I had some little hot-dog stands. I had six at one time. And I had a truck stop, and I had two poolrooms."

And this brings us to that *other* Weenie Beenie, Weenie Beenie the businessman, Weenie Beenie the chamber-of-commerce type. He lived an impractical and improbable double life, and in some ways that dichotomy came to define him. He recalls sometimes looking both ways before going into Lyles "just to make sure none of our country-club friends were watching." He and his brother grew one hot-dog stand into many, and then he ventured into other businesses. Even his hustling name spoke to his dual nature: "Weenie Beenie" was what he called his orange and yellow hot-dog stands. At first these stands supported his expensive poolroom habit; later, his billiards' winnings helped support the hot-dog stands.

A road trip in 1960 to Blytheville, Arkansas, was responsible for funding one of the stands, Weenie Beenie told me.

"I like to say I made over $1 million on that trip," Staton said. "I won $27,000, and I went home and wanted to invest it. . . . So I declared it on my income tax and then built a little hot-dog stand. It was twelve foot wide and twenty foot long. . . . The way I figure I made $1 million is from the rent I've collected."

That was his first big score, but others would follow. He made regular road trips down to Hot Springs and was a regular in Johnston City, Illinois, before George and Paulie Jansco contemplated even the first of their famous hustlers' jamborees. It was there, during the 1963 tournament, that Weenie Beenie was driven out to the woods by bandits and relieved of more than $1,000, but he also won and lost a fortune in Detroit, at the Rack. He claimed to have wagered and won big bets against Ronnie Allen and local D.C. players.

One such player—let's just call him "Al"—had received a reputation for being the biggest locksmith in Southwest Washington. Local player Dick Yates recalls one session down at Joe's poolroom with Al and Weenie playing a game of one-pocket. "As usual Al tried to lock up Beenie in a sucker game," Yates explained. "The rules for that particular game, Weenie had to make two balls in a side pocket while Al had to make eight balls in the lower two pockets. The game went in Al's favor for quite a while. Then the stakes were raised quite a bit.

"At that point Weenie won six expensive games in a row. Seems as though Weenie knew a thing or two about locking up a sucker. During the seventh game, Al accused Weenie of cheating and demanded all his money back. Weenie told him where to go, and Al came at him with a cue stick. Al, still with the cue in hand, chased Beenie from Seventh & D streets to G Street; from G to Eighth Street; then back to Seventh & D streets. At that point Weenie jumped into his car and waved bye-bye to Al. Not only was Beenie a smarter and better pool shooter, he was also a faster runner."

And as his reputation rose, so too did his fame. His national trick-shot career began in 1965, after AMF selected him for the company's "Staff of Champions." Eventually it led to appearances on ABC's *Wide World of Sports*, ESPN, and the popular game show *I've Got a Secret*, where he sank fifteen balls in one shot. On *The Tonight Show* Staton gave a trick-shot lesson to the buxom Mamie Van Doren, who exposed an eyeful of cleavage while bending over. Johnny Carson quipped "who cares" when she missed.

His winning personality likewise contributed to the popularity of Arlington's Jack and Jill Cue Club, which Staton sometimes described as the nation's most successful poolroom. I have no idea on what he based that claim, but it's true that Jack and Jill was *always* busy. Weenie Beenie told me that it didn't matter that he once lost the front-door key because the poolroom was never empty.

"The Jack and Jill Club opened up in 1967 and never closed for one minute in fourteen years," Weenie Beenie explained. "We had waiting lists at four in the morning. This was a thirty-table poolroom. One time I had a waiting list until 7:30 in the morning. My partner and I gave everybody action. It was in the basement of a drugstore, and it didn't have one window. Not one speck of light came in. There were no clocks on the wall, and nobody knew what time it was."

The room had bleachers twenty rows high, a tournament room, big action, top road players. Regular Billy Pullen remembers the room fondly. "If anybody came to the East Coast, that's where they stopped: Jack and Jill's," said Pullen. "They had the nine-ball championship. Ed Kelly won there. They had the U.S. Open there, and every player who was a player came through. Ronnie Allen used to hang around there; Lassiter was there. It had twenty-four tables and a two-table pavilion . . . that they'd use for tournaments and all-night matches."

Weenie Beenie lost his lease on the poolroom in 1981, and then the room eventually got torn down along with the building it was in. And that's when Weenie Beenie retired to Myrtle Beach, where, during the twilight of his life, he played golf. I've never had a Weenie Beenie hot dog, but next time I'm in Arlington, I'll be sure to get one. There, over at 2680 S. Shirlington Road, you can find perhaps the last of the businesses. It's about a hundred yards from the best poolroom in the area, Champion Billiards.

During seventy-seven years on earth, Bill Staton fathered three children, became a grandfather to four, helped run six hot-dog stands, won a national championship, traded jokes with Johnny Carson, won and lost tens of thousands of dollars, challenged the likes of Ronnie Allen and Jersey Red, stayed married to his beautiful wife Norma Jean for fifty-two years, and earned the respect of friends and strangers alike.

Even if you take pool out of the equation, he lived an enviable, wildly successful life. He may have started out as a sucker, but he left us as a lion.

Rest in peace, Weenie Beenie.

The Rainmakers: Norfolk Whitey and Cleo Vaughn

A stranger walks into a poolroom. "Is there anybody in here, anybody at all, with some money?" The challenge is astonishing. A fat man and a bald man look up from a game of one-pocket. Another snorts. There are four tables, all dusty 4 by 8, and a lunch counter. The place is a rattrap.

"Is there anybody here with any money?"

The stranger is young, reedy, cocksure. There's a pool cue, in a case, slung over his right shoulder. Those gathered eye the stranger with both amusement and avarice. "Boy," says one, "there must be four people in this room with at least $10,000 in their pockets."

Perhaps the stranger went a bit pale then. Perhaps the rebuke stunned him. But what is certain is that the stranger returned to his motel room, dug around for his bankroll, and then reappeared at that backwater room the very next day.

"Make that *five* people," he said.

Welcome back to "Untold Stories." This month's column touches upon a topic that lately has come to fascinate me—the poolroom gambling economy and the gamblers who fuel it. Much has been written about the big winners, about those who bring home thousand-dollar paydays. But the winners don't fuel the subculture's economy; rather, it's the losers. Their willingness to wager large sums feeds action like shit on mushrooms. And so on behalf of losers everywhere, I say: "You're welcome."

This month's column features a casino operator and a bookmaker. That means that by definition both are professional gamblers. Many rainmaker players are: They're men who know how to make games, are accustomed to winning and losing large amounts of cash, but who can't stand up to the top pros. And so they get a spot, make a game, and hope for the best. Sometimes it works for them; sometimes it doesn't.

And when it doesn't, the results can be spectacular. There's evidence that Norfolk Whitey, the second player referenced in this column, lost $10,000 to one player, $24,000 to another, and—if you're to believe one second-hand account—$123,000 to a third. And this was in 1946! That money then got redistributed to other gamblers, who used it to match up with still other players, who would then take it and gamble with the chumps . . .. and, voilà, a poolroom economy was born.

I mention two rainmaker stories in this column, but there are countless more. Bob Henning, in his book on Billy Joe Burge, *Cornbread Red: Pool's Greatest Money Player*, talks about such a player at a poolroom in Detroit, Michigan. Eddie Beuchene, also known as "Detroit Whitey," said he once hustled a Miami department-store owner out of $72,000. I've heard similar stories about rainmakers in Houston. In each case, the players lose big, keep losing, and then that money gets redistributed through additional betting up and down the gambler food chain.

The "stranger" in the story above is none other than Bill "Weenie Beenie" Staton, who by no means is a loser. Instead, Weenie serves as our narrator, recounting for us the story of Cleo Vaughn, a bookmaker, whose willingness to wager and lose a wad attracted joyful high rollers from D.C. to Tuscaloosa. When Weenie Beenie walked into Cleo's street-level poolroom during the winter of 1960, he found there gathered Rudolf "Minnesota Fats" Wanderone, Marshall Carpenter, Earl Shriver, and Hubert "Daddy Warbucks" Cokes. They'd all come for a piece of Cleo, but then ended up gambling with each other instead.

"And remember, this was a small ratty poolroom in this little town," said Beenie. "Everybody went out there to play this guy. He was a bookmaker, and he had a lot of money, and he spread it around. . . . He was the one who attracted people there. . . . They all congregated there, and there was action galore."

Cleo's poolroom was in Blytheville, in the upper northeast corner of Arkansas. So besides high-rolling nine-ballers, Cleo's place also drew big-time gamblers like Titanic Thompson, as well as lesser-knowns from the horse tracks in Hot Springs and West Memphis. Weenie also recalls the presence of pimply-faced teenage hangers-on, which eventually drew the cops. "We were in a tough place, and the action was so high, the chief of police said 'you got to take this somewhere else.' You know, the kids were coming in after school, and the money was exchanging hands."

"And so Cleo rented this place, out in the middle of nowhere, and he told everybody to meet up there, and they hired a policeman to keep guard on the whole thing. It was behind a gas station. It was like a carport, and they had a pool table and a card table. So we started playing out there, and it was around-the-clock action."

It was there, out behind a filling station, that Weenie Beenie played Cleo Vaughn for fifty-six straight hours. Beenie said it wasn't that Cleo couldn't play pool—he could, he played it top notch—it's just that Cleo was, well, a bit on the chunky side, and so he couldn't keep up during the long sessions. "At the end of forty-something hours, we were dead even. But I was slim and he had a bit of extra weight on him, and he just ran out of gas. I beat up on him pretty good for the next thirteen hours. I won, and I beat him pretty good. . . . Afterwards, after fifty-six hours, I said, 'Who's next?'"

Beenie also played one of the world's most renowned cheats: Titanic Thompson.

"I never will forget this: I would play this proposition game that I could make twenty-something balls. And Titanic, he was racking the balls, and he put glue on his hands. You know, he was a cheater. And so I'm trying to run the balls, and they wouldn't break up. There was fuzz on the table, and that was also sticking on the balls. He had put the glue on his hands, and it was just enough to make the balls stick together when you tried to break."

Norfolk Whitey Howard

Although the action at Cleo's place was rough and heady, it pales in comparison to that of Norfolk, Virginia, which during the 1940s became the greatest action town ever. There you could find all the top players: Wimpy Lassiter, Marcel Camp, Rags Fitzpatrick, Johnny Irish,

Minnesota Fats. I've written previously about the influence of the military during those days—how the shipwrights and the World War II recruits flooded the town with fast money. I've written about the bachelor culture that was in full bloom during those years. But eyewitnesses also note a much more direct cause for those Norfolk glory days. Many credit a single man: Charles "Norfolk Whitey" Howard, an excellent pool player, an excellent gambler . . . and a man unafraid of losing money.

And sweet Jesus, how he lost money. A full twenty years before Cleo Vaughn lost his thousands, Norfolk Whitey lost ten times that amount. He would gamble on *everything*: pool, horses, probably even the time of day. "It's pretty well documented that he bet three games of baseball, for $150,000 each, in one day, and lost all three," said Bob McKown, an old friend. "He said he wasn't worried about it. He said with the system he had, he'd bounce right back."

What do we know about Norfolk Whitey? Through interviews with McKown, veteran player George Rood, stake horse Rusty Miller, Rags Fitzpatrick widow Christine Schafer, and others, a picture begins to emerge. First off, Whitey likely made millions in Norfolk through the operation of speakeasy-style nightclubs. They have been identified variously as "The Commando Club," "The Zam-Zam Club," "Piney Point," or simply "Whitey's."

Those that remember them said they included floor shows, wide-open casino gambling, and food. Whitey was said to have drawn $10,000 cash money, each week, from those clubs. And that was in 1940s dollars—that equates to about a half million a year these days—making Whitey wealthy indeed.

Fats, in his autobiography, recalls one:

> "Back then, there were about 300 high rollers all told around Norfolk and when the good times started in the 1940s, Whitey happened to be one of the high rollers himself. But Whitey hit a real hot streak and won enough cash to buy a piece of property about 14 miles out of downtown Norfolk and he built a fabulous joint to accommodate the 300 genuine high rollers and nobody else.

"Whitey ran a very discriminating joint on account he wouldn't allow a sucker near it. He always said suckers were good for one thing: trouble. So by word-of-mouth he let it be known that suckers were not welcome at his place, which was a tremendous arrangement because if you happened to break a guy down to his alligator-skin shoes, you never had to worry that he needed the money to feed a wife and a half-dozen kids. Whitey only skinned his own kind.

"Whitey had every known gambling game at his joint and if you happened to be a pool player he even had a special billiard room where you could go broke in quiet and peace with as little pain as possible."

George Rood, now ninety years old, got to Norfolk in 1947. Although he didn't play Whitey directly, he credits Whitey for much of the high action in the city and the poolroom economy there generally. Rood said that he couldn't even get a game for less than $500 and that he won $1,900 on his very first day in town. Rood figured that much of that money came indirectly from Whitey's pocket.

"Everybody was down there, and they were all playing for big money, so that's why I went down. I went to one downtown pool hall—and there couldn't have been more than seven or eight tables—and they charged us time on the table according to how much we won. I remember he charged me $200 for one session. I was a little bit shocked by that.

"And it was his [Whitey's] money that was being redistributed by the time I got there, and so everybody had it. I heard from everybody that he had got this bankroll, and they all had a part of it. There was just a whole lot of money involved."

Reader Bob McKown, who knew Whitey during his final years in Norfolk, said he was also pretty sure that Whitey won his share.

"Whitey played one-pocket, gin rummy, and consistently beat the bookies at professional football and basketball. He had his regular pigeons that he played, and never did he ever bet with or play anyone that could not afford to lose the money. He never hustled the common man. He was above that. Rarely did he ever lose. He ran it like a business. I'm sure he knew to the dollar how much he won over the years. He was also very secretive and not one to ever boast or brag. . . . It is really no telling how much money he made over the years, but for sure he dealt in the millions."

And finally, stakehorse Rusty Miller tells us that "because of Whitey, when all the other players who weren't in the army and navy finally started getting out, they all migrated to Norfolk. Fatty was in Norfolk. Titanic Thompson was there, too.

"But the major draw was Whitey. I saw him lose $22,000 in one day. I'm talking about $22,000 in 1944 dollars. And the next day, the same guy who won that money lost most of it. Whitey was the centerpiece of the action. As a result I saw every famous pool player known to mankind. They all came in the hopes of playing Whitey."

APPENDIX II

14.1 STRAIGHT-POOL CHAMPIONSHIPS: THE WILLIE MOSCONI ERA

Year	Date	Location	Winner	Runner-Up
1940/1941	Nov 26–May 2	Eight Rooms in Five Cities	Willie Mosconi	Andrew Ponzi
1941	Oct 20–Nov 7	Town Hall, Philadelphia	Erwin Rudolf	Irving Crane
1942(n)	Mar 24–26	Philadelphia	Ralph Greenleaf	Andrew Ponzi
1942	May 7–9	St. Margaret Mary's Men's Club, Rochester, NY	Irving Crane	Erwin Rudolf
1942	Nov 30–Dec 5	Detroit Recreation Building Detroit	Willie Mosconi	Andrew Ponzi
1943	Apr 13–17	King & Allen's Kansas City, MO	Andrew Ponzi	Willie Mosconi
1944*	Feb 29–Mar 4	King & Allen's Kansas City, MO	Willie Mosconi	Andrew Ponzi
1945*	Jan 29–Feb 24	Four-City Tour	Willie Mosconi	Ralph Greenleaf
1946*	Feb 4–Mar 30	Ten-City Tour	Willie Mosconi	Jimmy Caras
1946	Dec 2–12	Town Hall Philadelphia	Irving Crane	Willie Mosconi
1947*	May 8–18	Two-City Tour	Willie Mosconi	Irving Crane

1947*	Oct 25–Nov 12	Two-City Tour	Willie Mosconi	Jimmy Caras
1948(n)	Feb 27–Mar 4	Navy Pier, Chicago	Andrew Ponzi	Arthur Cranfield
1948*	May 5–7	Navy Pier, Chicago	Willie Mosconi	Andrew Ponzi
1949(n)	Feb 4–10	Navy Pier, Chicago	Jimmy Caras	Irving Crane
1949	Feb 11–13	Navy Pier, Chicago	Jimmy Caras	Willie Mosconi
1950(n)[1]	Feb 10–16	Navy Pier, Chicago	Irving Crane	Willie Mosconi
1950	Feb 17–19	Navy Pier, Chicago	Willie Mosconi	Irving Crane
1951*	Jan 8–19	Two-City Tour	Willie Mosconi	Irving Crane
1951(n)	Feb 15–22	Navy Pier, Chicago	Joe Canton	George Chenier
1951	Feb 23–25	Navy Pier, Chicago	Willie Mosconi	Irving Crane
1952	Mar 24–Apr 5	Bond Billiard Room Boston	Willie Mosconi	Irving Crane
1953	Mar 2–12	Downtown Bowl San Francisco	Willie Mosconi	Joe Procita
1954	No Sanctioned Tournament			
1955*	Feb 21–Mar 11	Newby's Billiard Academy Philadelphia	Willie Mosconi	Joe Procita
1955	Apr 16–23	The Arena Philadelphia	Irving Crane	Willie Mosconi
1955*	Nov 28–Dec 2	Allinger's Billiard Academy Philadelphia	Willie Mosconi	Irving Crane
1956*	Jan 30–Feb 25	Six-City Tour	Willie Mosconi	Jimmy Caras
1956*	Mar 15–20	Les Bow's Billiard Room Albuquerque, NM	Willie Mosconi	Jimmy Moore
1956	Apr 2–16	Sportsman Billiard Room Kinston, NC	Willie Mosconi	Irving Crane
1956(n)	Oct 27–Nov 18	Judice's Billiard Academy Brooklyn, NY	Luther Lassiter	Mike Euphemia
1957	No Sanctioned Tournament			
1958	No Sanctioned Tournament			
1959	No Sanctioned Tournament			
1960	No Sanctioned Tournament			
1961	No Sanctioned Tournament			
1962	No Sanctioned Tournament			

*Challenge Matches   (n) National Title   Source: Charles Ursitti

[1] According to Charles Ursitti, this tournament was the first to feature the smaller 9 by 4½ table as the official tournament-sized table. Before that, the bigger 5 by 10s had been standard. That means there had not yet been any tournament records set on this smaller-sized table. Willie wasted no time in setting new ones, first with a run of 111; then he beat that new record with a run of 133, and then he beat that record with a run of 141. These new records all came during this 1950 tournament.

END NOTES

Chapter 1: The Champ

The description of Willie Mosconi's altercation with Fats in October of 1977 is based mostly on the recollections of Charles Ursitti. An affidavit attesting to Mosconi's high run is on record at the Smithsonian Institute. References to his first tournament victory come from various newspapers, including the *Chicago Daily Tribune*.

Chapter 2: The Usurpers

Willie's comments regarding pool's being a family game and that he played in plush billiard academies comes from a March 27, 1975, article in the *Houston Post*. The public-relations department at Brunswick Billiards provided much of the pool history in this chapter. Mosconi was quoted as saying "ours is an honorable game" in an undated "Morning Line" column by Mike McKenzie that appeared in Section D of an unknown paper. The author obtained the newspaper clipping from the private collection of Bill and Judy Mosconi.

Chapter 3: The TV Disaster

As noted, this chapter draws heavily from Ned Polsky's *Hustlers, Beats and Others* (Aldine Transaction, reprint edition, April 30, 2006); Melvin Adelman's *A Sporting Time: New York City and the Rise of Modern Athletics* (University of Illinois Press; reprint edition, January 1, 1990); and interviews with Charles Ursitti. The author also referred to an undated edition of the *Pittsburgh Press,* which came from Bill and Judy Mosconi's private collection. The author's conversation with Bruce Christopher, also referenced in the chapter, occurred in August of 2005.

Chapter 4: The Kingdom

This chapter draws from *A Sporting Time: New York City and the Rise of Modern Athletics*, by Melvin Adelman. The Mosconi genealogy information is from the family records of Bill and Judy Mosconi. These records include the birth and baptism certificates of Willie Mosconi. As noted, the author also drew from Willie Mosconi's published memoirs, *Willie's Game* (Macmillan Publishing Company, April 1993), written with Stanley Cohen, and again from Polsky's *Hustlers, Beats and Others*. Additional information regarding Willie's early years came from a 1984 interview with Mosconi by journalist Paul Jayes; an October 25, 1947, article by Clive Howard in the *Star Weekly* (published in Toronto, Canada); a 1988 article in the *Los Angeles Times*; an interview with Mosconi that appeared in a July 1962 edition of the *Bowlers Journal*; and an undated newspaper clipping from the Mosconi family collection.

Chapter 5: Odysseus and Eurymachus

Some of the details about the early life of Rudolf Wanderone were taken from his memoirs, *The Bank Shot and Other Great Robberies* (The Lyons Press, reprint, 2006), written with Tom Fox. Reference to the arrival of Rosa Wanderone at Ellis Island can be found at the American Family Immigration History Center, which can be accessed online. The author also reviewed census data and physically visited the childhood home of Wanderone in Washington Heights. Probate information in the *New York Times* provided the author a physical address: 403 West 148th Street, in upper Manhattan. A promotional poster in the possession of Bill and Judy Mosconi is referenced in a footnote. References to the Masked Marvel players come from the recollection of Wanderone and others, and photographs and references can be found throughout billiards literature, including at the Billiards Archives, which is curated by Mike Shamos. However, the Coca-Cola Company has no specific record of the early-twentieth-century marketing gimmick.

Chapter 6: Roadmen

Mosconi's observation that he had not contemplated pursuing pool as a lifelong profession came from a January 8, 1982, edition of the *Philadelphia Daily News*. The location of Jim Jacobs and Hal Cayton's office at 9 East Fortieth Street in Manhattan comes from Charles Ursitti. The promoter/historian also provided plenty of additional information about Jacobs and Cayton, including details about their background in the boxing world and Cayton's back injury. The reference to Mosconi's public challenge of Fats came from Willie's memoirs, written with Stanley Cohen, as cited above. Ursitti also spoke of the fruitless challenge, as did Willie Mosconi himself in various newspaper interviews. For instance, there's a reference to the challenge in a February 16, 1978, clipping provided to the author by the Mosconi family. The clipping does not reference the newspaper of origin. Ursitti described his road trip to the Mosconi home and his contact with Wanderone for the signing of a contract.

Chapter 7: A Nation of Rottweilers

Willie's observation that he was "not a poolhall guy" is cited from his interview with Gerry Dulac of the *Pittsburgh Press*. The undated newspaper clipping was provided to the author by the Mosconi family. The author draws observations about the Great Depression from *Only Yesterday: An Informal History of the 1920s,* by historian Frederick Allen Lewis (Blue Ribbon Books, 1931). Mosconi's observation that "it was like having a weight lifted from my shoulders" came from his memoirs written with Stanley Cohen, as referenced above. Various newspapers also included Mosconi's numerous observations about his family's plight during the Depression, including a February 26, 1984, interview with Maralyn Lois Polak in the *Philadelphia Inquirer,* in which Willie said, "Yeah, I was hungry. My whole family was hungry. And we had to eat. I did my damndest to win because we needed the money."

Willie's recollections of Beinfield's son were included in his memoirs, as cited above. The author also drew from an interview with Willie Mosconi by Mort Luby Jr. in a July 1962 edition of *Bowlers Journal* and a 1984 interview with Mosconi by journalist Paul Jayes and provided to the author by the Mosconi family. Mosconi's observation that "I always had access to a table, but it wasn't until my mother and father became sick that I took it seriously" came from a November 10, 1986, edition of the *Arkansas Democrat*. That newspaper is also the source of a later-referenced observation by Mosconi that he finds pool to be a "stupid game." The author also references an *Atlantic City Sunday Press* article from the Mosconi family collection. The date is unknown. Also included in this chapter are observations from Willie's family—son Bill Mosconi, daughter Candace Fritch, and wife Flora Mosconi—taken from interviews conducted by the author.

Chapter 8: Creation Myth

Some of the details of Fats's early life are taken from his memoirs, written with Tom Fox. The author has expanded on those facts and cross-referenced them when possible by reviewing census data and probate information in the *New York Times*. Many of the outlandish claims made by Fats, such as playing the kaiser and the shah of Iran and whatnot, were taken from an October 12, 1982, article in the *Philadelphia Daily News*. However, such claims can be found repeatedly in his interviews printed in scores of newspapers. His reference to not playing in a tuxedo and "jack-offs playing in tuxedos" is taken from a July 17, 1978, article in *Rolling Stone*.

This chapter also includes various references to Wanderone from the *New York Times* in 1931 and in Chicago's *Billiards Magazine* in 1932, as cited in the text. The description of Fats and Willie's first encounter comes from various journalistic accounts, including a 1982 interview with George Gamester that appeared in the *Toronto Star*. Both men's memoirs also provide descriptions—albeit contradictory ones—of the encounter.

Chapter 9: Fats versus Willie, Round 1

Frankie Mason's instructions to Willie to play Fats come from Willie's 1961 interview with Dave Lewis, the sports editor of California's *Long Beach Independent-Press-Telegram*. Descriptions of hustling techniques come from *Hustlers, Beats and Others,* by Polsky; through a review of newspaper clippings that include interviews with famous hustlers like Wimpy Lassiter; and through the author's interviews with famous hustlers, such as Jersey Red. Much of this material has been cited previously in *Hustler Days* (Dyer, The Lyons Press, 2003). Information about Jimmy Caras comes from a biographical piece about him by *Billiards Digest* columnist George Fels, published in 1993. Fels also set the author straight about the reputation of Babyface Whitlow during a conversation in Las Vegas on June 22, 2007.

Details about the initial matchup between Fats and Willie come from both men's memoirs and from newspaper accounts, including a 1961 edition of the *Long Beach California Independent-Press-Telegram,* a 1982 edition of the *Toronto Star,* and a January 1996 article in the *Los Angeles Times.*

Chapter 10: Jawing the Yellow Ball

The story of Willie's first appearance on the world stage draws heavily from journalistic accounts in several newspapers, including the *Chicago Daily Tribune,* the *Chicago Daily News,* the *Minneapolis Star,* and the *New York Times.* Research assistant Sofia Dyer helped her father review the microfilm. A footnoted reference to Greenleaf's 1931 world-tournament victory comes from a listing of world tournaments created by Charles Ursitti. The promoter/historian also provided additional insight into Willie's initial tournament foray. *Billiards Digest* founder Mort Luby Jr. also provided information about this tournament in a July 1962 piece on Mosconi.

Willie's memoirs provide more details of those early tournament days, including Willie's recollection of his first Ranbow cue and his recollection of sending money home to his father. References to Ralph Greenleaf and the World Tournament of 1931 come from research by historian Charles Ursitti, a column by George Fels, and the *New York Times*. References to Andrew St. Jean are taken from Ursitti, an interview with St. Jean expert Ray Desell of Massachusetts, a Ken Shouler piece for *Bowler's Journal,* and Mosconi's memoirs.

Chapter 11: *Wide World of Sports*

This chapter draws heavily from *Wide World of Sports: The First 25 years* (NYLAC Network, 1987). For instance, excerpts from Roone Arledge's famous letter outlining his ideas for the now-iconic sports program came from this book. The "long-time associate" referenced here is Dennis Lewin, former *Wide World of Sports* coordinating producer. He is quoted throughout this chapter.

Chapter 12: Ralph and Willie

As noted, this chapter draws heavily from the insights of Brunswick historian Joe Newell, who spoke on several occasions to the author. Also, this chapter draws from Brunswick's official history: *Brunswick: The Story of an American Company, the First 150 Years,* by Rick Kogan (Brunswick, 1995). The only references found to Mosconi's 112-day tour with Greenleaf come directly or indirectly from Willie Mosconi himself, from his memoirs, in his separate *Willie Mosconi's Winning Pocket Billiards* (Three Rivers Press, reprint edition, 1995), and in newspaper interviews. Willie's children also have recalled stories their father told them of his road trips with Greenleaf.

Specific references to Sylvester Livingston, the promoter, were included in Willie's memoirs and in *Winning Pocket Billiards*. Also, the author indirectly cites *The Encyclopedia of Sports* by Clement Trainer. Author John Grissim, in his book *Billiards,* makes reference to the book, although the author could not acquire an original copy.

Chapter 13: The Trickster

Descriptions of the ABC film crew in Little Egypt are taken from the author's interviews with several local residents, but most especially John Ogolini, Luciano Lencini, and Brad Holford. ABC's Dennis Lewin also recalls sending the film crew to Little Egypt. Promoter/historian Charles Ursitti also spoke to the author on several occasions for this chapter.

Chapter 14: The Prophet

As noted, much of the information from Willie's 1938 tournament appearance comes from the *New York Times*. Also, promoter/historian Charles Ursitti provided perspective, as did the introduction to Mosconi's book, *Winning Pocket Billiards*. That his victories in 1940– 41 came on 5 by 10 tables comes from a posthumously reprinted interview with Mosconi that appeared in the September–October 1981 edition of *Billiard Digest*. The same is true of Mosconi's observation that "in addition to position play, I was always a good defensive player" and that he had nine runs of 125 or better in the 1940–41 tournament.

Information about Willie's first wife, Anna Harrison, comes from brief references in his memoirs, family records, and sketchy recollections of Willie's children. In particular, Bill Mosconi spoke about his mother during interviews June 20–21, 2006. The detail that Anna was in New York before meeting Mosconi is surmised by a review of Bill Mosconi's birth record. Information about the King Edwards Hotel was taken from the library of the New York Historical Society near Central Park in Manhattan.

Willie's declaration that "when the hustlers came to town, they would have to play me because I was the youngest" comes from a June 21, 1989, *Los Angeles Times* article by Dan Le Batard. Observations about the Better Billiards Program were related to the author by historian/collectors Charles Ursitti and Joe Newell.

Chapter 15: Wagers Made with Suckers

The story of Rudolf Wanderone and the teenage Dorothy Hawkins comes from *Rage to Survive, the Etta James Story*, written with David Ritz (Villard, May 23, 1995). Some biographical information about Willie Best, the actor, comes from the IMDB.com Web site. Wanderone's boasting about his side betting on Willie Mosconi's first world-tournament victory comes from Wanderone's memoirs. Author/historian Mike Shamos reminds us that Arthur Thurnblad was a former billiards champion.

Chapter 16: Hermes and Krishna

The author's observations about the trickster archetype are drawn largely from two books: Lewis Hyde's *Trickster Makes This World* (North Point Press, 1999) and Charles Lemert's *Muhammad Ali: Trickster Celebrity in the Culture of Irony* (Polity Press, 2003).

Chapter 17: The Best Trick Yet

For further details about Fats's arrival in Little Egypt, see *Hustler Days* (The Lyons Press, 2003). The references here draw largely from the author's previous research for that book, including the author's interviews with local residents Jess Kennedy, Ron Lively, St. Nicholas Hotel owner Joe Scoffic, and Fats's first wife, Evelyn Wanderone. Historian Mike Shamos spoke to the author about Brunswick during an interview on July 10, 2006.

Chapter 18: Duty and Responsibility

The author reviewed articles by the Associated Press and the *Bowlers Journal*, as already noted in the text. Bill Mosconi provided the author with a description of Philadelphia's Town Hall. The discussion of the tie-breaker agreement in Philadelphia during the 1941 tournament was provided by *Billiards Digest* founder Mort Luby Jr. in his July 1972 profile of Mosconi.

This chapter also includes information from the birth certificate of William Mosconi Jr. and additional information from Willie's memoirs. References to Willie's marriage to Anna come from family records, provided by Bill and Judy Mosconi. Descriptions of Willie's character come from multiple sources, including his children, Bill Mosconi and Candace Fritch. This chapter also includes information from several major newspapers, but most especially a November 7, 1941, *New York Times* article and a November 19, 1942, *Los Angeles Times* article. Charles Ursitti contributed information to this chapter.

Chapter 19: The Fats & Willie Show

The folklorelike telling of Wanderone's supposed pool game with the shah of Persia is based upon Wanderone's numerous tellings of that fanciful story. Willie's story that he left hustlers penniless comes from a June 21, 1989, article in the *Los Angeles Times.* The story of Mosconi's matchup in Kansas City with Benny Allen and Walter Franklin comes from a conversation between the pool champion and Gerry Dulac, published in the *Pittsburgh Press.* That undated press clipping comes from the private collection of the Mosconi family.

The reference to Fats carrying the pool case for Babyface Alton Whitlow and Willie claiming to have beaten him badly comes from a 1982 article by George Gamester in the *Toronto Star* newspaper. That press clipping was also provided to the author by the Mosconi family. Fats's claims to have known Conrad Hilton when he was looking for work and playing Atlantic City before there was a boardwalk come from a colorful soliloquy by Fats recorded in the *Philadelphia Daily News* on October 13, 1982.

As noted, the author also interviewed George Rood for descriptions of the Norfolk glory days. This chapter also includes information previously reported in *Hustler Days* and in *Billiards Digest,* as part of the author's "Untold Stories" column (www.billiardsdigest.com/untold_stories/rainmaker.php). The chapter includes information about the sudden departure of Anna Harrison taken from various interviews with Bill Mosconi. Bill and his sister Candace Fritch also talked to the author about their experiences growing up in New Jersey. The author reviewed the record of Willie Mosconi's December 3, 1945, honorable discharge from the U.S. Army. That Willie Mosconi lived in Kansas City after 1947 comes from a reference in his memoirs, with supporting references from various newspaper accounts.

Chapter 20: Fats's No. 1 Helper

This chapter draws from several interviews with Du Quoin resident Brad Holford, mostly conducted in June of 2006.

Chapter 21: Penelope and Ithaca

Bill Mosconi told the story of his father's relationship with Madelyn O'Day. Willie Mosconi described his exchange with C. P. Binner in his memoirs. References to his numerous tournament victories between 1947 and 1952 were drawn from Charles Ursitti's research and contemporary newspaper accounts. Flora Mosconi also spoke at length to the author for this chapter. The author conducted numerous interviews with Flora Mosconi in 2005 and 2006, including one at her Haddon Heights home. Bill Mosconi also provided the author with further details about his father's courtship of Flora.

Chapter 22: Records

This chapter included information gathered through the author's September 2006 interviews with Judy Bruney, Ronald Collins, Dick Hatfield, Bud Fry, and Tom Stafford. Dick Hatfield's gracious assistance was especially useful. The Mosconi family provided the author with an affidavit attesting to his 1954 high run in Springfield, Ohio. That affidavit can be found online at the Smithsonian Institution. The chapter includes some of Willie's comments included in his memoirs.

The chapter references an October 25, 1947, article by Clive Howard in the *Star Weekly* (Toronto). It references several articles in the *Springfield News and Sun,* including the March 20, 1954, article that appeared the day after Willie's high run. Virginia Weygandt, senior curator of collections for the Clark County Historical Society, sent the author information about Springfield during the 1950s. The reference to Gloria's birth comes from Mosconi family records and a conversation between the author and Bill Mosconi. This chapter also describes Willie's 1956 victory in North Carolina and is largely drawn from references in the *Kinston Daily Free Press.*

Chapter 23: Polsky's Lament

As noted, this chapter draws from Grissim's *Billiards,* and from Polsky's *Hustlers, Beats and Others.* The author also included information from the Billiard Congress of America Web site. The chapter includes information gathered by Charles Ursitti, with details surmised from a review of all *New York Times* articles referencing billiards during the late 1950s. The chapter also references a July 7, 1959, article in the *New York Daily News*. As noted, details about the 1954 championship in Philadelphia, won by Luther Lassiter, were drawn from the *Philadelphia Inquirer*. For context, the author also consulted the *Billiard Congress of America's Official Rules and Record Book* (Billiard Congress of America, The Lyons Press, 2005).

Chapter 24: The Bite Artist

This chapter draws largely from the author's interviews with John Ogolini, conducted during the late 1990s, with some details courtesy of Du Quoin resident Brad Holford.

Chapter 25: The Stroke

This chapter draws largely from numerous interviews with Willie's family, including interviews with Flora Mosconi, Bill Mosconi, and Candace Fritch. As noted, Bill Mosconi recounted to the author several stories about his father's uncompromising nature. John Ogolini spoke about Evelyn Wanderone in Du Quoin. This author also interviewed Charles Lemert, who wrote *Muhammad Ali: Trickster Celebrity in the Culture of Irony*. The author also referenced his book. A February 26, 1984, article in the *Philadelphia Inquirer* by Maralyn Lois Polak provided more details about Willie Mosconi's stroke and his recovery. The author also reviewed the *Philadelphia Inquirer's* and the *New York Times's* coverage of the 1958 tournament. The sixth commemorative edition of the *Official Publication of the National Italian American Sports Hall of Fame,* published in 2000, provided additional information.

Chapter 26: *The Hustler*

The author watched *The Hustler* again before he wrote this chapter. He also spoke to Bill Mosconi and Flora Mosconi about their memories of

Paul Newman and the filming of the Robert Rossen movie in New York City. This chapter references a February 14, 1959, article in the *New York Times*; a March 19, 1961, article in the *New York Times*; a March 19, 1961, article in the *New York Herald Tribune*; a July 14, 1963, article in the *New York Herald Tribune*; a July 15, 1963, report by Ward Cannel for the Newspaper Enterprise Association; and a story about *The Hustler* published in the November 1961 edition of the *Bowlers Journal*. As noted, it also references John Grissim's book *Billiards* and various additional articles from the *New Orleans States-Item*, *Newsweek*, and the *Chicago Sun-Times*.

Chapter 27: Hustlers and Scufflers

The author drew from his previous interviews with Little Egypt residents John Ogolini, Luciano Lencini, and Dave McNeal. He also reviewed television news coverage of Johnston City he discovered at www.youtube.com and references an article in the *Long Beach Independent-Press-Telegram*. In a November 20, 2006, interview, former champion Ed Kelly spoke about Willie Mosconi's 1966 West Coast tournament appearance. For this chapter the author also spoke with promoters Jay Helfert and Charles Ursitti, with historian Mike Shamos, and with Willie's son Bill. The author reviewed contemporay newspaper accounts of the 1966 tournament, including those published by the Associated Press.

Chapter 28: Willie's Trap

Karen Fox has spoken to the author on numerous occasions about the creation of *The Bankshot and other Great Robberies,* the memoirs of Minnesota Fats. Fox's late husband Tom Fox wrote the book based on interviews with Wanderone and his then-wife Evelyn. This chapter references the book. Information from the author's interviews with Jay Helfert were included in this chapter. Willie spoke about an aborted lawsuit in his memoirs. The author spoke to Willie's son Bill and Willie's widow Flora for this chapter.

Chapter 29: Three Weeks in Johnston City

The author interviewed former champion Ed Kelly for this chapter. He also referenced Grissim's book *Billiards*. Information about Paulie Jansco was taken from interviews with JoAnn Jansco and Dave McNeal.

Chapter 30: The Death of Willie's Game

This chapter includes details about straight pool from Mike Shamos's *Illustrated Encyclopedia of Pool*. Fats sneering about old brokes playing for cigarettes was gathered from a 1978 interview with the hustler broadcast on ABC. The chapter likewise draws from a televised Johnston City news feature by Dick Kay of Chicago's News 5 TV. The news feature was obtained through the magic of youtube.com. The date of the interview is unknown, although it was probably conducted during a Johnston City tournament during the early 1960s. The author also interviewed former champion Ed Kelly for this chapter, as well as Jay Helfert, Charles Ursitti, Brad Holford, and the promotions director for table-maker Valley-Dynamo, Dave Courington. The chapter references a Matt Racki III article in the August 1973 edition of *National Bowlers Journal*. Willie Mosconi's description of Fats as a "big bag of no-show" comes from a November 16, 1982, newspaper clipping provided by the Mosconi family. The name of the publication was not included in the clipping.

Chapter 31: 1978

As noted, this chapter draws from an interview with Dennis Lewin, the former coordinating producer of ABC's *Wide World of Sports*. Brad Holford also spoke at length with the author about his trip to New York City in 1978. The chapter includes information from an interview with promoter Jay Helfert.

Chapter 32: The Great Shoot-Out

This chapter draws from an interview with Charles Ursitti and includes other details gathered from the author's conversation with Brad

Holford. The author also reviewed video tape of ABC's coverage of the Great Pool Shoot-Out. Mosconi's comments that Fats ". . . can't play. He's a phony" come from the October 18, 1982, edition of *USA Today*. This chapter also includes information from a February 16, 1978, newspaper clipping provided by the Mosconi family but from an unknown publication.

Chapter 33: Behind the Eight-Ball

This chapter draws from a videotape recording of the Great Pool Shoot-Out and from interviews with Brad Holford. Viewership information was provided by Nielsen Media Research and from an article in the June 1978 edition of the *National Bowlers Journal & Billiards Revue*. The author included comments from Dennis Lewin. Fats's challenge that he would take on Willie Mosconi at "any time, any place, for any amount living or dead!" came from an article in the *New Jersey Sunday Press* by Patrick Pawling. The undated article was provided to the author by the Mosconi family.

Chapter 34: Willie and the Trickster

The story about Willie's high run at the Flamingo Hotel in 1979 comes from two sources: the obituary of Mosconi written by Tom Shaw of *Pool & Billiard Magazine* and an interview with Charles Ursitti by the author. This chapter also draws from the March–April 1979 edition of *Billiards Digest*. Charles Ursitti and Flora Mosconi recounted the story of Fats sitting down with the Mosconis at the hotel restaurant. Flora Mosconi also spoke to the author about some of the later challenge matches between her husband and Fats. A videotaped compilation of various Fats and Mosconi challenge matches shows Fats coming within one ball of beating Mosconi during one of the annual events. That Fats won one of his challenge matches outright was recorded in the November 1984 edition of the *National Billiard News*. The author reviewed the transcript of an interview with John Ogolini that was conducted in the late 1990s. The anecdote of the Philadelphia bartender not recalling Mosconi's name but recalling that of Minnesota Fats was taken from a January 21, 1978, article in the *Philadelphia Inquirer,* written by Lee Winfrey. Again, the author drew some guidance with regard to the trickster in folklore from two books: Lewis Hyde's *Trickster Makes This World* (North Point Press, 1999) and Charles Lemert's *Muhammad Ali: Trickster Celebrity in the Culture of Irony* (Polity Press, 2003).

Epilogue

The information in the epilogue draws from interviews with Bill Mosconi and Candace Fritch. The mellowing Willie Mosconi admitted to liking Minnesota Fats in an October 12, 1982, edition of the *Philadelphia Daily News.* As noted, this epilogue references the *New York Times* obituary of Willie Mosconi and the *Los Angeles Times* obituary of Rudolf Wanderone. Flora Mosconi spoke to the author for the epilogue.

GLOSSARY

action: The presence of wagers or people willing to place wagers.

army: Betting money ("I've got an *army* with me.")

backer: A person who provides financial support for a pool player. He funds wagers and expenses and in return receives a percentage of winnings. See also *stakehorse*.

ball in hand: Placing the *cue ball* anywhere within a specified area of the table after a *scratch* or *foul,* generally used in *nine-ball.* This is opposed to the more traditional method of placing a *cue ball* behind the *string,* or behind the end diamonds, which is common after a *foul* in many forms of pool.

big action: The exchange of large wagers.

bird dog: A person who arranges matches and hustles, for a cut of the *action*.

bite artist: Moocher.

break: The initial shot of any pool game, usually with the cue placed behind the *string* or in the *kitchen*.

C-note: A one-hundred-dollar bill.

call shot: A shot that requires the player to tell others which ball he intends to shoot into which pocket.

cue ball: The white ball, used for targeting other balls.

dead nuts: Extreme skill. See also *nuts*.

diamonds: The markings, generally placed about a foot apart, on the *rails* of a table. These are used in various targeting systems and for judging the placement of the *cue ball* after a *foul.*

dumping: Intentionally and fraudulently losing a game, so as to divvy up a *backer*'s money with the other player.

easy action: Relative ease in finding pool players with whom to gamble.

fast action: The frequent exchange of wagers of any size.

foul: Any illegal move on the pool table, such as pocketing the *cue ball,* hitting the *cue ball* twice with the cue stick, or failing to hit a *rail* with the *object ball* or *cue ball* in *one-pocket.* Generally results in loss of turn and the *spotting* of a ball. See also *scratch.*

fun player: Amateur; tournament player.

G: One thousand dollars.

heavyweight: A topflight player.

high run: The number of balls pocketed consecutively, without missing, in one game or tournament.

jarring: Placing a Mickey in the drink of an opponent to foul his game.

jaw: The sides of the pocket (a *jawed* ball is an *object* ball that hits the sides of the pocket and bounces back and forth without dropping.)

kick: A shot in which the *cue ball* strikes a *rail* before contacting the *object ball.*

kitchen: The area on the far end of the table behind the *string;* that is, the imaginary line running between the two end diamonds on the table. This is the traditional placement area for *break* shots, for the *cue ball* after a *scratch.*

knife and fork: Hustlers' eating and sleeping money; i.e., money required for basic survival.

lemoning: A hustler's custom of not playing up to his full *speed,* or ability. This is done in order to fool a *mark* into increasing the wager. Also referred to as "playing on the lemon."

lock or **lock-up:** A game that can't be lost, because of an inferior opponent or an insurmountable *spot.*

locksmiths: Hustlers who specialize in playing *lock-up* games.

making games: (1) Convincing somebody to gamble; (2) Negotiating a wager, the form of pool, and any handicap.

mark: A pool hustler's potential victim. See also *sucker; pigeon.*

masse: Extreme English on a cue ball, requiring that the cue stick be held in an almost vertical fashion.

matching up: Negotiating the form of pool and any handicap on a money game.

miscue: A *scratch* or missed shot, caused by the cue tip's making inadequate contact with the *cue ball.*

money game: A game of pool on which players have set a wager.

nine-ball: A rotation game with nine object balls and the *cue ball.* The only permissible object ball in any inning is the lowest-numbered ball on the table. The first to pocket the nine wins.

nuts: Skill. (He had the *nuts* to win.)

object ball: The targeted ball, as opposed to the *cue ball.*

one-pocket: A game in which an opponent must sink eight balls, of any number, stripe, or color, in order to win. Each ball, however, must be pocketed into a predetermined pocket at the end of the table. Each player shoots for separate pockets, making one-pocket more defensive than other sorts of pool. Also known as "one-hole" or "pocket apiece."

OPM: Other People's Money—that which pool players try to win during money matches.

pigeon: A pool hustler's potential victim. See also *mark; sucker.*

poolroom detective: A person who can spot potential hustlers or *marks.*

rail: The cushioned edges of the pool table, often referred to as the banks.

railbird: A spectator during a money game. See also *sweator.*

roll: (1) A roll of money, often bound by a rubber band, held loose in the pocket of a gambler. Gamblers often don't use wallets, preferring to keep their money loose for easy access for the quick disposal of debts. (2) The trajectory of the cue ball or object ball; e.g., "You got a lucky *roll* on that shot."

safety: A defensive shot; a shot designed not to pocket a ball but to leave one's opponent without an easy shot.

scratch: A foul or illegal shot, in which the cue ball falls into a pocket. Generally results in the loss of a turn and the *spotting* of a ball.

selling out: Leaving an opponent an open table, allowing him to make balls at will. Usually used in reference to poor safety play in one-pocket.

shortstop: A player who can be beaten only by a top player.

side action: Betting between *railbirds* or *sweators*. See *side bet*.

side bet: Betting between *railbirds* or *sweators*. See also *side action*.

speed: A player's ability.

spot: A handicap.

spotting: Placing a ball on the spot on one end of the table after any foul.

stakehorse: A person who provides financial support for a pool player. He funds bets and expenses and, in return, receives a percentage of winnings. See also *backer*.

stalling: Occasionally losing a game to keep an opponent betting. See also *lemon*.

straight pool: A game in which any ball on the table can be pocketed and a player is awarded a point for each ball pocketed.

string: An imaginary line on the far end of the table from which the cue ball must be shot after fouls in certain games. In most games the cue ball must be placed behind the *string* for the opening *break*.

sucker: A pool hustler's potential victim. See also *mark*; *pigeon*.

sweator: A spectator during a money game. The term refers to the sweat that may form on the spectator's brow as he frets about the outcome. As noted in *The New Illustrated Encyclopedia of Billiards* (Mike Shamos, The Lyons Press, 1999), the word is spelled with "or" rather than "er" to distinguish it from apparel. See also *railbird*.

takedown: The amount of money won at the tables.

weight: A handicap. See also *spot*.

whitey: The *cue ball*.

who shot John: A pool player's unverifiable boast.

INDEX